Imagining the Postcolonial

Imagining the Postcolonial

Discipline, Poetics, Practice in Latin American and Francophone Discourse

JAIME HANNEKEN

SUNY PRESS

Published by
STATE UNIVERSITY OF NEW YORK PRESS
Albany

Printed in the United States of America

For information, contact
State University of New York Press
www.sunypress.edu

Production, Laurie D. Searl
Marketing, Kate R. Seburyamo

Library of Congress Cataloging-in-Publication Data

Hanneken, Jaime, 1978– author.
Imagining the postcolonial : discipline, poetics, practice in Latin American and Francophone discourse / Jaime Hanneken.
pages cm
Includes bibliographical references and index.
ISBN 978-1-4384-5621-8 (hardcover : alk. paper)
ISBN 978-1-4384-5622-5 (pbk. : alk. paper)
ISBN 978-1-4384-5623-2 (ebook)
1. Postcolonialism in literature. 2. Comparative literature. 3. Latin America—In literature. 4. French-speaking countries—In literature. I. Title.
PN56.P555H36 2015
809'.93358—dc23 2014023235

10 9 8 7 6 5 4 3 2 1

Contents

Introduction

Latin Americanism, Francophone Studies, and Identity Thinking

For those of us writing today, a full generation after "postcolonial" first gained popular usage in English departments as a descriptor and then a category of literature and culture, it is not considered particularly insightful to assert that postcolonial studies is at a crossroads—or, to put it in starker language, in crisis, even "dead."[1] Although conjecture on the end of the postcolonial from the past decade or so has appeared to imbue critical exchange with a renewed sense of urgency, in effect, one could argue that institutionally it has always moved along an axis of crisis and that it is precisely because of this movement that humanistic scholarship persists in discussing things in postcolonial terms at all.[2] Early polemics over the semantic and political intrigue or the rightful historical and geographic purview of the term are, in this sense, inseparable from more current concerns about its function as an organon of critique, in that both attempt to manage the conceptual identity of the postcolonial—what the postcolonial is as well as what it does.

This book deals with both senses of postcoloniality's identity: It reassesses some of postcolonial critique's common assumptions in its encounter with Latin American and francophone discourse, two areas that have largely remained on the sidelines of postcolonial studies's historical and critical panorama. The analyses I undertake here are thus preoccupied not only with the predilect themes and problematics of postcolonial identity in cultural and literary expression but also with disciplinarity's stakes in that identity, which are determined by the institutional and geopolitical places that house Latin Americanism and Francophone Studies as much as by the residual proprieties of postcolonialism as a metropolitan, anglophone, and twentieth-century construct. My analyses attempt to track these features simultaneously in theoretical approaches, regional historic cultural paradigms, and practices of recognition and valuation, keeping in mind how the same discursive properties work in tandem in each sphere. Through a combined inquiry into discipline, poetics, and practice, comparison may be able to pair the nominal or semantic decentering of the postcolonial—which has already removed a number of barriers to considering ecumenically what the postcolonial "is"—with a theoretical shake-up that has been slower to arrive.

Prospects of Postcolonial Comparison

It cannot be denied that the metacritical interrogation of what the postcolonial "is," both as a project and as a corpus, has substantially dynamized its faculties: Some twenty-five years after it first circulated in English departments to theorize literary and cultural practices common to recently decolonized populations of the anglophone world, the postcolonial serves more as an intersectional site where scholarship on colonialism and imperialism in an ever-larger number of historical moments and places, read through the lenses of anthropology, geography, area and ethnic studies, feminism, and languages and literatures, finds common ground. So strong is the impetus to use the postcolonial label as a tool of comparison, in fact, that it has the aura of an antidote to pessimism about the term's continued usefulness. Many roundtables, edited volumes, and conference panels that ponder the death of postcolonial theory seem to find the answer in interdisciplinary conversations and strategic or radical adaptations of its reticulation.[3] A central focus of postcolonial comparativism is the dialogue among marginalized or "minor" areas of study: In this vein of research one finds, for example, Françoise Lionnet and Shu-Mei Shih's volume *Minor Transnationalism* or Gayatri Spivak's essays in *Other Asias*, both of which are dedicated to excising Europe and the United States as the ground of comparative intelligibility. Their projects are aligned with Comparative Literature's own reformulation into what Rey Chow has called "post-European Comp. Lit": This entails wresting analysis from the European "grid of reference," where the non-European becomes visible only as an ancillary element, and learning to "judg[e] the value of things horizontally, in sheer approximation to one another" (298).

My comparative study of francophonist and Latin Americanist uses of the postcolonial stems from a conviction of a piece with the post-European vision of these critics. But if we are to take seriously the assertion, implicit in the horizontal grid Chow speaks of, that comparison is good when it changes the operational as well as the thematic mode of the postcolonial—not just what it means but also how it means—then bringing these areas together must involve a new way of engaging their specificities: In other words, comparison should not simply add more examples to the same list of traits and practices readymade for the postcolonial; it must aim above all to transform the concept itself for the better. This is not the same as sizing up the differences between Latin Americanist, francophone, and mainstream postcolonial ideas about imperialism or opting between global and local theory. Rather, my objective is to mobilize those elements of the texts examined here that defy the equalizing gesture associated with the postcolonial in order to think the postcolonial against its identifications. For a provisional definition of the fundamental problematic of postcolonial identity as *equivalence*—both the individual equivalence invoked between people or things and their representations and the ordering of heterogeneous elements into uniform constituencies for knowledge, control, and exchange—it is useful to recall Graham Huggan's influential distinction between postcolonialism and postcoloniality.[4] The first term refers to "a local assemblage of more or less related oppositional practices" (*The Postcolonial Exotic* 6) that "posits itself as anti-colonial, and that works toward the dissolution of imperial epistemologies and institutional structures" (28); the second is "a global apparatus of assimilative, institutional/commercial codes" (6) that "is more closely tied to the global market, and that capitalises both on the widespread circulation of ideas about cultural otherness and on the worldwide trafficking of culturally 'othered' artifacts and goods" (28). Signaling the differences between the postcolonial's two main "regimes of value"—in Bourdieusian terminology, the mechanisms by which various agents and institutions assign and endorse cultural capital—serves the larger purpose of unmasking how each is bound up with the other: The point, in Huggan's words, is "that in the overwhelmingly commercial context of late twentieth-century commodity culture, postcolonialism and its rhetoric of resistance have themselves become consumer products" (6).

Huggan's phrasing, to my mind, captures the core issue of contemporary debates in anglophone postcolonial studies. But one need not assume an exceptionalist stance to acknowledge that paradigms like Huggan's "postcolonial exotic" grasp only partially the tensions of value-coding underlying the postcolonial tenor of Latin American and francophone discourse. The categories of postcolonialism and postcoloniality set up by Huggan, sedimented in multiple generations of Third World literature mass-produced for anglophone multicultural audiences, pertain to an established structure of recognition that gathers representatives of a territory coextensive with nineteenth-century British imperial holdings, who are groomed to frame their craft within a set of problematics—politics of language and translation, travails of decolonization, migration, racial and religious difference—that bind them collectively to the postcolonial apparatus. This structure only unevenly addresses Latin

American or francophone postcoloniality's own binding features, a fact that tends to be muddled by the way texts and thinkers from these areas have come to be seen as "postcolonial" largely as auxiliaries of pre-existing anglophone corpuses within postcolonial studies's expanded avatar of global or world literature. But rather than continuing to inventory the absence or mishandling of non-anglophone regional-historic traditions in mainstream venues, or to accentuate their distance from the Commonwealth postcolonial model, comparison does better to substantiate the horizontal correspondences among them: In a word, the common ways that postcolonial identity as a claim to defiance and postcolonial identity as market position are bound together in Latin American and francophone production.

For the two areas of concern in this study, such commonalities are rooted first in their very titles. In fact, Francophonie and Latin America are both inventions of colonial ideology that attempt to name and unify unmanageably heterogeneous groups of nations, cultures, and histories in defense of the universal pretensions of fading empire (an empire that, even in Latin America, is as French as it is Iberian for post-independence societies, as the vintage of the region's "Latin" identity reminds us). What is more, in both cases the artificial unity imposed by imperial design yields a diachronic mapping of coercion and resistance: From the nineteenth-century decline of French and Spanish political influence through the zenith of U.S. hegemony and global capitalism, this mapping allows one to read how the supranational shells of Francophonie and Latin America, riven on the inside by linguistic hierarchies and ethnic oppression, nonetheless serve for the outside as a heuristic for cultural agglutination and collective opposition: Although the "idea of Latin America," as Walter Mignolo (2005) argues, originates in a Creole suppression of the non-white, non-Iberian make-up of new American republics, it also provides an effective front for those republics against the other, Yankee America, a front whose successes include José Martí's "Nuestra América" as well as *The Motorcycle Diaries*. Francophonie, likewise, wavers between the sense of its ghettoization as an accessory to French language politics and the subversive, humanitarian positionality it claims to afford member nations against the more monolithic gestures of U.S. global politics, going so far as to brand itself as a "defender of the weak and powerless" (Majumdar 170).[5] Such ambivalences of identification, present in today's university configurations as much as in their historic development, provide the signposts for identitarian movements between postcolonialism and postcoloniality in these fields. The dominant optics they produce in the academic moment of the postcolonial might be summarized as autochthony and globality: For the autochthonist, the most compelling path toward liberationist self-expression is promised in locationist, telluric, or indigenist reasoning, while the global and postcolonial labels are equated with ruinous equivalence; for the globalist, on the other hand, participation in the broad international circulation of goods and ideas represents freedom from the restraints of national or bilateral center/periphery channels of exchange, a timely cosmopolitanism that breaks away from old imperial and postcolonial national hierarchies alike.[6] Intellectual practices associated with Francophone Studies and Latin Americanism historically have confronted similar quandaries over their native or global identities: While Latin American postcolonialism has gravitated more toward autochthony, francophone postcolonialism tends to be self-consciously globalist. If the disciplinary origins of the postcolonial in each case present a more or less divergent set of histories, the historical variation between them is, nonetheless, helpful for documenting the ways all outcomes of the global-local debate ultimately facilitate postcolonial identity as equivalence.

Postcolonial Latin Americanism and Francophone Studies: A Disciplinary History

Latin Americanism originates in the Creole intellectual tradition of the nineteenth and early twentieth centuries, much of which was dedicated to the articulation of a singular regional civilization that opposed the Northern "anglo" utilitarianism associated with the United States' increasingly predatory foreign policies. After World War II, the propulsion of Latin American literature onto international markets introduced regional archives and debates into North American and European university classrooms, where interest in the representation of "Third World" voices rose, starting in the 1970s, as the coinage of the multicultural humanities. Historically, the field was built across the very fault lines of hemispheric domination: Particularly after the political radicalization of scholarship and the turn away from literature that marked the late 1970s, it was molded by competing ideas about where, institutionally or geopolitically, the study of Latin America could be considered authentic, informed, and committed, and where it served as handmaiden to one or another ideological program. Therefore, the question of whether Latin America was postcolonial beyond a straightforward historical sense, first raised in the early 1990s, played out on a plane of contention previously occupied by postmodernism, poststructuralism, and Cultural Studies, where devotees of a locally or natively produced Latin Americanism discovered additional proof of the ways theories from the United States or Europe had consistently painted Latin America, in Mabel Moraña's words, "as an object to be (re)presented from outside, that is, as an image that verifies the existence and function of the eye that watches it" (647).[7] The artificial cleavage between a metropolis-based, theoretically complex Latin Americanism and an autochthonous form of criticism centered in a canonical literary tradition colored from the beginning Latin Americanist interest in the postcolonial. As a result, the specific historic discordances of postcolonial studies vis-à-vis Latin America—namely, the differences between Enlightenment-era colonialism and the expansionist phenomenon that in the Iberian world dated to 1492—as well as the theoretical inconsistencies resulting from these discordances were filtered through other iterations of the century-long local/metropolitan Latin Americanist conundrum.[8]

The relationship between Francophone Studies and what is now often called Francophone Postcolonial Studies is heir to a center/periphery configuration trained more on French imperial history and its legacies than on the bugbear of postcolonial studies's metropolitan alliances. The creation of French-language literature outside the hexagon, before it was the subject of scholarly interest, was managed under the ideological aegis of Francophonie, the cultural institution that was charged with promoting the colonial *mission civilisatrice* and later, under the guise of postcolonial French-periphery cooperation, aimed to defend global French language use against the rise of English.[9] Thus the original dynamic of francophone literature, or in fact any item one could label "francophone," underscores its existence as a lack and supplement of Frenchness: Although this literature did not meet the racial, geographic, or cultural threshold to be simply French, its very insufficiency was used to bolster the measure of Frenchness, at the same time that its commercial production guaranteed the domain of French as a universal language.[10] The longstanding effect of these arrangements within academic study of French is what Réda Bensmaïa has described as a "scotomization process" or interdict that made francophone literature unmentionable despite its well-known existence ("Francophonie" 19). The status of Francophonie, asserts Bensmaïa, is that of a trace on the self-presence of French national and linguistic identity (20). The historic distaste for postcolonial studies in French academia mirrors a wider reversal of fortune in the defense of republican universalism that several commentators tie to the ethno-racial violence subtending recent initiatives like the banning of face veils in public or the government-sponsored 2011 debate over *"l'identité nationale."*[11] As Nicholas Bancel and Pascale Blanchard have argued (2009), the same French rigor of *longue durée*-style analysis and strict disciplinary delineation that objects to postcolonial studies's tendency to make fluid connections across time and space (a tendency it largely considers an intellectual cohort of Anglo-Saxon "communitarianism") also resists analyzing issues internal to France in conjunction with the colonial history of Africa, Asia, or the Caribbean. Academic failure to link these legacies to contemporary disputes surrounding immigration, marked in particular by the explosion of tensions in minority communities during the riots of 2005 and 2007, is seen as symptomatic of a wider intellectual ambivalence toward the critical revision of colonial history.[12] It is, therefore, no surprise that the development of Francophone Studies as a "postcolonial" field in British and North American literature and language departments over the past twenty years has gone hand in hand with the adoption of Anglo-Saxon–style cultural interpretation and a virtual reinvention of the francophone appellative, swapping its longstanding association with humanist universalism for a worldly cosmopolitanism that is more easily absorbed into the multiculturalist cant.

In keeping with this historical density of investments of location and identity woven into their disciplinary study, the versions of Latin America and francophone literature selected for postcolonial inflection offer an object lesson in the unpredictability of the forms that postcolonialism's complicity with global capitalism may take. The preferential—and oftentimes exclusive—identification of Francophone Studies with postcolonialism has been the product of abundant academic publishing, including the creation of journals, edited volumes, and book series conceived under the proprietary framework that names the francophone postcolonial field and establishes its objectives.[13] For authors who access this publishing network, being postcolonial is largely a reflection of the markets it opens to their work outside the marginalized niche francophone writing is accorded in French book culture: The opportunities for wide distribution, translation into English, and teaching and research positions that follow the postcolonial reincarnation of Francophone Studies symbolize liberation from the imperial sensibilities of the hexagonal publishing edifice, which is seen to relegate francophone literature to the office of serving French language politics. The influential project of "*littérature-monde*," launched by a collective manifesto published in *Le Monde des Livres* in 2007, mobilizes this same opposition between the perceived recidivism of French literary sensibilities and the ebullience of a beckoning cosmopolitan connectivity. The manifesto's forty-four signatories—which include Québécois and European as well as African, Asian, and Caribbean authors—profess to shed the otiose constraints of Francophonie in favor of the unfettered horizon of "world" literature, reporting that "the center . . . is from now on everywhere, in the four corners of the world" (Le Bris et al. 296). *Littérature-monde*'s emphasis on the classically postcolonial themes of migration, translation, and cultural cross-fertilization suggests that, as the circulation of francophone literature overtakes that of Franco-French texts and as the global French-speaking population acquires more characteristics of diaspora rather than North-South binarity, the mechanisms of recognition for francophone cultural products resemble more and more those of anglophone postcolonial studies, together with the marketing acumen they generate.[14]

Contrary to the francophone postcolonial authors who jubilantly, as Abdourahman Waberi writes, "cultivate the wide world" [*jardinent le vaste monde*] (70) from U.S. university campuses, for the Latin Americanist body of work best represented within mainstream postcolonial studies, referred to as "decoloniality" or the "decolonial option," the physical and geopolitical locus of enunciation of the global periphery is vital to epistemological critique.[15] Drawn from sociologist Aníbal Quijano's notion of the coloniality of power and Enrique Dussel's philosophy of liberation, and developed mainly by anthropologist Walter Mignolo, decoloniality is animated by the primacy of location in questions of knowledge and power.[16] Using the arguments of Quijano and Dussel, decoloniality first concludes that the purview of postcolonial studies within nineteenth- and twentieth-century colonial dynamics only magnifies one subsection of the entire enterprise of modern colonial logic dating from 1492, whose key features are found in the singular imperial history of Latin America.[17] Decoloniality is not, then, one variant of the postcolonial concept but is its metacritique and conceptual correction.[18] As expressed in an ever-expanding lexicon, which besides decolonial terminology includes the closely related concepts of post-Occidentalism, border epistemology, colonial difference, and the colonial wound, Mignolo's endeavor is to show that the place from which one speaks—in a bodily as well as geopolitical sense—determines the kind of knowledge best suited to one's interests. This means not only that the Cartesian universe of modern Western philosophy that is instrumental to colonial projects is "invalid" for people living in postcolonial societies, but also that local thought traditions displaced by the colonial knowledge-power matrix have an epistemological profile separate from the coercive function inherent to First-World ways of knowing and are, therefore, capable of changing the very terms under which the conditions of life are brokered for Third-World inhabitants or First-World postcolonial immigrants.[19] The "decolonial option" promotes using the knowledge generated by firsthand and historic communal experiences of coloniality to "delink" from capitalism and Eurocentric epistemes, through scholarship as well as in political activism and aesthetic creation.[20]

Postcolonial Critique and Identity Thinking

I have been arguing that postcolonial comparison among non-anglophone areas of cultural study must go beyond common motifs and tropes toward the material factors that mediate postcolonial identity as resistance and as product. Taking together the two cases highlighted here, one finds a set of mutually inverted itineraries in which the adoption of a postcolonial framework can involve the migration from provincialism to cosmopolitanism, from the old-fashioned assertion of identity to the embrace of hybrid indeterminacy, from dogged empiricism to discourse-based politics, or their exact opposite. Indeed, if the vagaries of Latin Americanist and francophone movement toward postcolonial studies indicate anything, it is that there is no disciplinary approximation of postcoloniality that is not also an approximation of its market logic. In light of that conclusion, it is less interesting to meditate on the elusive transfer of postcolonial identity between solitary resistance and acquiescence than to examine the elements that always reach beyond its identitarian gesture, the part of Latin Americanist and francophone postcolonialism that, so to speak, says more than it means to say.

In attempting to pinpoint this constellational portion of postcolonial identity, my project is inspired by Theodor Adorno's understanding of identity thinking: His negative dialectics is premised in the identity of all thought, in the inevitability that "to think is to identify" (*Negative Dialectics* 5). The universal scheme of identity thinking that preoccupied Adorno from his first lectures at the University of Frankfurt until the posthumous *Aesthetic Theory* was composed of the matrix of economic and epistemological processes, starting with the early modern waves of European expansion, that work ceaselessly toward converting the totality of social and natural life into exchange value. The postcolonial names a durable residue of these processes, although as a concept it is both complicit with and opposed to the forces it would like to arrest: In an Adornian view, its challenge is to "use concepts to unseal the nonconceptual with concepts, without making it their equal" (*Negative Dialectics* 10). The principal objective of his negative dialectics is to elaborate a practice of thought oriented to the activity of the nonconceptual, or non-identity, within subjective reflection, understanding this activity as an integral part of historical development and thus as a present indicator that an alternative to universal rationalization is possible and necessary. The goal is to compose a catalyst for social transformation from the negative imprints of non-identity palpable in existing, damaged structures of thought. Even though a nonconceptual meaning undistorted by our concepts is currently impossible, Adorno insists that the responsibility of thought lies in anticipating a future mutation of thought able to dissipate the subjective regime, using the material remnants that contradict it.

The utopian dimension of negative dialectics signals both its ample congruence with and its points of departure from the predominant deconstructive apparatus of postcolonial critique. Like deconstruction, this is an aporetic mode of thought animated by its own impossibility: Its stimulus, as postcolonial studies also foregrounds, most visibly in its subalternist formulations, is the irretrievability of the manifold particulars extinguished by colonial and neocolonial technologies of representation. However, from an Adornian perspective, the incommensurability that severs the writing subject from what she studies is historically, not absolutely, posited. That is, the prohibition on reaching the thing itself that occasions dialectical reflection does not hold irrevocably for all thought, as it does in *différance*'s structural conditions of impossibility, but only in all thought as it has existed until now. The exigency of the work to be done in the name of the postcolonial is then given in the current poverty of its concept: The promise that postcolonial studies could actually change the world cannot be outlined in any positive way but becomes legible negatively in the historically measurable distance between the subjective labor that suffuses its formulas and nagging reminders of how these have missed their mark.

Because of their facility to connect theoretical abstraction to questions of material injustice, negative dialectics, and early Frankfurt School cultural theory in general, have for a long time supported a Marxist counterpoint within anglophone postcolonial studies, a critical position with which my proposals here are largely resonant. For example, I find it not only useful but necessary for comparative postcolonial practice to ask, as Asha Varadharajan does in her Adornian excavation of postcolonial theory, why "if the discourses of postmodernism and poststructuralism have been responsible for decentering the patriarchical and imperialist subject, . . . has this perception not produced the emancipation and self-acceptance of the object?" (*Exotic Parodies* xi). If there is any takeaway from the failure of postcolonial studies not just to expose the racialized and gendered forms of power that underwrite the rapid metamorphosis of imperial global capital but even to explain to itself adequately how those forms are present in its own institutional and theoretical formats, it must be sought in the index of its particulars, hence in the conviction that "the split between subject and object is not inherent but historically produced and negated" (xviii). But I do not think properly executing this materialist dictum requires us to end up, as Varadharajan does, in a "staged confrontation of dialectics and *différance*" (xi); on the contrary, recognizing up close the parallel threads of deconstruction and Critical Theory, particularly regarding the messianic promise that appears in the interlocking ambits of existing and unachieved reflection, sharpens our appreciation of the intermingling between deconstruction as promise and as act: In other words, a materialist outlook helps us to recognize how the endless demand issued by deconstruction is fused with the neutralization of this demand through the thematization of deconstruction, for example, in palaver about the decentering function of postcolonial critique. Even when the most common sort of deconstructive reading degenerates into a mere tropology of difference, critique gains less in declaring outright its wrongheadedness than in dissecting the conditions of its reification: For Adorno as well as Derrida, the debilitation of the deconstructive injunction in actual practice, as in the perfunctory "Othering" of the imperial archive, is also the renewed possibility of a future deconstruction that is still unimaginable. Deconstruction, in this sense, is one of the faces of the promising substrate of the postcolonial, not merely a register of its shortcomings.

A critical practice that combines the best insights of deconstruction and negative dialectics could be characterized, following Adorno, as a "wishful" mode of thought. As I argue in chapter 1, "wishful thinking" is based in the awareness that a transformation of reality cannot come from the empirical understanding of things as they are nor from metaphysical abstraction, but must be sought in the entwinement of material and metaphysical realms. Wishful thinking, like Derrida's deconstructive injunction, is generated from a need internal to reflection, a need constituted by the fact that the present errors of thought also prove thought's continued possibility and necessity. Attuned to both the material and the abstract components of critique, wishful thinking holds the processual, experiential dimension of postcolonial identification to be inextricable from its drive to fix and equalize. Starting out from the theoretical premises shared by dialectics and deconstruction can offer comparative study a much-needed exit from the ongoing polemics between materialism and high theory: Indeed, the best outcome for the reprioritization of historical mediation may be to draw us away from postcolonial studies's wars of position, by helping us, in Keya Ganguly's words, to "resis[t] the demand that one must choose between keeping a naive though ideological faith in the authenticity of origins, being, and experience, or conversely, avowing a more self-consciously 'anti-essentialist' and 'decentered' view of the world in which everything and everybody is remitted to the ineffabilities of signification and textuality" (241). In piecing together the stories of how the postcolonial label has cathected different symbolic economies of Latin Americanism and Francophone Studies, it becomes difficult to tell just where "essentialism" is not lurking, given the way postcolonialism's commercial annex welcomes decentered and naive ideological viewpoints alike. For that reason, comparing uses of the postcolonial in different fields should not be a matter of rooting out essentialism or determining at what point "going" postcolonial means selling out. Rather, the liberationist potential of the postcolonial concept—the release it represents from the uniformizing clutch of different imperial networks—is contained in the variation among the concrete paths that historic experiences beat toward it. This is true as much for decoloniality, which has been fashioned as the postcolonial concept's more committed alternative, as it is for Francophone Studies's overt assimilation to it: The historic signature behind both, extracted from the commodity character of the criticism that expresses it, is the measure of the life left in the term *postcolonial*. Because the historic movement built up in Francophone Studies and Latin Americanism is not fully captured by their conscious intentions and informational content, their formal as well as constative gestures must be of interest for comparative study: In short, it is important to heed not just the political or ideological profile but also the aesthetic dimension of these discourses.

The Aesthetics of Discourse

Materialist postcolonialism's relative disengagement with questions of aesthetics, responding perhaps to a desire to avoid the conservative strain of modernist-era ideas about the autonomy of art, has nonetheless shortchanged critique of sustained inquiry into the productive overlap between art and society. This overlap, as Adorno's theories recognize, involves not only how formal conditions of art register external social contradictions but also how discourse as a whole is subject to the dialectic of context and form usually identified with the aesthetic realm. In *Native Intelligence*, Deepika Bahri argues forcefully for the reinstatement of aesthetic considerations to postcolonial criticism as the analytical vector lacking for a fuller assessment of postcolonial literature's political relevance. As proof, Bahri offers Adorno's insistence that only the aesthetic lens properly detects the tension between the formal and societal portions of art that, from a postcolonial perspective, are often artificially divided into poles of commercial acquiescence and political resistance. Particularly when it comes to the issues surrounding postcolonial studies's "bogey of authenticity" (19), Bahri remarks, aesthetics offers the nuance required to avoid falling into the "assumption either of irrelevance because of the text's success—and therefore complicity with the market—or its inherent radicalism by virtue of category alone" (7). The specific value of aesthetics for the postcolonial context—where cultural production is often construed haphazardly as revolutionary manifesto (and the de facto site of politics) on one hand, or as multicultural decoy on the other—is to recall that neither the exchange value nor the producer's "message" sum up the work of art. There is thus a sense, in Bahri's view, that the absence of aesthetic reflection is itself "a measure of criticism's inadequate resistance to the status quo logic of exchange society" (7). What Bahri, in her focus on anglophone postcolonial bestsellers, is unconcerned to add here is the way the dialectic of aesthetics is also a condition of language in general. Indeed, for Adorno, just as in art the contextual elements embedded in the formal composition harden against the artwork's reduction to a commodity, in language there is an almost hieratic history inhabiting words, which counters their will to identify and subsume particulars as information.[21] Even if language, as the primary tool of subjective mastery, obeys the demand to transfix the heterogeneity of the world for the sake of communication, its elements nonetheless retain impressions of the discrete contexts of their iterations, which supplement the transparent meaning of words with a non-subjective voice, what Adorno calls "expression."[22] The truth that appears in language, as in art, is composed of the force field between its service to utilitarian logic and the memory of concrete usage that adheres to it because "language as expression of the thing itself and language as communication are interwoven" (Adorno, *Hegel: Three Studies* 105).

One of my intentions in this study is to explore aesthetic dialectics as a component of art strictly defined and implicitly as a feature of discourse writ large. For the francophone and Latin American contexts, it seems especially important to interpret aesthetics as broadly as possible because the division between art and philosophy or criticism is traditionally blurred in these areas and because of the tendency to judge the credentials of their disciplinary representatives based on their political commitment, where this is evaluated on the basis of transparency and identity. If the real pertinence of the postcolonial concept for francophonist and Latin Americanist critique, as I am arguing, has less to do with these fields' overt position taking than with the constellational quality of their digestion of postcolonialism's existing apparatus, then it is worthwhile to read them, at least in part, as aesthetic constructions. Understanding aesthetic mediation in this incorporative sense, we appraise the postcolonial as a transversal intelligence spread across the axes of politics, theory, and creative production, those of communication and expression, as well as across the contextual boundaries of Latin Americanism and Francophone Studies. The three-part focus of this book on discipline, poetics, and practice is not meant to provide a trenchant ordering of the sites of academic-regional discourse, but it is intended to demonstrate the flow of similar aesthetic, historic, and political preoccupations throughout its various layers. It shows, for example, how the main dilemma for a theoretical practice of the postcolonial—namely that discourse itself is caught up in the irreducibility of language's identitarian compulsion—is reflected in philosophical and aesthetic meditations on specifically Latin American or Caribbean models of expression and how market-driven literature ultimately also can be seen to exist in tension with these constraints.

Chapter 1 is framed by the materialist critique's contention that postcolonial studies is posited in the shrouding of its historic conditions of emergence. I evaluate the possibility for a comparative theoretical practice scrupulously oriented to the material conditions of its own production, analyzing Alberto Moreiras's influential formulation of "double hybridity" from *The Exhaustion of Difference* together with Adorno's final meditations on metaphysics in *Negative Dialectics*. Hybridity's double articulation, loosely modeled on Derrida's democracy-to-come, achieves a turning-back on theory's claim to totalization by tactically separating its identitarian gesture from the unprogrammable opening to radical alterity, thus thinking hybridity simultaneously in what Moreiras calls its "cultural" and "savage" registers. Dialectics, on the other hand, understands theoretical abstraction as a site of subjective thought's confluence with alterity: At the intersection of metaphysical projection and materialist empiricism, in what Adorno dubs a "wishful" mode of thinking, conceptual reflection is reoriented to its material objects. I argue that double articulation and wishful thinking, despite their disagreement over the theoretical apprehension of the diremption of subject and object, ultimately rest on a similar notion of experience. Thinking them together allows us to conceive a critical practice based on an experience of the undeconstructible, defined as the contingent and sensible register of conceptual thought's encounter with non-identity.

Chapters 2 and 3 delve into the shared problematics of Latin American and francophone efforts to articulate a legitimate expression of place through parallel discussions of José Lezama Lima's assertion of "American expression" and Édouard Glissant's "archipelic" poetics. My study of Lezama focuses on the role of baroque poetics in the suspension of historical causality and the affirmation of an autochthonous American subject in *La expresión americana*, with the aim of demonstrating how they may lead us to an understanding of historical consciousness driven by non-identity. Lezama envisions an American practice of historical agency through the poetic counterpoint of images occasioned by the magnetic encounter of far-flung visual fragments of history: The chance spark of these encounters activates a mythic process of history as a continual capture and dissolution of form. I contend that Lezama's repurposing of the tropes of landscape and myth offers an American historical consciousness based, much as Walter Benjamin's theses on history, in constellation—that is, in the fragments that drive the image's waxing and waning form as a measure of history. In privileging non-identity, not as an ineffable difference but as so many crystallizations of the resistance to history that fuels historical vision, American gnosis also suggests a way to read the creative negation of Latin America's identifications as an index of its postcolonial expression.

The discussion of Glissant in Chapter 3 traces a triangulation of place, poetics, and history from his early emphasis on art's probe of second nature—in what I call his "monadic" period—to the theories of Relation and Tout-monde, during his "nomadic" period. The relationship between place (*lieu*) and thought in Glissant's poetic career functions both as a misunderstood cipher of the transformative capacity he grants to art and as a key indicator for Glissant's own gradual move away from localized historical and political commentary toward a rhizomatic idiom of globality. Noting the way Glissant's theories retain residues of his "monadic" thrust even within their adoption of Deleuze and Guattari's rhizome and chaos theory, I evaluate the ways the connection between place and thought, throughout the production of "late" Glissant, leaves intact the potential of social transformation he imagines for poetics.

Although the individual treatments of Lezama and Glissant are separated to give full attention to the contextual specificities their poetics involve, each also highlights their strikingly similar preoccupation with arriving at a discursive communication with place—namely, with nature and landscape—through poetic action. The two chapters are followed by an excursus that extrapolates from their conclusions to suggest some wider consequences these may hold for approaches to the theorization of postcolonial locality. Insofar as the advent of the postcolonial academic framework has presented Latin Americanism and Francophone Studies with a referendum on the proper place for their disciplinary bounds—catching them, in the end, in a false choice between historic-regional autochthony and an intrepid globality—reflection on their relation to the postcolonial concept must also consider the concomitant relation these disciplines brook with globalization. The two options presently pursued by prominent Latin Americanist and francophonist contingencies—to promote a localized version of postcoloniality or alternatively to celebrate the eclipse of the local in the embrace of a worldly scale of cultural belonging—in fact deliver critique to the same final outlet of global capitalism. A primary interest for disciplinary thought in this state of affairs must be to articulate itself within its inevitable accession to globality, but in flight from its reifying overtures. This thinking from the "need" in institutional thought, what Moreiras calls "delocalization," resides in the maneuver of the minimum distance between aesthetics and politics, the "and" that Jacques Rancière posits as the sole guarantor of the dissensual capacity of aesthetics. Viewing Latin Americanism and Francophone Studies also as a "politics of aesthetics" roughly akin to Glissant's archipelic thought or Lezama's American expression, I argue, prevents us from elevating the aesthetic troping of the heterogeneity of these discipline's objects as their political stand-in for global markets.

Chapters 4 and 5 examine the symbolic and material economies that circulate value between centers and peripheries of the Latin American and francophone imaginaries, first in the symbolic value of Paris as capital of cultural modernity and second in the reception of "minority" writing in U.S. and French literary markets. Chapter 4 reexamines the fetishization of Paris as capital of modernity from a pair of peripheral contexts related to disparate vicissitudes of the French imperial enterprise. For Spanish American *modernistas* faced with the rapid professionalization of the regional literary sphere at the turn of the twentieth century, Paris became a destination and a key topic of journalistic writing. Similarly, contemporary Congolese *mikilistes*, among the most disenfranchised youth of post-independence Kinshasa and Brazzaville, maintain a ritual cult of fashion and dandyism through *sape* clubs (Sociétés des Ambianceurs et Personnes Élégantes), which culminates in a voyage to and triumphant return from Paris. Analyzing Rubén Darío's chronicles and Alain Mabanckou's novel *Bleu blanc rouge*, this chapter traces the "cultural biography" of the Parisian fetish object as it is imported and circulated in local Spanish American and Congolese economies. Both in the dialectic of commoditization apparent in Darío's stylization of Parisian consumer society and in the *mikiliste*'s diversion of symbolic prestige goods from a strictly capitalist context of exchange to a cult of "wealth in people," it becomes clear that the paths traveled by the import object of Paris include numerous exits from market-driven exchange value, hence also from a straightforward reading of peripheral societies' insertion in global symbolic and political economies.

Chapter 5 investigates the polemics surrounding Rigoberta Menchú's *testimonio* that roiled mainstream and academic media in the United States in 1999 and the plagiarism scandal over Malian writer Yambo Ouologuem's novel *Le Devoir de violence* in early 1970s France. Previous scholarship on both cases has examined this impasse by dismantling monolithic categories of truth and autonomous subjectivity, pointing to the ways "truth effect" and the autobiographical pact in fact establish truth as simulacrum. I argue that truth effect is unable to register the flexible modes of identification and exchange that link minority "truth," as a good of multicultural tolerance, to the preservation and extension of capital's overdetermination of social life. My reading of Menchú and Ouologuem attempts to recuperate an awareness of this inevitable relation from within the content of their works, in what Adorno called their "truth content." Truth content appreciates the fact that artworks, from under the commodified schema of their reception, still harbor a disagreement with the historic antagonisms that block their transparent expression: What works like *Me llamo Rigoberta Menchú* and *Le Devoir de violence* profess is indeed a falsehood, a mere effect of truth bartered in the multicultural regime of authenticity, but their falsehood is an illusion of a non-illusionary totality of the conflicts barring an eventual, direct truth. Reading their content for the negative imprint of this non-illusionary forces critique also to read through its own, contradictory relationship to the difference recognized under the commercial category of minority literature.

The selection of texts explored in these chapters, far from offering an exhaustive view of the contiguities of Latin American and francophone discourses in the sphere of postcoloniality, is meant to provide a representative sampling of how the problematics of these two areas may be brought together. The point sustained throughout is that a transformative approach to comparative postcolonial practice must refigure scholarly commitment as an exercise in negativity. This means, to begin with, that no solidarity with efforts to change reigning power dynamics will be guaranteed by the declarative or thematic allegiance with the postcolonial object of study; positive commitment of this sort is ultimately confronted with the same condition Adorno painstakingly illustrated in the phenomenon of politically "committed" art, that when suffering "becomes part of the cultural heritage in the themes of committed literature, it becomes easier to play along with the culture that gave birth to [it]" ("Commitment" 85). But the inevitability that academic discourse, like art, is cut from the same cloth of exchange logic it hopes to defy will not be resolved by a shift from direct advocacy against suffering to the affirmation of the ambivalence it introduces into identity. Commitment against the omnipotence of conceptual thought, of which the postcolonial concept also unambiguously partakes, is given only minutely and cumulatively, in the distance between the postcolonial's claim to arrive flush with the objects it speaks for and the context that in each instance belies that claim. In this the aesthetic and experiential qualities of critique become decisive, as the frequencies contained within critique are best able to record what arrives from without. The priority of a negatively derived commitment is the priority of the postcolonial object, the task of preparing for the moment when it may speak without prematurely breaking the existing restraints of subjective thought.

Chapter 1

Double Articulation and Wishful Thinking

It has come to be axiomatic of the term *postcolonial*, especially when it refers to a disciplinary construct, a theoretical standpoint, or a reading practice, that it denotes a critique of identity. As any summary review of its academic lineage will point out, its subfields, concepts, and categories are all fundamentally concerned with the noncoincidence between European representational schemes and the various forms of signification these elide or subsume in discourses of imperialism. The expository overview of *The Empire Writes Back*, the most consciously institutional forerunner of postcolonial studies, describes how "the syncretic and hybridized nature of postcolonial experience refutes the privileged position of a standard code . . . and any monocentric view of human experience" (Ashcroft, Griffiths, and Tiffin 41). Disciplinary paradigms of postcolonial studies since Ashcroft, Griffith, and Tiffins's initial stance have followed suit, elaborating theories of hybridity, migration, and subalternity to scope out the violence that subtends the fiction of self-presence in colonial thought, mining its texts' constitutive foreclosures of other, incommensurable histories or voices. The foil of this hallmark critique of identity is the materialist denunciation of postcolonial studies's failure to cognize existing conditions of imperialism, a set of social relations anchored in the globalization of capital and the fortification of U.S. hegemony to which the proliferation of postcolonial criticism itself is adduced as a product, if not an accessory.[1]

This book argues that a main task for comparative uses of the postcolonial concept is to transform its existing paradigms, rather than to adapt them to new contexts. To that end, the theoretical labors of comparative study cannot be carried out in isolation from longstanding disagreements over postcolonialism's political valence, in particular from enduring questions about the postcolonial's detachment from, or complicity with, present forms of domination. No viable future of the postcolonial, in this sense, will be divorced from its disciplinary past. For Neil Lazarus, for example, the genealogical connections between the theoretical alignments of postcolonial studies and the moment of its disciplinary inauguration are key to understanding its present-day failures: He signals a transformation between uses of the term *postcolonial* in social scientific parlance of the 1960s and 1970s as an empirical descriptor, a neutral identifier with no stake in the heated debates over underdevelopment, Three Worlds theories, or even anticolonialism, and its repurposing in the early 1990s as "a fighting term, a theoretical weapon, which 'intervenes' in existing debates and 'resists' certain political and philosophical constructions" (19). Lazarus finds the positions claimed for the postcolonial particularly telling, namely its refusal of "an antagonistic or struggle-based model of politics in favour of one that emphasizes 'cultural difference,' 'ambivalence' and the 'more complex cultural and political boundaries that exist on the cusp' of . . . determinate categories of social reality" (19). The reconfiguration of global processes of domination that occurs during the highlighted period, punctuated by the international debt crisis of the 1980s and the end of the Cold War, is by no means unrelated to this striking metamorphosis of the term; on the contrary, its newfound conceptualization constitutes a "pragmatic adjustment," a "rationalization" of the misfortunes of socialist ideologies, which then stands astride the unfurling hegemon of unilateral capital. In other words, postcolonial studies so far has been unable to diagnose concrete forms of imperialism because its own idiom is posited on an epistemic supersession of the "old" ways of knowing that consider the current state of capitalism a visible and urgent case for critique.

As bids for interdisciplinarity and comparativity sound the new clarion call for sustainable humanistic scholarship on issues related to the postcolonial, whether or not one continues to use that term at all may depend on how well the critical edifice can rebut the charges laid out by Lazarus. His study, published in 2006, is directed at an assessment of postcolonial studies in the aftermath of the second U.S. invasion of Iraq; it aims to substantiate the ties between the lethargic academic response to the escalation of injustices exercised in the name of the global war on terror and the postcolonial's foundational abjurement of Marxist categories of analysis. Lazarus identifies how the evolution of the term *postcolonial* bespeaks the defining problematic behind its signature mode of thought and the historic conjuncture that gives it theoretical relevance. The postcolonial's fatal flaw, on his reading, is that the translation of the political question of academic responsibility to a program of cultural position-taking becomes the alibi for scholarship's implicit endorsement of imperialism's current course. My argument in this chapter first will draw out the consequences of the points he raises for an eventual comparative postcolonial endeavor by attempting to read popular formulations of what is generally called a "strategic" or "double register" of deconstruction, in counterpoint with Adorno's negative dialectics. Second, it will outline a mode of thought that weighs Lazarus's own materialist view together with the deconstructive theories that so trouble him. Although deconstructive insights are useful against the teleological register of certain dialectical ideas about the fall from or imminent return to a fulfilled, self-present society, dialectics reminds us that deconstruction's endless dissolution of self-presence is itself materially conditioned: As regards the supposed political haplessness of postcolonial studies, this is the reminder that where ambivalence, hybridity, and other concept-metaphors become self-contained figures for political intervention, postcolonial critique has effectively abdicated the historic scene of its conditions of production. My objective is to locate an approach drawn from the assumptions both of these philosophical stances share about the experiential nature of critique, what could be called the experience of the indeconstructible or, in Adorno's words, wishful thinking. A postcolonial reading conceived as the experience of the distance between conceptual thought and alterity, I argue, may be able to reorient disciplinary reflection to the priority of the disciplinary object. To demonstrate how a wishful mode of critique can alter accepted interpretations of canonical postcolonial texts, I conclude with an analysis of Moroccan author Abdelkebir Khatibi's notion of the *bi-langue*.

The Introduction explained that the incidence of postcolonialism in Latin Americanism and Francophone Studies is structured by historic struggles between the centrifugal consolidation of cultural and political identity and the exodus of identity into orbits of worldly, global, or cosmopolitan discourse. Latin Americanism, at least its existence in language and literature departments of the English-speaking world, stems from an investment in the cultural production of a region in "development," beginning during the 1960s Boom generation, whose scholarly circuits have replicated for over four decades the same North-South trajectory of import/export, migration, and frequent interventionism that have shaped Latin America's world role in the post–World War II era. The largely bilateral inscription of Latin Americanism charges place with a definitive role in its study, at times hypostasizing thought from Latin America or Latin Americans into a fey insight into the object, meant to countervail appropriative theoretical overtures from the North. Francophone Studies, born from the map of Francophonie and measured from the beginning in its distance from France, has found in the global, comparative, and postcolonial idioms of anglophone academia a set of discourses able to upend the identification of francophone as the detritus of Frenchness. Although the postcolonial label extends to Francophone Studies a critical agenda capable of unearthing the racial, linguistic, or epistemological underpinnings of its own constitution, these same gifts may distract from legitimate concerns about how francophone literature and culture avoid being filed away as the latest addition to an arsenal of "minority" representation. What comparison between francophone and Latin Americanist postcolonialisms immediately reveals is the flexibility of the postcolonial concept as a repository for global capital, in short, its ability indifferently to generate multiple forms of identity thinking. Thus if collaboration between the two areas is to reinvigorate studies of postcoloniality, as assured by so many placets of comparative or transnational inquiry, it needs to go beyond recalibrating its historical or pragmatic parameters and reconsider how the theoretical apparatuses at hand broach their ties to a determinate moment of thought. This is the need Lazarus exposes when he outlines the changing valence of the term.

Double Articulation

Although Latin Americanist-francophone cross-references remain fairly scarce in literary and cultural criticism, Michael Syrotinski's *Deconstruction and the Postcolonial* posits an important theoretical connection between them that suggests, as well as anything else, an avenue of future engagement. Syrotinski's book reviews the historical and epistemological confluences of deconstruction and the condition and theorization of the postcolonial. Intent on the salutary realignments each might offer to the other, he constructs a series of contemporary genealogies of the two title topics in order to "dwell between" them in search of a position that can counteract both the postcolonial's vulnerability to ontopological claims and deconstruction's tendency toward textualism: He finds a good example of this middle ground in the double articulation of hybridity promoted by Alberto Moreiras as a tactical approach for Latin American cultural studies. Syrotinski sees in double articulation a chance to steer through the critical impasse whereby "either the postcolonial is taken as the experiential realm that affords deconstruction the opportunity to move out of its textualist Eurocentrism . . . or the local singularities of the postcolonial are subsumed under the generalizing logic of deconstructive reading" (37). Moreiras's adoption of double hybridity comes at the end of *The Exhaustion of Difference*, one of the most thorough examinations of failed Latin Americanist cultural theories of difference from the vantage point of the late 1990s. The book is concerned to recover a "properly politico-epistemological project" for critical reason from the dominant chain of conceptualizations for Latin America's particular experience of modernity which, trained on a national-popular or local stratum of inquiry, fail to register the globalization of spatial and discursive movement. It is thus an argument against locational and identitarian thinking in favor of an aporetic mode of thought along broadly Derridean lines.

There are many reasons to accept *The Exhaustion of Difference* as a starting point for comparative postcolonial critique, not least of which is the fact that the atopic gesture of the book's arguments are also present in certain variants of francophonist thought: The work of Cameroonian anthropologist Achille Mbembe, for example (which Syrotinski also discusses as a combined thinking of deconstruction and the postcolonial), has long been committed to moving theoretical formulations of the African postcolony beyond anti-imperialist nationalisms and meditations on French republican universalism toward an *Afropolitanisme* focused on the aporias of continental identity. Peeling back the various inventions of Africa administered by colonial, nationalist, or pan-Africanist projects, Mbembe avers, reveals nothing but a continuous movement of peoples and ideas into and out of the continent, so that "Africa itself is from now on imagined as an immense interval, an inexhaustible citation subject to manifold forms of combination and composition. The reference is no longer made to an essential singularity, but to a renewed capacity for bifurcation" [*L'Afrique elle-même est désormais imaginée comme un immense intervalle, une inépuisable citation passible de maintes formes de combinaison et composition. Le renvoi ne se fait plus en relation à une essentielle singularité, mais à une capacité renouvelée de bifurcation*] (210). Mbembe's *Afropolitanisme*, like Moreiras's reconfigured Latin Americanism, relays implicitly to the making of a future community free of filiative jealousy, something akin to Derrida's democracy to come. But beyond its resonance with the most rigorous brands of francophone cosmopolitanism, *The Exhaustion of Difference* has the distinction of issuing, more than any other single title, the prognosis of a necessary radicalization of the Latin Americanist critical enterprise: From its proposals can be traced a decade of scrupulous revision of the foundations of Latin American singularity, but also fresh renditions of old polemics over the political allegiances of theory that have sprung up in the wake of new Leftist Latin American movements, including the allegation, reminiscent of Lazarus's own complaints, that Latin Americanism qua deconstruction "involve[s] in fact a renunciation of actual politics" (Beverley, *Latinamericanism after 9/11* 59).[2] Insofar as comparative postcolonialism is likely to unfold within the context of this debate, the double articulation of hybridity is an apposite place to begin deciphering its theoretical investments.

The Exhaustion of Difference starts out from the dilemma that locationally inscribed politics—something like Walter Mignolo's decoloniality—amounts to nothing more than an "optimistic wager" against hegemony that is "always essentially open to hijacking by the movement of global capital itself" (279). When the organic fictions of national popular culture, regional singularity, or subaltern expression are finally revealed as appropriations of capital, and thus as expropriations of Latin Americanist identity, there is no more telling "whether Latin American cultural studies, and its particular fostering of the production of regional difference, is a genuinely productive enterprise and not the mere byproduct of a global phenomenon that is reading us all" (57). Over several chapters, Moreiras lays out a Latin Americanist praxis strong enough to resist the expropriative pull of global capital and to remain open to the unforeseen alterity of its object in an active effort to curtail its pretensions to "serve as the mimetic-discursive assistant to social power" (158); this critical regionalism, as he calls it, thereby labors to acknowledge the claims of alterity, the excess or ur-object of Latin Americanist thought, so that activating that desire becomes itself the field's critical faculty. A critical regionalist approach to Latin America is proposed as a "systematic exploration of the fact that no systematic exploration can today be understood as something other than a ruse of universal reason—even if and when such (latter) systematic exploration believes itself to be merely local or subaltern" (53).

Hybridity, the subject of Moreiras's last chapter, offers a prime monitory example of the constitutive risk of cultural theory in the way it moves through the machine of cultural coding under the sign of flexible accumulation and emerges the empty signifier of heterogeneity for contemporary politics. In order to recoup the force of hybridity as a reserve for subalternity, understood as that which remains outside hegemony at any given moment, Moreiras insists on theorizing it in two turns. Along with the constative cultural hybridity that is necessary but insufficient to maintain the possibility of an alternative to hegemonic articulation, we must attend also to hybridity's savage side, the remainder that is by definition excluded from cultural politics. Savage hybridity prevents the closure of politics around the commodified hybridity of cultural heterogeneity; it is "the site of an abyssal exclusion, beyond any principle of reason, and it marks the (im)possible locus of enunciation of the subaltern perspective" (294).

Moreiras's rendering of hybridity is composed of a series of theories of cultural difference from a variety of contexts brought into constellation. The notion of double articulation is borrowed from Paul Gilroy's proposals regarding the politics of cultural diaspora in the black Atlantic, which distinguish at the outset between politics of fulfillment—a cultural politics "mostly content to play occidental rationality at its own game"—and politics of transfiguration, which is exemplified by Gilroy in black musical expression and "strives in pursuit of the sublime, struggling to repeat the unrepeatable, to present the unrepresentable" (37).[3] The hybrid's cultural/

savage dynamic comes from Homi Bhabha's discussion of the postmodern and the postcolonial, a discussion similarly aimed at the articulation of the fleeting material of experience with the temporalization of discourse in the emergence of political subjects. This involves, following Barthes, a doubleness of writing that is "at once very cultural and very savage": The experience of language "outside the sentence," as Barthes says, demands an "art of guiding one's body into discourse, in such a way that the subject's accession to, and erasure in, the signifier as individuated is paradoxically accompanied by its remainder, an afterbirth, a double. Its noise . . . makes vocal and visible, across the flow of the sentence's communicative core, the struggle involved in the insertion of agency . . . into discourse" (184). The thrust of both of these intertexts is echoed in Spivak's strategic essentialism, refigured by Moreiras as tactical essentialism, which in her later-disavowed introduction to *Selected Subaltern Studies* postulated a method for "breaking" theory strategically to speak of a subaltern consciousness that nevertheless remains the "absolute limit of the place where history is narrativized into logic" ("Deconstructing Historiography" 16). In gathering these theoretical instances, all committed in one or another way to prising open the limit of historical and political representativity, Moreiras hopes to outline a program of subalternist affirmation able to work in two registers at once, maneuvering the negative or savage side of hybridity over against the positive as an "automatic corrective": "The relation between the tactical essentialism contained in subalternist theoretical fictions and the radicality of subalternism as a thinking of negativity . . . is to be thought not dialectically but through the notion of a double articulation or double register whereby the subalternist will be able to engage both radical negativity and tactical positivity simultaneously and distinctly" (*The Exhaustion of Difference* 285).

Disciplinary Aporetics

The tenor of Moreiras's arguments, as well as the general idiom of the texts it places in conversation, owes to certain core features of conceptualizations of democracy to come prominent in Derrida's later work. Like democracy to come, savage hybridity expresses the holding open of thought to an always as-yet-indefinable change "to come," an opening, as Derrida states in *Specters of Marx*, "of [the] gap between an infinite promise . . . and the determined, necessary but also necessarily inadequate forms of what has to be measured against this promise" (81). Because political cynosures like justice, democracy, the promise, or the messianic spill over the claims made by any particular redress—and, in fact, make particulars possible in that very spillage—they serve as their own limit, offering an autocorrection of any rampant fiction of self-presence. For this reason, Derrida holds that political concepts are im/possible: They give currency to discrete demands that can be heard and satisfied thanks to the infinite responsibility of the idea, its openness to the sheer heterogeneity of items to come into its care, yet this satisfaction (the notion, for example, that "justice has been done") is only a murky ersatz of the idea, a base homage that paradoxically answers to the concept's potential through its insufficiency.[4] The aporetic relation between referent and concept thus becomes the latter's possibility and limit. The defense of the name *democracy* in *Politics of Friendship* formulates this principle:

> One keeps this right strategically to mark what is no longer a strategic affair: the limit between the conditional . . . and the unconditional which, from the outset, will have inscribed a self-deconstructive force in the very motif of democracy, the possibility and the duty for democracy itself to de-limit itself. Democracy is the *autos* of deconstructive self-delimitation. Delimitation not only in the name of a regulative idea and an indefinite perfectibility, but every time in the singular urgency of a here and now. Precisely through the abstract and potentially indifferent thought of number and equality. This thought certainly can impose homogenizing calculability . . . but it perhaps also keeps the power of universalizing . . . the account taken of anonymous and irreducible singularities, infinitely different and thereby indifferent to particular difference, to the raging quest for identity corrupting the most indestructible desires of the idiom. (105–6)

The passage contains all the components of aporetic political concepts as well as the relevant grounds for their transposition to disciplinary thought, to conceiving objects like Latin America, Francophonie, or the postcolonial also as an autodeconstruction. Strategically wielded, the name of democracy harbors the myriad differences that outrun its appropriative reach but which, in their resistance to the "raging quest for identity" of the name, open a space for political practice here and now. The promise afforded democracy by its unfulfillable instances, its to-come-ness, is the measure of its autodeconstructive capacity. In the ambivalence of the qualifier "to come," Derrida highlights the risk and adventure of deconstruction, which at once enjoins one to proceed confidently in the name of democracy and chastens those claims by holding out for uninstantiable difference: The "to" of the "to come" is an undecidable limit that "wavers between imperative injunction (call or performative) and the patient perhaps of messianicity (nonperformative exposure to what comes, to what can always not come or has already come)" (*Rogues* 91).

The attempt of Moreiras's double articulation of hybridity to infuse disciplinary practice with the basic insights of autodeconstruction resonates with the direction of cultural and literary critique at large in the decade since the publication of *The Exhaustion of Difference*. The most influential model of this trend may be Spivak's bid to reconceptualize Comparative Literature in *Death of a Discipline* along the lines of Derrida's use of teleopoiesis, imagined as a turning back of the Euro-U.S. focus of literary comparativity through a planetary community "imaginative[ly] ma[de]" (31) in the active acknowledgement of the discipline's "definitive future anteriority, [its] 'to-come'-ness, [its] 'will have happened' quality" (6). Her more recent *Other Asias* takes the same move further afield, attempting to name "Asia" as the "instrument of an altered citation" for an interdisciplinary space of thought flexible enough to eclipse metonymic renderings of the region in restrictive correspondence with the West, so that India-, China-, or Asian-American-centered Asias give way to pluralistic continentalism. Spivak's "critical regionalism," molded largely of a piece with Moreiras's examination of Latin Americanism, is also inherently aporetic: "We are looking at the claim to the word 'Asia,' however historically unjustified. To search thus for an originary name is not a pathology. Yet it must at the same time be resisted. The desire is its own resistance" (213).[5] In Latin Americanist debates, Moreiras's own conclusions are reiterated by David Johnson, who opens a 2007 special issue of *South Atlantic Quarterly* dedicated to Latin America with a long detour through Derrida. For Johnson, too, the most pressing obstacle to thinking Latin America is the reliance on an assumption of an irreproachable conveyance of the will and consciousness of such an object; dismantling this assumption (Johnson specifically targets the philosophy of Enrique Dussel) requires one to preface Latin American Studies with the lessons of spacing and autoimmunity that peg singular expression, any statement of a "Latin American" subject, to iterability and temporization, with the result that "Latin American studies is impossible, but no less necessary for this impossibility, because it is unlocatable" (16).

The impetus for disciplinary aporetics, particularly as they are credited with having a sharper acumen for the study of cultures wrought along old imperial lines and under the international division of intellectual labor, is the conviction that autodeconstruction in the vein of democracy to come can muster the best effort for the ongoing critique of identity at the heart of cultural and literary fields today. What must still be determined is if, or how, that conviction can achieve the desired metamorphosis of postcolonial studies comparative scholarship hopes to deliver. Much of the probity of the theorization of difference in a double register, as opposed to earlier thematizations of ambivalence or subalternity, appears to find a certain guarantee in the strategic nature of its undertaking.[6] Read in a straightforward manner, strategy denotes an intervention of calculated risk in a game of political stakes: The act of naming thus takes a chance of gain or loss pursuant to the contingencies of the field in which it intervenes. Yet, as Derrida's passage on democracy quoted above illustrates, the status of any given conceptual referent is no longer a question of strategy; it is the "limit between the conditional . . . and the unconditional," which is already overwrought by the movement of self-deconstruction. It is precisely this elevation of matters of historical contingency—the "gamble" imputed to democracy to come—to an unconditional that provokes materialist critics to signal deconstruction's indifference to, or even masking of, theory's real relationship to politics. Adornian critics, in particular, express irritation at what they see as Derrida's expulsion of the mediation of subject and object from the stage of political action: Asha Varadharajan, for example, remarks upon the oxymoronic phrasing of *différance* as a "strategy without finality" in Derrida's earlier work, musing that it announces its operation, elaborated in the notion of play, as a self-contained economy. The circularity of a strategy with only itself as end, she points out, effectively neutralizes the range of historical consequences that follow success and failure: Thus rendering its material repercussions indistinguishable, *différance* is easy to understand as an "endless calculus" that animates the necessity of strategy for its own sake in which "one wins and loses each time." "Because the subject and object in question have been dismissed from the indifferent scene of différance, Derrida is not obliged to explain who loses and who wins and in what historical circumstances this game of chance and necessity is played" (*Exotic Parodies* 32). There where the sum of possible outcomes of political decision in the realm of action are folded "from the outset" into the realm of thought, as this view has it, critique no longer seeks to change but to comprehend the situation of identity and difference within existing arrangements, and in perfecting its understanding of such arrangements, to maintain them.[7]

What relevance do these objections have for the double articulation of disciplinary aporetics? That depends on how one understands the distinguishing qualities of a decision designed to intervene in a set of im/possible relations. For Derrida, identity's every self-constituting act must cite its spectral, non-present iterations: No identity without this contamination, but also, because of this contamination, no identity. The fundamental movement of Derrida's "autoimmunity" is at once to hearken identity into existence and to prevent its complete existence "as such," thereby providing both the ground and limit of thought. For a knowledge irreparably bound by this movement, action, decision, and responsibility—in short, everything involved in "real" politics—must remain unconditionally vulnerable to the heterogeneity that may alter or nullify its positive content, while avoiding turning said vulnerability into a program for thought. As Derrida writes at the end of *Rogues*, an appropriate decision along these lines is "a transaction that is each time novel, each time without precedent . . . between, on the one side, the reasoned exigency of calculation or conditionality and, on the other, the intransigent, nonnegotiable exigency of unconditional incalculability" (150). It is the aporetic nature of any decision that impossibly deliberates between calculation and the incalculable, as on the unconditional ground of decision that, in Derrida's words, "strategically . . . mark[s] what is no longer a strategic affair." As regards the foregoing points, I think materialists have been hasty to misconstrue democracy to come and related concepts as hermetic and essentially conservative exercises, especially in the failure to recognize the ways they are predicated on locating the ground of knowledge in the current irretrievability of its heterogeneous particulars (the insurmountable divorce from subaltern, animal, or natural worlds required for knowing) and, more important, in the demand to transform that state of things. The acute discomfort with defining deconstructive thought as a "strategy," however, remains well warranted, inasmuch as this definition invites us to view the interruption between calculable and incalculable navigated by the aporetic decision as a mastered terrain. In other words, precisely because the conditions of knowledge are not available to knowledge, because every decision, so to speak, is a jab in the dark of what it decides upon, the breach between thought and its unconditional grounding cannot be grasped objectively and thus subordinated to subjective knowledge. If all calculation necessarily dissipates the unpredictable force of the "to-come," then there is strictly no stepping outside that fact to guarantee its truth: Even the im/possible is damaged by our cognition of it. The mediation between knowledge and its other will not be isolated and extracted, for it is already, as Adorno says, "in the innermost cell of thought" (*Negative Dialectics* 408). Brought to light, it becomes an absolute for itself, an appendage to critique rather than its motor.

Herein lies, I believe, the error of double articulation. As we know, the notion of the hybrid that has become popular for studying cultural difference in Latin Americanism and related fields remains susceptible to reabsorption and reification within the constraints of hegemonic cultural-political value coding, under which it no longer contests but reaffirms reigning power dynamics. For Moreiras, it is thus necessary to think hybridity simultaneously and separately in two registers: The cultural hybridity that inhabits the grid of ideology is distinguished from its negative, savage side, which exists to "reveal its limits" and "ideological character" (*The Exhaustion of Difference* 267). The latter is proposed as a "corrective counterconcept" (267) for hybridity in its dominant sense, one meant to "preserv[e], or hol[d] in reserve, the site of the subaltern" as well as "the site of a subalternist politics" (294). Rather than hand over the defiant capacities of hybridity to its unruly market translations, in which they always take a gamble on being captured and recoded as exchange value, Moreiras clears a space figuratively to house hybridity's negative side. It should be noted that the proposal of double hybridity is positioned specifically to counteract the underlying premise of academic models of identity politics that proliferated during the 1990s, which were legitimated by the belief that collective identities based on ethnic hybridity or local singularity could withstand the pull of neoliberal logic. Such programs, Moreiras argues, lose sight of the fact that oppositional identities can only respond to this logic through its logical inversion: Defined by its resistance to capital, hybridity remains trapped within its structure, represented politically by the transcendental subject. By separating the positive fiction and negative flight between which hybridity wavers, double articulation means to recall conceptually how politics acts beyond subjectivity, how subjects are always split. Its dual registers offer a place to think "the conditions of possibility for the constitution of the sociopolitical subject as at the same time conditions of impossibility" (291). Together they form an "abyssal foundation for subjective constitution" that is "a nonsite" or "ambivalence itself" (291).

But ultimately, only the subject can benefit from cognizing its own splitting, by exteriorizing for knowledge non-identity's unforeseeable share in its self-expression. Once the relation between hybridity's cultural and savage faces is thus circumscribed, once we have adjudicated, however tactically, on their compenetration, we become prescient to their oscillation and regard objectively what is really a matter internal to thought. For the subject that anticipates and performatively holds in reserve the savage substrate of its own im/possibility, decision can no longer be, as Derrida envisions it, "a transaction that is each time novel, each time without precedent" (*Rogues* 150), but a prefiguring of its undulating perhaps, over which the deciding subject now presides. Staking a claim in double articulation's positive register for hybridity, the postcolonial, or a Latin Americanist or francophone object of study, we can avoid falsely pontificating about the rightful stance of our intervention this side of multicultural capitalism, but only if the ground of our claim is already posited above the commingling it speaks for. From there it is a short step to confirming, *pace* all of Moreiras's efforts, the identity of hybridity, to admitting "the delusion that [the hybrid] is but a specimen" (Adorno, *Negative Dialectics* 408) of this commingling. The tactical separation of double articulation imperceptibly segues to a gesture of identity thinking: In Derrida's terms, it would thus neutralize the eventfulness of the event to come that the defense of critique guards unconditionally, "by securing for itself . . . the power that an ipseity gives itself to produce the event of which it speaks [and] appropriat[ing] for itself a calculable mastery over it"

(*Rogues* 152). From the negative dialectical standpoint, it risks falling into the Heideggerian ruse that projected Being as something in abeyance of its particular beings, as something added to being rather than enmeshed in its instances. The unassailability of Being, Adorno insists, ends up reinstating the omnipotence of the subject that it wished to foreclose, by curtaining off the supplement Being provides to objects as an entity. It "conserves . . . what it is rising against: the screening thought structures for whose removal its own program calls. On the pretext of bringing to light what underlies them, those structures are once more, imperceptibly, turned into the 'in itself' which a reified consciousness makes of them anyway" (*Negative Dialectics* 85).

Wishful Thinking and Metaphysical Experience

From either position—as well as from Moreiras's way of seeing things—the core issue is how one accounts for and gives measure to the responsibility of critique. Rephrased in the framework of Lazarus's quarrel with postcolonial studies: On what philosophical basis does critique derive the possibility and the demand that academic names for the postcolonial not be converted into an envoy of imperial logic? It is agreed that the current indigence of our concepts, insofar as we are able to think it, proves the absence of and need for a noncoercive relationship between subject and object, and that the silencing of the object is itself the best indication of our distance from a world where it could speak. But the falseness of existing representations, as Adorno has it, cannot be remedied in any positive maneuver through the tactical withdrawal of identity; rather, the only way around identity is through it. If indeed identity cannot be helped, this does not mean that it is all wrong; on the contrary, a totally false identity would have no reason to be because thought itself originates as a response to some material need. Thus, for any name given to an object, although its concept cannot be said to be "real," "there would be no conceiving it if we were not urged to conceive it by something in the matter" (*Negative Dialectics* 404). The urge tethering thought to the world provides a historical index of negative dialectics: Both its kernel and its trajectory are intimately linked to society's ills, though neither is exhausted by social mediation.[8] For this reason, as Fredric Jameson points out of Adorno's sociological discourse, the flaws in knowledge exist because contemporary society, the object as well as the subject of knowledge, is itself animated by contradiction (38); addressing the shortcomings of knowledge is only possible through a fundamental transformation of society. This primary guarantee and injunction of critique is the defining quality of "wishful thinking," brought up in the conclusion of *Negative Dialectics*. The wishful mode of thought

> cannot be a deductive context of judgments about things in being, and neither can it be conceived after the model of an absolute otherness terribly defying thought. It would be possible only as a legible constellation of things in being. From those it would get the material without which it would not be; it would not transfigure the existence of its elements, however, but would bring them into a configuration in which the elements unite to form a script. To that end, metaphysics must know how to wish. . . . [T]hinking, itself a mode of conduct, contains the need—the vital need, at the outset—in itself. The need is what we think from, even where we disdain wishful thinking. The motor of the need is the effort that involves thought as action. The object of critique is not the need in thinking, but the relationship between the two. (407–8)

How is wishful thinking different from double articulation?[9] The second, as we have seen, strives to be accountable to difference by equipping thought with an awareness of its own instability, thereby acknowledging in a positive register its entanglement with the nonconceptual others of its negative register. Desire, the vehicle of this strategy—as in the desire for "Latin America" or "Asia"—extends a reticent invitation for its object's expression, reticent because no good-faith anticipation of achieving the object itself is available within its representational scheme. My argument is that this cedes to identity thinking when, in advancing a conceptual figure for the entwinement of representational labor and its objects, critique posits a vantage point privy to that entwinement from which disciplinary practice would excise its own involvement in the historical development it contemplates. Wishful thinking also denotes a desire to understand difference in full awareness that the path to the object is hopelessly distorted by false conceits, but rather than attempt to render those obstacles directly (as though the "need in thinking" were itself the object of critique), it accrues minute impressions that point negatively to what lies outside of reach, so that the expression of what is as yet illegible becomes legible through the composition of its instances. The "wish" of wishful thinking is to overthrow the conceptual regime in which it is caught by compiling instances of non-identity into a script. This can only be carried out, of course, through experience, precisely the "effort that involves thought as action." Indeed, as Simon Jarvis defines it, negative dialectics is "thought's repeated experience of its inability finally to identify what is non-identical to it" (173).

To understand why wishful thinking is ultimately an experience, and in what it consists, we must go briefly to the main points of the last section of *Negative Dialectics*, "Metaphysics after Auschwitz." The pressing concern here is to determine what, if any, future remains for transcendental philosophy in the wake of World War II. If Auschwitz has any meaning, Adorno says, it resides in the proven nonexistence of any reasoning able to digest the horror of recent history. When the winning transcendental formulas of the day fail to make coherent the reduction of human life to a mere quantity slated for extermination, only the sensible alerts us to their incapacity; only on "the somatic, unmeaningful stratum of life [which] is the stage of suffering" (365) is philosophy's poverty exposed. Thus "the course of history forces materialism upon metaphysics" (365). Adorno's point is that the encounter with material exclusively attests to the need from which thinking occurs: Where ideal categories parade as the authority on finding the lesson in unthinkable tragedy, only the blind residue of the sensible tells otherwise. On the other hand, no reprieve from the fact of suffering will result from the comprehension of things solely as they are: The relegation of our cognition to pure immanence becomes just as much a prison overseen by existing ideological structures as its opposite. The feebleness of both metaphysics and materialism taken alone make inevitable what Adorno considers the fatal scourge of identity thinking, the "withering of experience": the total encroachment of institutional and/or discursive precalculation on worldly encounter. After the colonization of exchange value has so engulfed life forms that we no longer retain a bodily index for its alternative, there is no more sensing how given reality differs from what it could or should be: A life thus falsely fulfilled is death, total exchange without remainder, completed identity.

To bring thought back from the brink of the disastrous end of experience requires an understanding of experience in which the metaphysical and the material supplement each other, what Adorno calls "metaphysical experience." The clearest illustrations of this notion involve moments of discovery about the diremption between subject and object, between idea and material, which communicate the possibility and need for something unprecedented: The child who imagines the singular delights of a whimsically named village will be disappointed by the reality, but "his mistake creates the model of experience, of a concept that will end up as the concept of the thing itself, not as a poor projection from things" (*Negative Dialectics* 373)[10]; likewise, the dogged nothingness of the nihilist will ultimately be found lacking when the memories of ephemeral kindnesses "make the ideal of nothingness evaporate" (380). Metaphysical experience is speculative, but negatively so: From particulars it recollects the echoes of an absent whole. One of Adorno's most Benjaminian statements reasons that "grayness could not fill us with despair if our minds did not harbor the concept of different colors, scattered traces of which are not absent from the negative whole" (377). Experience provides the negative proof of non-identity, the proof that thought has not yet reached its closure—that without imagining color, grayness would be meaningless—and that it therefore can and must create a new society to make experience equal to its longing.

Experience of the Undeconstructible

Adorno's arguments regarding the relationship of thought, non-identity, and experience encapsulated in his idea of wishful thinking allow us to pinpoint the potential fallacy of double articulation as a comparative disciplinary approach to the postcolonial concept. I hope I have made that point. But, at the same time, wishful thinking's comparison with double articulation reveals deep convergences in the way each orients thought to its others: In both cases, significantly, experience becomes the proper site for this effort. Indeed, although experience is not explicitly theorized in *The Exhaustion of Difference*, the book's very first asseveration is that "Latin Americanism lives, if it is living, in a certain precariousness of experience . . . unleashed because the waning of the critical subject involves the dissolution of the critical object itself" (2); even savage hybridity is referred to at one point as "an experience of thought" (290). Not coincidentally, the theoretical antecedents of double articulation drawn upon by Moreiras are also characterized by an experiential, nondiscursive base for critical thought. Gilroy's transgressive politics "exists on a lower frequency where it is played, danced, and acted, as well as sung and sung about, because words . . . will never be enough to communicate its unsayable claims to truth" (37). Bhabha's elucubrations about the savage side of writing, similarly, are geared to capture the production of social subjects outside of words, their "corporeal exteriorization of discourse," through his idea of the time lag: His sensuous appeal to Barthes's carnal stereography envisages a theoretical description of "a form of cultural experience and identity . . . that does not set up a theory-practice polarity, [or make theory] prior to the contingency of social experience. This 'beyond theory' is itself a liminal form of signification that creates a space for the contingent, indeterminate articulation of 'social experience'" (257). The common thread running through all of these moments, what Moreiras, Gilroy, and Bhabha all consider essential to theorizing the radicality of postcolonial objects, is the attempt to resituate the trace that sets off discourse at the heart of their determinations not as something placed in reserve, but as the nongraspable particle that grates experience from within, driving thought to an awareness of social mediation's failure to exhaust the things it identifies.

Part of the supposed rift between apparatuses of cultural and postcolonial studies influenced by deconstruction and the world of material interests can be explained by the underemphasis on the role of experience in their vision of critique. Against the almost absolute dearth of critical formulations of Derrida's idea of experience, Roland Végső has recently analyzed deconstruction's philosophical engagement with politics against the grain of dominant interpretations that cite its inadequate consideration of political subjectivity. Végső signals the ways deconstruction itself is, in fact, an experience.[11] Not only are the major terms of deconstruction (the promise, mourning, friendship, justice, aporia, etc.) qualified as experience at the crucial points of their delineation, but Derrida's theoretical discourses even from before his "political turn" are centered on an aporetic relation that makes deconstruction possible precisely as an experience.[12] Because the unique insight of deconstruction is the inclusion of im/possibility as the limit of all spatial formations, the "necessary heteronomy of all discourses," deconstruction cannot count itself exempt from this condition but advances through reflection on its own limit, the "undeconstructible condition of deconstruction." As Végső submits, "what makes deconstruction the exceptional case is that it claims to coincide fully with its very own heteronomy . . . its extraphilosophical outside" (138). In other words, unlike other philosophical viewpoints that are subjected to deconstruction, so to speak, from outside, deconstruction denotes the realization of the im/possible condition of all thought, in which that realization is first and foremost included. Deconstruction cannot simply subject this undeconstructible condition that inhabits it to infinite deconstruction because it is not itself universalizable; rather, its existence requires the minimum distance between the structural place accorded undeconstructability and the sense of it in a given situation, a distance that is available only in experience. Without a doubt, it is this distance in which, as Derrida writes, the im/possible "announces itself, . . . precedes me, swoops down upon and seizes me *here and now* in a nonvirtualizable way" (*Rogues* 84). For Végső, deconstruction is thus the "experience of the conditions of experience" (130), the point of nonclosure in thought where subjectivization and the decision emerge. If deconstruction will not permit an authentic experience of fully present subjects, neither can it tolerate the endless deconstruction of experience, for only the self-limitation of deconstruction "here and now" allows it to survive: Experience thus provides deconstruction's crucially political dimension. It is not illogical to conclude, on these grounds, that the deconstructive elaboration of experience proves the responsibility of thought precisely as the last frontier against the "withering of experience," in which "the reified, hardened plaster-cast of events takes the place of events themselves" (Adorno, *Minima Moralia* 55).

If double articulation and wishful thinking, despite their divergences, touch in the notion of experience, is there a disciplinary practice able to adapt one to the other?[13] It would be something like an experience of the undeconstructible, but one whose savageness retains its contingent volatility. In restituting to the conceptual realm the priority of the non-identity it names, wishful thinking cannot be content to appoint the savage side of its object to an absolute limit but insists on opening itself to the savageness sensible, however negatively, in actually existing suffering and inequality: It pursues the same goals of double articulation by other means. Thus although negative dialectics, like democracy to come, activates a certain messianic desire, the temporalization that opens its messianic horizon is not absolute but historic: It is not given structurally but in the imprint of non-identity in its contextual distribution. In this it differs from Derrida's messianic each time he insists, as he does in *Rogues*, on the "absolute interruption" between the calculable and incalculable, between knowledge and "the moment and structure of the *il faut*" (145). Experience, for Adorno, is nothing other than the sensible record of injustice, which witnesses an alternative temporal index by urging us toward a transformed state of affairs. Dialectical im/possibility deconstructs historicity by recognizing how historical time is constituted by the unfulfilled, the unfinished or violated instances of the past that supplement the present, demanding from our own Now their recompense—but anticipating that recompense, it anticipates its own birth into a time that would be real. A disciplinary postcolonial practice could establish itself in that waiting for the real, starting with the premise, for example, that "the concept [postcolonial/Latin America/Francophonie] is not real . . . but there would be no conceiving it if we were not urged to conceive it by something in the matter." Not only would disciplinary study then have to reconnect with its historical conditions of emergence, it would confront its ethical political responsibility as a matter of risk renewed in every encounter with its objects, where "fearlessly passive, it entrusts itself to its own experience" (Adorno, "Subject and Object" 506).

Conclusion: Khatibi's Bi-Langue

It remains to be asked whether the amendment of double articulation through Adorno's negative dialectics makes a worthy respondent to Lazarus's and Syrotinski's questions about the postcolonial, particularly as the spread of that term becomes a comparative and perhaps universalized terrain.[14] That is, can it satisfy the conflict between deconstruction's challenge to postcolonial thought "to leave its grounding in socio-historical reference . . . by taking seriously the epistemological uncertainties that deconstruction has so rigorously articulated" and deconstruction's need to "provid[e] convincing responses to claims about its lack of relevance to . . . the so-called 'real' world" (Syrotinski 4)? I would like to return to a more specific focus and explore one possible answer with a closing excursion through the work of

Moroccan author Abdelkebir Khatibi. Khatibi makes a suitable figure for this purpose both because he is one of a handful of francophone intellectuals—along with Edouard Glissant and Frantz Fanon—with a wide, if epidermic, appeal in Latin American studies, and because his poetic and narrative concerns are articulated at the dead center of deconstruction's imbrication with postcoloniality.[15] His hallmark concept of the *bi-langue*, developed in the essays of *Maghreb pluriel* and enacted in his novel *Amour bilingue*, revolutionized the relationship of francophone authors to the French language by putting maternal North African language(s) to work in the French text—not in confrontation with it or assimilated to it but as an infiltration that dismantles the self-sufficiency of the language from within. The *bi-langue* thus does not restore any original native language but travels around wreaking havoc on the proposed propriety of all language. Critical studies of the *bi-langue* almost without exception hail it as an exercise in deconstructive unmooring of subjectivity and identity, a theoretico-poetic process informed more or less autobiographically by Khatibi's own experience entering the French language from the colonial heteroglossia of mid-century Morocco. The writer's well-known friendship with Derrida and public admiration for his theories has no doubt inflected this reception: Indeed, it is impossible to deny the consanguinity of Khatibi's main narrative topics and a work such as *Monolingualism of the Other*, in which Derrida famously announces, "I only have one language; it is not mine" as the dictum of the "appropriative madness" of all language. The thematization of exile and translation in critical readings circles around a certain summation, as that found in *Monolingualism*, of the way all appropriation of language is engulfed by language's own jealousies "without appropriation," the sheer madness of language (24). This madness destroys in Khatibi's writing any consistent assertion of a subject "I": For Réda Bensmaïa, probably the most cited reader of Khatibi apart from Derrida himself, the *bi-langue* displayed in *Amour bilingue* announces that "there is no longer any self-presence [of the narrator and the reader]," but only "infinite permutation, endless reverberation, and the play of blinding mirrors" (*Experimental Nations* 115).

Certainly these elements are a central feature of the *bi-langue*, as Khatibi's own critical engagement with Derrida affirms.[16] Reading a book like *Amour bilingue* through this intertext is all the more edifying for studies oriented to postcolonial issues because it ropes the former's decidedly abstract narrative acrobatics back into the historical relations among Berber, Farabé, and French in Maghrebi colonial society, a prospect that has also attracted plenty of attention to autobiographical writing by Derrida or Hélène Cixous.[17] For readings which collate the *bi-langue* in an already familiar register of translation and untranslatability, of the endless slippage of origins, the primary conclusion is that the *bi-langue*, as the site where other languages work away at the surface of French, is the bridge between deconstruction and the postcolonial. Living at the limits of language's intelligibility, the *bi-langue* silently mines the quiddity of French: it *is* this undermining. It is easy here to place such conclusions in counterpoint with the oversights of double articulation I have outlined by observing, for example, how they make Arab and Berber into admixtures rather than agents of the *bi-langue*. This would mean that these languages' haunting of Khatibi's French narrative, raised to the level of motif, already speaks for any resistance or nonidentity they might deliver into it. Any singularized contradiction is thus bundled up beforehand, calculated into a risk without hazard.

This understanding of the *bi-langue* portrays as a state or condition what Khatibi emphatically describes as a struggle on the order of experience. For the bilingual author, it is the struggle to answer somehow to the untranslatable currents of the maternal (oral) language, the life of that language, at work in the French text: The untranslatable, as he states in *Maghreb pluriel*, "is not that unsayable, inaudible and forever closed-off beyond, but a labor of sleep and insomnia . . . , hallucinating all translation and which dreams for its own account from language to language, and in which the particles spring up day and night in the waking dream of every writing" [*L'intraduisible n'est pas cet au-delà indicible, inaudible et fermé à tout jamais, mais un travail du sommeil et de l'insomnie . . . , hallucinant toute traduction et qui rêve pour son compte de langue en langue, et dont les parcelles jaillissent le jour ou la nuit dans le rêve éveillé de toute écriture*] (197).[18] This characterization of the *bi-langue* fundamentally as a waking dream, a kind of suffering and joy, is best seen in the prose poetry of *Amour bilingue*. The novel tells of the love affair between a French woman and a Moroccan male narrator, but more than anything it is occupied in the painstaking rendering of how it feels to live in multiple languages and write in only one. The unnamable, innumerable fragments of language that, in many scenes, flood the protagonist's imagination overtax the supposed organicity of Frenchness, but their chaos also negatively invokes a hidden clearness, "an impossible clarity, a clarity that suffers in the text, a clarity of thought struck by the unthought of" [*une clarté impossible, une clarté qui souffre dans le texte, une clarté de pensée frappée par l'impensée*] (*Maghreb pluriel* 197). The characters' carnal passion symbolizes the strenuous quest for this clarity: It makes them sick, it is even lethal, but the *bi-langue* is also intense pleasure, expressed—as language always is by Khatibi—by a masculine heterosexual erotic idiom.

The sine qua non of the *bi-langue* is the flight from identity, to write against one's name, as Khatibi often says. The characters of *Amour bilingue* try to disappear in language; at times they consider suicide, simply to detach from who they are said to be. After the break-up, in a final *compte rendu* of his ex-lover's life upon her return home, the narrator triumphantly relates how she learns to live against language, seizing on its errors and tiny truths, with a "devouring energy" that nevertheless is not silent: "To float above the universe and above language? No one is imaginary. No one! She was the countenance of the uncountenanceable, around which this other-thought revolved ceaselessly. As far as the unthought of was concerned, she felt this obsession only to differentiate herself, whatever it cost, from any concept that brought her to her knees" [*Flotter au dessus de l'univers et de la langue? Personne n'est imaginaire. Personne! Elle était la figure de l'infigurable, autour de laquelle tournait et tournait cette pensée-autre. De l'impensé, elle ne sentait que cette hantise de se différencier, coute que coute, de tout concept qui la mit à genoux*] (*Love in Two Languages* 110; *Amour bilingue* 122). The *bi-langue* lives against itself discretely and minutely in the contradictions that afflict French expression of the Maghreb. Its goal is not to denounce violence in silence but to speak, to produce language and literature ("[to] continue in this set direction, this other-thought, which invites me to speak, again and again. What expectation of life!" [*continuer sur ce point fixe, cette pensée-autre, que m'invite à prendre la parole, encore et encore. Quelle espérance de vie!*] *Love in Two Languages* 113; *Amour bilingue* 125), in order to conduct thought to an entirely new form, a *pensée autre*. The wonderful thing, says Khatibi, would be to write in all languages at once, a translation that is not even a translation because it touches everything at once (*Maghreb pluriel* 205).

At a moment when Khatibi's work has settled among French Studies critics to the status of a "first-generation" postcolonial approach to language issues, I think reading the *bi-langue* against the deconstructive troping that seems to overwhelm its reception can offer an incisive apparatus to gauge popular discourses of cosmopolitanism and translation, especially given that the international visibility of authors from North Africa, as Emily Apter has explained, oscillates between black-out and white-out, between an absolute absence from the market and the smooth "translationese" favored by distributors of global literature (108).[19] I imagine such a reading running parallel to Adorno's comments on the potential of foreign words: Against the organicist veneer of language, he claims, these foreign assailants express an alienation that "strikes the stream of language, which gleams painfully in it" ("On the Use of Foreign Words" 290). The contradictions embedded in language's self-sufficiency cannot be resolved by assimilation but only by a change in society itself, the way society "names itself along with things" (289–90). Writers of foreign words, regardless of the importance they ascribe to them, in fact access "the power of an unknown, genuine language that is not open to any calculus, a language that arises only in pieces and out of the disintegration of the existing one" (291).

Adorno asserts the dissident force of foreign words as so many pieces of a disaggregated key that, compiled from their disaccord with the fiction of organic language, glimpse its undoing. I have suggested that a similar tack can prove fruitful for the postcolonial in its venture into comparative terrain by focusing critique on the experience of antagonism which prompts it to transform the conditions it intends to name. Oriented to the protest the objects they stand in for ply against them, savage hybridity or *bi-langue* serve to fulfill the dual responsibility of thought, not to pawn what it thinks as totally knowable but not to foreclose it as unknowable either. Through deeper bilateral investigations of Latin Americanism and Francophone Studies, this kind of practice can build a variegated terrain of vectors for the postcolonial, testing its purchase beyond the usual historical and epistemological identities claimed for it and working to compose its script. This is how postcolonial studies knows how to wish.

CHAPTER 2

José Lezama Lima and the Gnosis of American Expression

The last chapter ended by suggesting that a method of critical practice drawn both from Alberto Moreiras's double articulation and Theodor Adorno's wishful thinking could be beneficial for comparative studies of postcoloniality because it retains the skepticism of deconstructive approaches already popular with postcolonial critique without removing academic thought from the field of historic action where it encounters and apprehends its objects. This method, I concluded, would involve an experience of the undeconstructible, the experience of the limits of thought where the preponderance of the object becomes palpable and determinate. This chapter and the next explore the possibilities of wishful thinking in the poetics of Cuban José Lezama Lima and Martinican Édouard Glissant, analyzing specifically the efforts of these authors to articulate an expression of place in their discussions of "America" and the Caribbean, respectively. Neither Lezama nor Glissant is concerned to present a political program; rather, their determinations of Latin America and the Caribbean promote a poetics of place that, in retraining the imaginaries connected to these objects, would be capable of transforming the roles and configuration of regional-historic models of identity. My interest in examining these poetics is to unearth their consequences for material history, something that is rarely, if ever, addressed in the work of Lezama or Glissant. That is, can the properly cultural or poetic investigations of autochthony teach us to orient geopolitical constructions to the non-identities they suppress—the mute victims, subaltern histories, and environmental and social destruction that compose these areas in so many indecipherable ways? And if so, can they steer clear of the identity thinking of both essentialist regional and commodified globalist claims? I rely on a set of Benjamin and Adorno's elaborations of dialectics to delve better into the more recondite material plane of Lezama and Glissant's work: Here, in particular, Benjamin's theses against the homogeneous time of history and certain of Adorno and Horkheimer's cogitations on myth will help me extract from Lezamian American expression a challenge to the axis of locationist thought, in a baroque aesthetic experience of time and place that in properly Adornian style attempts "to be entranced in one place without squinting at the universal" (*Negative Dialectics* 373).

Lo difícil: Expression of the Imago

José Lezama Lima (1910–1976) produced one of the most prodigious and notoriously difficult corpuses of Latin American twentieth-century literature. The trajectory of his work spans more than three decades and pursues, through several volumes of poetry and essays, two novels, and the journal *Orígenes*, the ongoing treatment of aesthetic, philosophical, and religious themes whose intersection is best captured in his famous "poetic system." Conjoining mystic Catholic gnosis with the counterpoint of a dazzlingly broad sphere of intertextual references, Lezama's work leads readers through meditations on the possibility of human knowledge and redemption predicated, in neobaroque fashion, on the accumulation of images, allusions, and poetic excess. In *La expresión americana*, these pursuits coalesce in the attempt to trace the contours of an autochthonous American expression. The five essays of the book were originally delivered in a series of lectures in La Habana at the beginning of 1957: Proceeding more or less chronologically from the sixteenth-century Spanish Conquest through the twentieth-century avant-garde, through examples taken from many parts of Spanish America as well as Brazil and North America (hence Lezama's "American" purview), they weave an historical consciousness activated by a poetic logos that is positioned to challenge both Hegel's famous exclusion of America from the becoming of History and the "terrible complex" of identity that weighs so heavily in modern Latin American letters as a result of that exclusion. *La expresión americana* thus takes its place as a celebrated specimen of a well-developed genre of Spanish American essays on cultural identity whose contemporary genealogy begins with José Martí's "Nuestra América" and includes, among many others, José Enrique Rodó's *Ariel*, José Vasconcelos's *La raza cósmica*, the historical labors of Pedro Henríquez Ureña and Alfonso Reyes, and the fiction of fellow Cuban Alejo Carpentier.[1] Lezama's rhetorical nucleus, comparable in many ways to the argumentation of these authors, focuses on the gnostic space of American expression, the creative links between man and land that are articulated by two commonplace figures of

Latin American autochthony: myth and landscape. A quick perusal of the texts and authors just mentioned would suffice to illustrate the enthusiastic reception the tropes of myth and land have enjoyed as instruments for Latin American cultural identity. Numerous intellectual currents throughout the twentieth century reprised one or the other as an auratic link to the land and to pre-Iberian civilizations, as an assimilatory encoding of Latin America's nonwhite populations through anthropological schematics, or as an analogue of magical realism.[2] Indeed, the well-worn path of these tropes has made them into exhausted myths of autochthony in their own right, which in the Latin American context have traditionally serviced identitarian narratives of essential telluric bonds or primitivist "rhythms" and whose collusion in hegemonic orderings of modern identity is amply documented. The challenge for a reading of these themes in Lezama, then, is to consider whether and how they are rendered any differently here, whether they can upend said orderings and perhaps provide a way to think the historical consciousness of Latin American expression without falling into the old ruses of spirit and essence or into the new ruses of language, play, and strategic relationality.

In Lezama's writing, myth and landscape are cultivated through the poetic counterpoint of images into elements of an American practice of historical agency. In dialogue with the imago, the "image participating in history" (*La expresión americana* 49), American expression launches a reaggregation and dispersal of meaning through the magnetic encounter of far-flung visual fragments of history: The chance spark of these encounters activates a mythic process of historical vision as a continual capture and dissolution of form. The epistemological and stylistic rebellion of Lezama's thought has made it a hallmark of "counterconquest" and "countermodernity" for contemporary critics, who place it in a postcolonial arena because of its refiguring of historic modernity and cultural hierarchy; however, critique of Lezama has yet to work through the symbiotic entwinement of myth or magic and landscape with the possible postcolonial attachments of his work to determine, for example, how it does not simply reincarnate earlier forms of exceptionalism but bears ties to material life in Latin America.[3]

La expresión americana begins, tellingly, with what Lezama calls "*lo difícil.*" "Only the difficult is stimulating," he writes; "only the resistance that challenges us is capable of raising, provoking, and maintaining our potential for knowledge" [*Sólo lo lo difícil es estimulante; sólo la resistencia que nos reta es capaz de enarcar, suscitar y mantener nuestra potencia de conocimiento*] (49).[4] The concept the essay uses to envision *lo difícil*, the resistance confronted by American expression, is gnostic space, which obtains between the expanse of landscape and the intervention of the imago through Lezama's metaphorical subject: The counterpoint of images launched by this subject—which in his own examples regularly moves among references as disparate as gauchesca poetry, the medieval Book of Hours by the Limbourg brothers, or the Lydian conquest of Persia—summons a historical vision not determined by any of the usual attributes of historical causality, autonomous subjectivity, or progressive self-consciousness; this is a history literally "knitted by images" [*tejida por imágenes*]. What issues historical significance, then, is not the weight of genealogical legitimacy or precedence, but quite the opposite: the illustrative force of expression here and now to create new meaning. It is in this sense that Lezama sees American thought as a space where old stories and images can shake off their conventional, calcified definitions: where old myths slide ineffectively like "tube feet of deflated sea cucumbers" [*pedúnculos de holoturias desinfladas*] toward the oblivion of "geological ash," gnostic space catches them as "verbal prey" [*presa verbal*] in its nets of possibility (55). In the reinvention of myth, American expression ripostes the dominant contemporary thought of T. S. Eliot or Oswald Spengler, "crepuscular" thinkers for whom the vitality of modern culture is always an echo of ancient civilizations, progressing through a finite and calculated revival of its forms. We can begin to see here how Lezama aims to dispel the complex of American culture by nullifying its anxieties over original and copy, countering the dim linearity of historical time with the unexpected causalities of gnostic space. Lezama's first essay announces these principles with the force of manifesto:

> Our point of view starts from the impossibility of two similar styles, from the negation of disdain toward imitators, from the non-identity of two apparently conclusive forms, from the creativity of a new concept of historic causality, which destroys the temporal pseudo-concept that everything leads to the contemporary, to a fragmentary time [*Nuestro punto de vista parte de la imposibilidad de dos estilos semejantes, de la negación del desdén a los epígonos, de la no identidad de dos formas aparentemente concluyentes, de lo creativo de un nuevo concepto de la causalidad histórica, que destruye el pseudo concepto temporal de que todo se dirige a lo contemporáneo, a un tiempo fragmentario*]. (63)

The passage just cited encapsulates all the elements of Lezama's main quarrel with the Hegelian format of history, namely, the forward march of an omnipotent universal Spirit that adduces causes and effects to a predetermined idea about historical becoming. This idea, writes Lezama, does not correspond to reality but rather molds facts and events to "his previous ideologram, the irritated exigencies of his conceptual world" [*su ideolograma previo, las irritadas exigencias de su mundo conceptual*] (*La expresión americana* 172). The poetic logos of *La expresión americana*, as Irlemar Chiampi's introduction to the book states, permits us to "signal the *possibility of being* (the imago) and broach, contrary to the Hegelian logos, multiple forms of the real, without the constrictions of a rigid a priori to which all facts must submit" [*señalar el* poder ser *(la imago) y abarcar, contrariamente al logos hegeliano, las múltiples formas de lo real, sin las constricciones de un* a priori *rígido al cual deben someterse todos los hechos*] (15). The poetic logos thus delivers a veritable "dialectical shot" [*disparo dialéctico*] (166) to Hegelian logic, in that it does not merely insert America into the progression of history, or invert the terms of progress by affirming the historic participation of America's prehistoric nature. Instead, it takes the primordial nature associated with America, the Spirit radiating from European history, and other remnants of Hegel, and rearranges them through a piecemeal portrayal of four centuries of American culture meant, at every turn, to show up the shortcomings of his very idea of history by demonstrating its noncoincidence with the images it weaves.

In this sense, we could call *La expresión americana* a determinate negation of traditional historicism. The early Frankfurt School theorists differentiated determinate from abstract negation, averring that the former "does not simply reject imperfect representations of the absolute . . . by confronting them with the idea that they are unable to match [but rather] discloses each image as a script. It teaches us to read from its features the admission of falseness which cancels its power and hands it over to truth" (Horkheimer and Adorno 18).[5] In line with Adorno's negative adaptation of dialectics, this means that the negation objects offer to the coercion of conceptual thought does not merge with the latter in a new, positive unity, but becomes a ledger in which to read the falseness of concepts through negation's silent protest. Determinate negation teaches one to read the distances between subject and object, much as Benjamin's *The Arcades Project* sought to "educate the image-making medium within us" to better "see into the depths of historical shadows" (458). Although Lezama is not in any traditional sense a dialectical thinker, the characteristics of his oeuvre overlap in interesting ways with those of Frankfurt School Marxists, not least because it also functions as a series of lessons in image-making (his monumental *Paradiso*, after all, narrates the preparation of the young protagonist José Cemí for his entrance to poetic creation). In viewing his imagistic historical vision as a determinate negation of historicism, I intend to highlight that the compilation of images in *La expresión americana* is meant, above all, to exercise a process of imagination, one whose poetic staging neither counters Hegelian notions of history directly nor preens as complete, correct, or definitive in its concepts or outcomes; on the contrary, the history engendered by poiesis is riddled with silences and failures, "made more of possible absences than impossible presences" [*hecha más de ausencias posibles que de presencias imposibles*] (130). Poetry's obeisance to possible absence, I will argue here, is its blind but determinate link to nonidentity and its chance to be useful for a materialist thinking of history. Because Lezama's deployment of the tropes of primitive magic and landscape is central to the poetic process he enacts, it also determinately negates their conceptual scions: Unlike many variants of modern Latin American "primitivism," such as *negrista* poetry or Brazilian *anthropofagia,* his poetics does not appropriate the thesis of innate American primitiveness as a positive attribute, embracing, as it were, the "savageness" of American culture, nor does it presume to give a voice to its "savage," subaltern and Other positionalities; rather, it recruits the idea of the primitive to an entirely different experience of thought, whose conduits resemble primitive logic but whose conclusions point up the falseness of its ideological underpinnings. Let us see now how myth and nature describe the path of the imago.

Myth and Image in History

The first essay of *La expresión americana,* "Mitos y cansancio clásico," details rather esoterically the participation of the image in historical vision: It explains that the imago surges from a field characterized by "a force of warp and gravitation . . . that lends it extension [with] animistic force in relation to [the] entities" it claims [*La fuerza de urdimbre y la gravitación . . . que le presta la extensión hasta donde ese espacio tiene fuerza animista en relación con esas entidades*] (54). The expanse of landscape supplies the animistic force or gravitational pull put in play by the imago: Each depends on the other in a kind of dual axis that echoes the spatiality evoked in Lezama's poetic and religious ideas about Dionysian descent, resurrection, desire, and knowledge. Through its tension with extension, the infinite field of possibility, the historic image is conjured in the chance encounter of two data in a sleight of memory; it reveals a momentary confluence between what is familiar or proper and an invading "surprising datum" [*dato sorpresivo*], which not only violates the propriety of the first, thus confounding the notions of origin and sequence, but also gives a glimpse of ungraspable knowledge:

> The most unknown, which makes memory undulate like an ungraspable wheat field, has to be fixed by the most embedded and even buried fact. In that way, it seems that memory, in settling on a fact it has well adorned, is as though lying in wait to be paired with another fact more distant and challenging . . . the surprising datum, surprise of spark in a macrocosmos, that anxiously seeks its mate, that launches itself to complete the extension of a skin, that vision cannot wrap itself around but that

> the memory of germ accustoms us to greet as an absolute [*Lo más desconocido, que hace ondular la memoria como un inasible trigal, tiene que ser fijado por el hecho más enclavado y aun soterrado. De esa manera, parece como si la memoria al afincarse sobre un hecho por ella muy bien guarnido, está como en acecho de ser emparejada con otro hecho más lejano y retador . . . El dato sorpresivo, sorpresa de chispa en un macrocosmos, que busca ansiosamente su par, que se lanza a completar la extensión de una piel, que la visión no puede ceñir, pero que la memoria del germen nos acostumbra a saludar como un absoluto*]. (61)

The spark of the imago involves three kinds of knowledge or being: the everyday knowledge of memory (*el hecho más enclavado*) is sighted and threatened by its double in an uncanny extension (*el hecho más lejano y retador*), which is itself recognized and accepted by a primordial memory, the *memoria germen*. It is this last kind of memory that drives the imago in its capacity to negotiate the other two, to engender something that is constantly transformed and also eternal. In his poetic exposition of gnostic space, both in *La expresión americana* and in other essays on the historic image, Lezama recurs to a language of the primitive and magic that lends insights into the way the imago captures this mutating eternal being, as well as the way it relates to America's reinvention of myth. For not only are the key moments of American expression moments of "magic"—as in, for example, the duel won by Moctezuma's artists who come to "capture" Cortés's men by painting their portraits, or in the trickery that defeats the evil señores de Xibalbá in the *Popol Vuh*—it would also seem that the imago's activity is essentially primitive: It is, as Lezama puts it, "*la magia del análogo metafórico*" [the magic of metaphorical analogy] (62).

The frequent references to animism and magic in *La expresión americana* invoke the dubious intertext of early anthropology, which mapped the magical and animistic practices of non-Western, usually colonized groups, in close alignment with an agenda of domination and acculturation. When Freud, in *Totem and Taboo*, explains the similarities between hysterics and savages through their common magical psychic processes, he takes as a matter of fact the distance, temporal and spatial, of the latter, who "ha[ve] a telepathic disregard for spatial distance and treat past situations as though they were present" (106). The non-personhood of savages and hysterics, their figurative and literal banishment from the space of modern subjectivity, is given in their failure to register the dimensional structure that grounds it. For the Western ethnographer, the logic of the savage is only conditioned by the absence of scientific causes; his existence is paradoxically ordered by chance, as Lucien Lévy-Bruhl indicates in *Primitive Mentality:* "since [the primitive mind] has not the most remote idea of [the determinism of phenomena], it remains indifferent to the relation of cause and effect, and attributes a mystic origin to every event which makes an impression on it. Since occult forces are always felt to be present, the more accidental an occurrence seems to us, the more significant it will appear to the primitive mind. There is no necessity to explain it; it explains itself, it is a revelation" (44). The hieratic understanding of primitive man clearly distinguishes him from the Cartesian ego, but it also retraces the humanist cosmology in its triangular communication of man, god, and nature. James Frazer points out in *The Golden Bough* that "the savage, failing to discern the limits of his ability to control nature, ascribes to himself and to all men certain powers which we should . . . call supernatural . . . over and above this general supernaturalism, some persons are supposed to be inspired for short periods by a divine spirit, and thus temporarily to enjoy the knowledge and power of the indwelling deity" (37). I offer these examples from early anthropological treatises because they enumerate the same primitive qualities that recommend Lezama's metaphorical subject. This subject, too, is beholden to a secret causality, and also awaits a divine revelation. In "La imagen histórica," an essay published shortly after *La expresión americana*, Lezama reaffirms the redemptive power of the image, which through faith "extracts from enigma a glimmer, with whose ray we can penetrate, or at least live in wait for resurrection. The image, in this acceptance of ours, thus attempts to reduce the supernatural to the transfigured senses of man" [*extrae del enigma una vislumbre, con cuyo rayo podemos penetrar, o al menos vivir en la espera de la resurrección. La imagen, en esta aceptación nuestra, pretende así reducir lo sobrenatural a los sentidos transfigurados del hombre*] (330). Indeed, not only *La expresión americana* but Lezama's entire oeuvre is infused with an appeal to the primitive, in terms more or less redolent of the commonplaces of New World discourses—from an early essay on poet Julián del Casal which, as Arnaldo Cruz-Malavé argues, establishes the figure of the "imploring primitive" as a touchstone of Lezamian "*americanismo*" (53), to his later affirmations, in *Tratados en la Habana*, that "the primordial act" becomes a "canon of conduct" [*el acto primigenio trasladado a canon de conducta*] (*Obras completas* II 569) for American poetry, or that Creole language consists of "amazement of animism" [*pasmo de animismo*] (567).

Existing critical studies of Lezama dedicate almost no attention to these sidelong echoes of the clichéd anthropological version of American culture, preferring to interpret his "mythic" side through the classical and Eastern references to Greek, Roman, ancient Chinese and Egyptian, and Hindu cosmologies that form much of the visual matrix of his poetic system in key essays and in *Paradiso*.[6] Margarita Mateo Palmer's exhaustive study of myth in *Paradiso* signals how the near total absence of African or syncretic Caribbean myths from Lezama's literary repertory, his neglect of precisely those mythic elements of most interest to the "anthropological imagination" of twentieth-century Latin American letters, marks a "violent contrast" with *negrista* poetry and other primitivist trends of his contemporaries (70)[7]; certainly it is true, as Roberto González Echevarría quips, that Lezama "did not engage in identity politics" (par. 16).[8] But though Lezama may not have subscribed to, or even appreciated, the ethnographic vein of poetry popular during the 1930s and 1940s, there is still no doubt that he both read anthropological works and was keenly aware of their influence on the array of modernist turns of Latin American literature, through which authors such as Miguel Angel Asturias, José Carlos Mariátegui, Fernando Ortiz, and Lydia Cabrera effectively "discover" and revalorize indigenous or Afrocuban cultures through the eyes of European or American institutional frameworks for the study of primitive societies.[9] *The Golden Bough*, in fact, is one of Lezama's sources for *La expresión americana*. There would seem to be, then, another silent "*disparo dialéctico*," however buried or unintentional, contained in this inherent barbarity of American expression.

In one of the best-known essays in recent times on *La expresión americana*, Gustavo Pérez-Firmat discerns a dual orientation of Lezama's primitive character, caught between the joyful creation of cultural crossroads—what he calls the "strut of the centipede"—on one hand, and on the other the ecstasy and aphasia occasioned by otherworldly nature, the "squirming" of human thought before its tremendous scenes. Thus while the señor barroco, for Lezama the first autochthonous subject of America, gathers a feast of culture from Spanish, colonial Spanish American, and contemporary baroque artists, strutting across the crossroads that connect them, the "primitive" prose of the first conquistadors feels squeamish in the face of the encounters it describes: Rather than dominating nature it is "dictated" by it (Pérez-Firmat 324–26). What is more, these two threads of the primitive summarize the main lineaments of discourses of modern American particularity as a whole: "Claims of American exceptionalism have always invoked one or another version of these two options: we are either centipedes at the crossroads, or we are centipedes in the wilderness; we strut, or we squirm" (331). For Pérez-Firmat, these alternatives sum up the central mechanisms of primitivism for Americanist thought: It can rearrange the heterogeneity of American culture through authoritative play, or it can recede into wonder at its sublime display. In Lezama's work, critics have also identified these options in the alternation of metaphor and image. Cruz-Malavé notes that Lezama's most devoted critics part from an interpretation of his poetic system as an alternation between these two poles, between the unified spark of the image and the "metonymic impulse itself: displacement, fragmentation, substitution; impulse that unfailingly goes toward the image in which it is resolved and justified" [*el impulso metonímico propiamente dicho: el desplazamiento, la fragmentación, la sustitución; impulso que va indefectiblemente hacia la imagen en que se resuelve y se justifica*] (6).

Despite the prominence of these interpretations of the dual or alternative operations of primitive control and primitive wonder, I do not think Lezama aims to keep the two distinct; for him, rather, they are simultaneous facets of the act of poetry as a primitive act. Metaphor, or "likeness," and image are fleeting companions of poetry, they have the power of "the question of the beginning and of the farewell" (*Obras completas* II 152) of poetry's momentary penetration into the world. In the essay "Las imágenes posibles," Lezama provides a thorough treatment of his poetic system, which can be seen precisely as a fusion of image and metaphor: the act of naming, of sympathetic associations whereby humans exert control over the world, is married to the image it provokes much as "fire and the fringe of its colors" [*como el fuego y la franja de sus colores*] (152). Although the labor of analogy fuels the image, it cannot instrumentalize it to a unified control of the object because the ephemerality of the image carries the lesson of its very impossibility, the fact that "the closer we come to an object or the untouchable resources of the air, we will derive with more grotesque precision that it is an impossible, a rupture without Mnemosyne of what came before" [*cuanto más nos acerquemos a un objeto o a los recursos intocables del aire, derivaremos con más grotesca precisión que es un imposible, una ruptura sin nemósine de lo anterior*] (152). The image does not grant a verifiable reflection of reality but a repeated experience of its unverifiability, over which presides no Mnemosyne, no goddess of memory to provide a successive link to the past. The image bears the reminder of its singularity against the inevitable urge to unify and to reproduce its effects: "For always in imitation or likeness there will be the root of an impossible progression, because in likeness it is known that we cannot even pair up two analogized objects. And that its urge to continue, to penetrate and destroy the object, advances only accompanied by the horrible vanity of reproducing" [*pues siempre en la imitación o semejanza habrá la raíz de una progresión imposible, pues en la semejanza se sabe que ni siquiera podemos parejar dos objetos analogados. Y que su ansia de seguir, de penetrar y destruir el objeto, marcha solo acompañada de la horrible vanidad de reproducir*] (156). Poetry's magic, then, is set in motion by the inextricable faculties of metaphor and image, whose limitations constantly place their powers in check. While the instant of clairvoyance of the image justifies the act of metaphor, to create new connections and analogies, it also insists upon the impossibility of the metaphor's task to seize and appropriate a coherent whole, warning against the false achievement, the "horrible vanity of reproducing," that it invites us to pursue.

Lezama's primitive is not, then, an alternation of control and wonder but an act that contains both: In the language of the Frankfurt School, it participates in both myth and Enlightenment, but it does so in order to ward off the exhausted, "crepuscular" logic of Enlightenment thinking. When Max Horkheimer and Theodor Adorno lay out the trajectory of Enlightenment in *Dialectic of Enlightenment,* they locate its roots in the first primitive myths that channel the fear of nature and the unknown into sympathetic rituals of control: circumscribing the haphazard world beyond man in the order of magic, they begin to submit it to human dominion. The scientific logic of the Enlightenment scorns the irrational fears of myth that cast the subjective impulse over fate and nature, and sets out to eradicate them through the total, logical elucidation of the world, yet, as the authors' famous argument insists, Enlightenment's own impulse to equate and identify merely perpetuates magic through the absolute division of the world's "abundance of qualities" into the omnipotent subject, mind or Spirit, and the unified objectivity it opposes and distances: "It is the identity of mind and its correlative, the unity of nature, which subdues the abundance of qualities. Nature, stripped of qualities, becomes the chaotic stuff of mere classification, and the all-powerful self becomes a mere having, an abstract identity" (6). In its compulsive separation and distancing of the objective world from the enlightened self, Enlightenment becomes "mythical fear radicalized," a "universal taboo": "Nothing is allowed to remain outside, since the mere idea of the 'outside' is the real source of fear" (11). In the impetus of equation, identity, and homogenization proper to Enlightenment thought, primitive myth survives but is also impoverished. Myth's radicalization ironically liquidates its potential for enlightenment: For magic, in all its untruth, nevertheless accommodates the variation of the world's elements rather than subsuming and distancing them under one mass objectivity. "Magic implies specific representation. What is done to the spear, the hair, the name of the enemy, is also to befall his person; the sacrificial animal is slain in place of the god. . . . the sanctity of the *hic et nunc,* the uniqueness of the chosen victim which coincides with its representative status, distinguishes it radically, makes it non-exchangeable even in the exchange" (6–7). Magic retains the capacity to apprehend the extreme specificity of its victims—what Adorno will later call *non-identity*—not through abstract figuration but in direct experience of it: "What the primitive experiences as supernatural is not a spiritual substance in contradistinction to the material world but the complex concatenation of nature in contrast to its individual link" (10). Despite their clear disdain for myth, Horkheimer and Adorno concede this opening it leaves to the kind of critical knowledge they pursue.

The idiosyncratic fusion of control and wonder, likeness and image, that mobilizes Lezama's poetic system may be said to exploit the same opportunity for critical knowledge *Dialectics of Enlightenment* perceives in primitive myth, precisely by steering thought away from the ruthless division of the world into subjective and objective halves. On this view, his challenge to the encroachment of abstract progression advanced by the myth of enlightenment—exemplified in *La expresión americana* by the historicism of Hegel—consists in seizing upon the possibility for knowledge harbored in primitive myth, in its capture of irreducible specificity. The "magic of metaphorical analogy" performed by the imago puts that possibility to work in a delicate maneuver of the twin energies of metaphor—the subjective intervention in material realms—and the image, the spark of vision it elicits. The restriction the imago places on analogy's rapacious urge to identify, to reduce its object to likeness and thereby penetrate and destroy it, is what separates poetic knowledge from philosophical Being: Lezama's suspicion of the mid-century trend to approach poetry "dialectically"—a fashion on display in the Afrocentric movements of Négritude and *negrismo* from which, as we have already mentioned, he maintained a guarded distance—echoes the same objections Adorno raised throughout his career against metaphysical idealism, arguing that by inserting dialectics into "the sinusoidal zone of existence" poets end up "throwing philosophy outside its fundamental limitations," seeking "less a real explanation of things than an intellectual epic, a sort of drama of spirit, a subjective poem" [*menos una explicación real de las cosas que una epopeya intelectual, una suerte de drama del espíritu, un poema subjetivo*] (*Obras completas* II 248). From the praxis of contemporary poetry, Lezama identifies the same "boiling danger" [*peligrosidad hirviente*] (248) of subjective hubris that Adorno condemned in contemporary philosophy, the danger that the power of a consolidated Mind over the exterior world reduce objectivity to the prison of sterile conceptuality and ultimately to the subject itself, the very "horrible vanity of reproducing" awakened in every poetic act.

La fijeza: The Now of History

On the reading I have been elaborating of Lezama's poiesis, primitive myth becomes cortical to *La expresión americana*'s determinate negation of Hegelian logos, insofar as it helps define the philosophical underpinnings of the imago's historical vision. Because the memory contained in the imago is singular, impossible to trace in any linear or accumulative progression, it allows us to index the workings of history through a different sort of causality: Its spark knits the most distant facts together with the most familiar independently of the explanatory force of cause and effect, bringing an instant of recognition of historical meaning that refuses narration as succession. Comparison with Walter Benjamin's framework will be instructive here to flesh out further this understanding of historical time. Benjamin's investigations of history also seek to envision it through the medium of images, backed by the author's conviction that "history decays into images, not into stories" (*The Arcades Project* 476). Discontent with the hypocrisies cloaked by historicism—for example, the notion that "progress" moved modernity continually forward despite that fact that it did not lessen the suffering of people or halt fresh catastrophe but only propagated the same unfreedom in ever-changing forms of the "new"—Benjamin combed through the shells it left behind—the arcades of Paris, the universal expositions, the dandy—to find clues that could blast apart the fiction that held their emergence and atrophy to be the natural steps of historical progression. Because he recognized the speciousness of this fiction, the "empty, homogeneous time" of historicism, Benjamin hoped to unlock an alternative historicism from the dustbin of history itself, through a montage able to "spring [its objects] loose from the order of succession" (475). With the fragments culled from decrepit forms of history Benjamin also assembles an image, a momentary vision that "flashes up" in the tension generated by a collection of citations, defying the logic of chronological time: "It's not that what is past casts its light on what is present, or what is present its light on what is past; rather, image is that wherein what has been comes together in a flash with the now to form a constellation. . . . For while the relation of the present to the past is a purely temporal, continuous one, the relation of what-has-been to the now is dialectical: is not progression but image, suddenly emergent" (462). For Benjamin as well as for Lezama, the goal of historicism is a unique, rather than eternal, experience of the past ("Theses on the Philosophy of History" 262), one that, as the primitive magic repudiated by Enlightenment thought, forges an entirely singular relationship between what has been and "now," which cannot be subsumed under any classificatory regime.

Suppressing the ruse of progression, the image provides an individual, if fleeting, link with the past. This link depends, for both Benjamin and Lezama, on the tension among items brought into a constellation, which suspends the movement of thought in a "standstill," a "cessation of happening": the standstill of the image, commensurable with what Lezama calls *la fijeza* [fixity], does not simply arrest history but actually submits that historical meaning happens only in the image, in the possibilities it brings to the surface of experience.[10] "The historically understood contains time," Benjamin writes, "as a precious but tasteless seed" ("Theses on the Philosophy of History" 263). For both thinkers, this conception of history, of image as possibility, is explainable only as a kind of messianic power. We have seen, in a passage quoted above, that Lezama's image offers hope for resurrection, which in his mystical idiom refers to an experience of the infinite: Paradise itself, he asserts in one of the poems of a collection titled *La fijeza*, is "extasis of participation in the homogeneous, intemporality" [*éxtasis de participación en lo homogéneo, intemporalidad*] (*Obras completas* I 857). Yet this access to the infinite does not transcend finite life on earth; in fact, it only obtains through it, by virtue of the image, which acts as proof of the existence of resurrection (*Obras completas* II 1215).[11] Benjamin's version of this argument is also ultimately pinned on hope: He holds that the image's temporal index derives from the unfulfilled possibilities of the past, which place the demands for their correction and actualization on today's Now. This is Benjamin's "*weak* Messianic power," the expectation past suffering places on us to recognize, reverse, and redeem it. It is not that we hold the power of historical time, as Werner Hamacher points out, but that "there is historical time only in so far as there is an excess of the unactualized, the unfinished, failed, thwarted, which leaps beyond its particular Now and demands from another Now its settlement. . . . Time—historical time—is nothing but the capability of the possible to find its satisfaction in an actual" (41). As the realm of the possible, the image becomes a repository of historical time: It is our only means to realize the need for change and to imagine it outside the prison of history's continuum.

Landscape and Gnostic Space

So far I have tried to show how primitive myth and magic are fundamental to the historical vision of the imago as a determinate negation of Hegelian logos. What remains to be seen is how this vision relates to the autochthony of Latin America, how it communicates a specifically American expression. For this we must turn to landscape, the American gnostic space, for, according to the author in his initial formulation of the Latin American cultural complex, "the only thing that creates culture is landscape, and that we have in masterful monstrosity" [*lo único que crea cultura es paisaje, y eso lo tenemos de maestra monstruosidad*] (*La expresión americana* 63). Indeed, as many critics have already indicated, landscape forms the backbone of Lezama's elucubrations in *La expresión americana*, although its centrality to his arguments is teased out explicitly only in the closing chapter. It was the flora and fauna Columbus and other cronistas encountered in their first treks to the New World, for example, that fecundated their Old World mythic imaginations into a properly American expression by "dictating" their primitive prose (74). And this magical force of landscape is by no means exclusive to the insertion of European elements: The cosmology and folklore of Tawantinsuyo, whose god Viracocha moved seamlessly between the divine and natural worlds, transforming stones into warriors and sustaining himself on libations of gold, serves as a powerful influence of gnostic space, which independence leaders like Simón Bolívar and Francisco de Miranda strove to recapture. American primitiveness is thus deeply imbricated with its land, although not in the usual way primitiveness is associated with nature. In *La imagen de América Latina*, largely a redux of his ideas in *La expresión americana*, Lezama describes how the *cronistas'* jumble of historical references, from Muslim and

Borgoña presences in medieval Spain to Marco Polo's tales of Çipango and Genghis Khan, are enchanted through American spaces: "It was no longer primordial chaos, when the wind rippled the water, but historic dispersion seeking an escape granted finally by chance, that was their true primitivity and what we have called gnostic space, the dimension that engenders the tree, the space that engenders and knows as the Taoists saw it, the force germinating in empty space" [*Ya no era el caos primigenio, cuando el viento rizó las aguas, sino la dispersión histórica buscando una salida entregada al fin por el azar, esto era su verdadera primitividad y lo que hemos llamado el espacio gnóstico, la dimensión que engendra el árbol, el espacio que engendra y conoce tal como lo veían los taoístas, la fuerza germinando en el espacio vacío*] (10). What defines the primitiveness of America, Lezama explains with another indirect reference to Hegel, is not the endurance of a primordial nature—that is, not the Spirit of God ruffling the water, as in the Book of Genesis—but the turbid movement of disperse historical fragments that are magnetized across America's spaces in the chance emergence of new images. From the first encounters of the Spanish expedition, the significance of America as historical entity resides for Lezama in the production of challenges to the actors' imaginations: Thus the prison sentence imposed upon Columbus after his trips to the New World, Lezama muses, allows the respite necessary for the marvelous images of his encounters to collect and settle, like a quiet pool along the margins of a river, as though a period of contemplation were called for to shuffle and recombine the myths and landscapes of the Old World with the physical experience of the New (7). So too, in a kind of blind contemplation, do Moctezuma's soldiers draw the invading army, down to their horses and the thunder of their cannon fire, the better to incorporate their strangeness into the native topography. It is the imaginative training forced by encounter, the distillation and recomposition of images, that serves American expression as a "magic safeguard and security of selection" [*un resguardo mágico y una seguridad de elección*] (11–12) in its historical existence.

The vision of Latin America, what Lezama calls its "imaginary era," is composed not only of the new causalities the imago grants to historic dispersion, but also the space from which they are engendered, a knowing and germinative space. The moments featured in *La expresión americana* all respond in one way or another to this sort of space: The *señor barroco*, surveying with delight his lands and interiors, begins to "knit his surroundings," throwing "honeyed shade" over the outskirts of his holdings (81); the rebellious plutonic thought of romantics like Fray Servando Teresa de Mier or Simón Rodríguez, attempting to break free of colonial order and behold the "new landscape" of independence, condemns them to wander endlessly through hostile lands—Rodríguez in particular figures as a wretched prophet, rambling in the oblivion of his old age around remote forests and lakes of the American interior (130); and the Argentine *estanciero*, confronting the "dangerous distance" of the pampa from under the shelter of the "canopy house of the ombú," begins the new domination of national space in the void left by the defeat of the Viceroyalty (151). Although it accompanies quite literally a physical process of colonization, Lezama maintains that gnostic space does not result from a taming of the land but a dialogue with it: Landscape has its own sowing [siembra], its own "arborescence" (169), which attracts and transforms outside elements into autochthonous vision. The germinative qualities of landscape explain why Lezama's favorite images so often pair a horizontal plane with some vertical structure, like the castles and houses that shape the horizon of young José Cemí's education in *Paradiso* or the many trees that appear in *La expresión americana:* The Argentine ombú, for example, is the "house of the desert . . . like a tender protection from the grandeur" [*casa del desierto . . . como una protección tierna ante la grandeza*] (170). It offers shade from the terrific spread of the pampa, generating the nineteenth-century songs and poems that arc a popular culture in consultation with landscape. Similarly, the "generational" silk-cotton tree of Cuba "calms the fecund womb and safeguards the homestead in unity of place" [*tranquiliza el vientre fecundo y resguarda la estancia en unidad de lugar*] (170). These have all the trappings of genealogical trees, "elaborate trees, respectable leaves, that in the American landscape acquire the value of writing where a ruling is dispatched on our destiny" [*Arboles historiados, respetables hojas, que en el paisaje americano cobran valor de escritura donde se consigna una sentencia sobre nuestro destino*] (170).

Such tableaus of American landscape seem to clash with the animistic attributes of the imago, particularly since trees, the premiere symbol of stasis, rootedness, and sequence, embody all the characteristics of cultural identity that gnostic space supposedly defies. Herein lies the apparent paradox of *La expresión americana*, the fact that a work scornful of identity and linearity should nonetheless insouciantly promote the idea of an American way of being, and be read as representative of it. A number of critics remain uncomfortable with Lezama's seemingly unqualified movement between the performative, deconstructive action of the metaphorical subject that knits historical images and the more transparent, essentialist assertions about American culture, especially where these imply that America is always already baroque.[12] In our current task to consider Lezama's gnosis as a way to reconceptualize the postcolonial, this is paired with a perhaps graver concern, namely, how does gnostic space account for the violence of Latin American history, not just the imposition of European forms of architecture and poetry but the silencing of subaltern experiences and voices, the destruction of pre-Conquest lifeworlds? If we begin by accepting that Lezama never partook of, or even found terribly interesting, the sort of political revalorization along the lines of race, class, and gender that we tend to see as the sine qua non of a postcolonial intellectual profile, I think we may glimpse their emergence, however negatively, by following landscape to its material objects.

One cannot understand how Lezama's treatment of land does not invoke a telluric or ontological bond of the sort so common in the Spanish American tradition without reaching once more into its metaphysical armature. Indeed, for Lezama nature does not exist in any legible way in itself but only as a mediated material in cultural dialogue, brought "to the height of man" [*a la altura del hombre*] in landscape: "When we say nature the *panta rei* gobbles man up like the Leviathan of extension. Landscape is nature that man has befriended" [*Cuando decimos naturaleza el* panta rei *engulle al hombre como un leviatán de lo extenso. El paisaje es la naturaleza amigada con el hombre*] (*La expresión americana* 167). He often affirms with Pascal that "since true nature has been lost, everything can be nature," meaning that the grasp of the abundance of nature through language or vision is already irremediably warped, cutting down to size and specimen what is "naturally" infinite and indomitable. What is left, then, is what he calls supranature: "an act that is produced and a choice that is verified by countercipher in nature" [*un acto que se produce y una elección que se verifica a contracifra en la naturaleza*] (*Obras completas* II 1213). With the term *countercipher,* Lezama suggests that supranature incurs against the infinity of impenetrable nature, conjuring with the magical forces of metaphor and image a glimpse of what is lost but only incomprehensibly. Supranature gives the negative of nature's cipher, "an answer to a question that cannot be formulated" [*una respuesta a una pregunta que no se puede formular*] (1213). As a countercipher to nature, landscape does not pretend to act as its proxy or spokesperson: It does not replace or represent nature but merely initiates its dialogue with man, facilitating "the palpatory consciousness of the blind" [*la conciencia palpatoria de los ciegos*] (1212) through the properties of image and metaphor we have already analyzed. Contrary to the idea of landscape as a domestication of nature, Lezama's landscape acts as a blind response to an indecipherable call: the gnosis of gnostic space orients poetic thought through the wilderness of infinity, though the path it provides is unknown to thought itself. Hence the appearance of landscape as a "friendship" between man and nature, a relationship based on the blind attempts to answer to an incommunicable order.[13]

This dimension of the gnostic space of American expression has important consequences both for the way Lezama arrives at his conclusion about the autochthony of American culture and for our probe into its connections to material history. Cintio Vitier's exegesis of Lezama's poems in

Lo cubano en la poesía captures perhaps better than any other these subtle elements of his poetic system. To answer the challenge issued to poetic expression, Vitier writes, Lezama envisions a partnership between physical and intellectual or spiritual life, between ideas and things, which does not view the two as antithetical but as secret sharers that bring together disparate parts of an ultimate reality. The poet works as an artisan with clay "who knows he cannot do without the material, although not giving up either to the laws of its resistance, which would make creation impossible. The artisan and the material have to enter into a respectful ignorance of resistance, to reach new gravitations, like a new innocence, of creation" [*que sabe que no puede prescindir de la materia, aunque tampoco rindiéndose a las leyes de su resistencia, que harían imposible la creación. El artesano y la materia tienen que entrar en un respetuoso desconocimiento de la resistencia, para alcanzar las nuevas gravitaciones, como una nueva inocencia, de la creación*] (454). To find the expression of material within its resistance, the subjective gesture—the poet or the artisan—cannot renounce itself to the former as to a hermetic enigma, just as it cannot imagine it to be open and transparent to manipulation, something the artist can recreate in a purely subjective realm. The material expresses itself in our respectful ignorance of its resistance—it speaks through the creation of new forms that emerge from its gravitation of the poetic impulse. This is why, Vitier explains, the answers poetry provides to the challenge of the unknown never take the form of idealistic pronouncements but are answers of art, made in discrete ritualistic forms: Like the artisan's pitcher, or the musician's fugue, Lezama's poems are "symbolic answers, outside all determinism, in a sort of transcendent lordly gentility, where creation acquires the transmutative distance of a rite" [*respuestas simbólicas, fuera de todo determinismo, en una especie de señorial Cortésanía trascendente, donde la creación adquiere la distancia trasmutadora de un ceremonial*] (446–47). Through the creative distance that magnetizes the unknown to the most familiar forms, in an operation that for Vitier also seems to take on the features of primitive ritual, poetic thought manages to speak a knowledge that is not its own.

Vitier's analogies offer a useful interface through which to read the pivotal role of landscape in American expression. The material of autochthony—the land, but also the histories and ways of knowing America has cultivated before and beyond its European colonization—exerts a gravitational pull on the imagination that greets it: this is exactly the "force of warp and gravitation" that lends the imago "animistic force" over the fragments of history it knits together, as we saw at the beginning of this chapter. In its attempt to intuit the guiding force of its material toward a historical vision embedded in *lo difícil*, Lezama's landscape assumes the same difficulties as the poet/artisan described by Vitier: its possibilities of meaning draw from the unknown substance of American spaces to transform old myths and histories into new images, whose fulgurations summon a dark, ephemeral reflection of its material bases. The creation of landscape requires subjective intervention—otherwise, as Vitier points out, creation would be impossible—but it frustrates the urge to fashion from gnostic space any coherent, definitive narrative to define a constant of American identity. The tension between gnostic space and landscape, much as the symbiosis of metaphor and image, both attracts thought and thwarts its pretension to order and dominate its objects. Just as the historic causality generated by the imago rejects the linear plotting of causes and effects, the flash of recognition in landscape's dialogue with nature eschews the comfort of a lasting identity of place: the stuff of autochthony here is nothing like an eternal or ontological link to land, but only the renewed effort to penetrate the extension of nature again. This is the function of storied trees like the silk-cotton and the ombú, not to anchor an essential and legitimate domination of the land but to mark as a "momentary column of the telluric" [*momentánea columna de lo telúrico*] (*Obras completas* II 1213) the subject's repeated overture to the expanse of space:

> [Man ascends] by way of an act, which reworks constantly over the germ, seeking through this act to turn over once more his germ in a new extension. That reworking of the act over the germ engenders a causal being, nourished with the immense resources of oblique living and a suddenness, that make extension creative, giving a tree to that extension, making of the tree a One, . . . and here commences the new festival of poetry . . . possibility in infinity. [*[El hombre asciende] por medio de un acto, que reobra constantemente sobre el germen, procurando por ese acto volcar de nuevo su germen en una nueva extensión. Ese reobrar del acto sobre el germen engendra un ser causal, nutrido con los inmensos recursos de la vivencia oblicua y un súbito, que hacen la extensión creadora, dándole un árbol a esa extensión, haciendo del árbol el uno, . . . y aquí comienza la nueva fiesta de la poesía, . . . el posible en la infinitud*]. (*Obras completas* 817)

Together, the imago's instant of illumination, a sudden concentration of meaning, and the oblique experience of extension—an intimate yet mute contact with material and spiritual infinity—are able to reseed a germ of poetic creation: in the "tree," as in landscape more broadly, the poet essays a countercipher to nature, generating a dialogue with land that is nonetheless never sequential or cumulative but only a "reworking" of the hope of restoring material, human, and divine realms to their lost plenitude, which for Lezama is the hope of resurrection.

The Material of American History in *La expresión americana*

Taking this process of countercipher as the index of history as I have just articulated it, one may read in the creative journey of *La expresión americana* the way material experiences register negatively in the "possible absences" that make up America's historical vision. Such a reading departs from the common interpretation of Lezama's thought on America as a performance and endorsement of "creative assimilation"—where the differences between original and copy, "first" Western culture and "second" American imitations, are befuddled—in that it seeks to account for the object as an undefinable but determinate participant in culture creation. We can appreciate the subtleness of this difference through a brief comparison with Brett Levinson's arguments regarding *La expresión americana* in *Secondary Moderns*. Levinson's book centers on the pivotal role resistance plays in the poet's stances on the historical position of Latin America: The thrust of these, he postulates in a treatment too long and detailed to summarize here, is to tease out the possibilities of meaning caught in the gaps between lost objects and histories of New World societies—both Amerindian civilizations and the troubled attempts to affirm something like an original Latin American culture—and the scriptural representations imposed on them by European teleologies. The result is a process very close to the readings of trace and erasure carried out in deconstruction: Indeed, Levinson goes so far as to dedicate a short section to the parallels between Lezama and Derrida, locating their philosophical affinity in the latter's thesis that "Since the trace is not a presence but the simulacrum of a presence that dislocates itself, displaces itself, refers itself, it properly has no site—erasure belongs to its structure." For both thinkers, Levinson concludes, "difference is neither truly present nor truly absent but is something radically other, 'absolute alterity'" (*Secondary Moderns* 83). This principle of structural erasure is operative in an extended analysis Levinson offers of Lezama's exegesis of the *Popol Vuh*, the first "native" topic addressed in *La expresión americana* and a supreme example of resistance as he understands it. A product of colonial transcription and adaptation of Quiché cosmology, as a "book" the *Popol Vuh* presents a labyrinth of erasures: Lezama detects in it the textual metamorphosis of Amerindian myth through narrative influences from the Bible to the Indian epic *Bhagavad Gita* to *The Odyssey*. Because isolating the original, authentic elements of Quiché lore in the textual morass of translation and citation is virtually impossible, the "real" history preserved in the *Popol Vuh* can be found only by prising open the layers of its intertextuality, where Levinson posits that Quiché tradition has been "preserved—preserved, however, as a silence, an interruption, an erasure, or an awaiting that never appear in the texts as readable presences, but only as the inexpressible" (*Secondary Moderns* 75).

It is not difficult to arrive at a conclusion like this, by way of the characteristics of Lezama's thought I have highlighted here or through Levinson's apparatus, as a plausible exposition of *La expresión americana*. My interest in delving momentarily into Levinson's study is not to refute his reading in toto but merely to point out how his arguments foreclose the portion of historical vision emitted by the "lost" material and natural world running through Lezama's commentary. Perceived only as a preserved silence, these objects exude none of the gravitation or animism that machinate gnostic space: In short, they figure more as "impossible presences" than as the "possible absences" that compose historical images. Because the poetic orientation of Lezama's writing often leads the reader into a realm of ethereal mysticism where anything concrete seems, if not unthinkable, at least negligible, it is easy to lose sight of the importance he gives to real objects and real experiences, not as fodder for representation but as partners in poiesis that furnish the "possibility" of possible absence. Poetry, Lezama writes in "Pascal y la poesía," is a "forest without trees, where, paradoxically, the fire receives a prodigious combustion that requires as inexorable raw material resins and branches" [*bosque sin árboles, donde, paradojalmente, el fuego recibe una prodigiosa combustión que exige como inexorable materia prima resinas y ramajes*] (*Obras completas* II 565). Paradoxically, in the absence of physical trees, poetic thought yet draws from the "evaporated perfume" of their matter.

The raw material of history, both natural and cultural, is similarly embedded at the heart of the essays of *La expresión americana*. Just after his ruminations on the *Popol Vuh*, Lezama turns to the first exchanges between Moctezuma and Cortés chronicled by Bernal Díaz del Castillo: Before Cortés meets the emperor in person, he carries out a tentative diplomacy with a group of imperial envoys and receives from them extravagant gifts including two large calendar discs, one a rendering of the sun in gold and the other a moon in silver, which Díaz can only describe as "wheels." Lezama imagines the perplexity of Cortés, dazzled by the richness and impenetrable majesty of these objects. "Vacillating to try to match those bewitchments" [*Vacilando para lograr la igualdad con aquellos hechizos*], he finally presents Moctezuma's men with a crystal chalice from Florence "etched and gilded with many orchard and hunting scenes" [*labrada y dorada con muchas arboledas y monterías*] (75). In his gloss on the exchange, which just as the *Popol Vuh* is irretrievable "as it really was," forever colored by the interests of a scribe of conquest, Lezama's focus is on the possibilities awakened in our imaginations by the meeting of the objects. These provide a snapshot that visually cues us to the overflow of meaning in the episode: the mixed messages of material and spiritual power, the spellbound attempt at achieving commensurability between radically incommensurable lifeworlds, which Cortés, impotent in his physical and imaginative poverty, rather blindly makes with the gilded chalice of idyllic European pastorals, these intrigues and many more undetectable encounters are revivified by the simple juxtaposition of the objects. The history of the matter, here, lies in the facets of the imago, which speaks like the perfume of an expunged forest.

The literary "banquet" Lezama weaves around the figure of the *señor barroco* in the book's second chapter, "La curiosidad barroca," reiterates and reworks this possible dialogue with absent, conquered, and natural worlds, praising in a flourish of images the incipience of regional expression. The first American subject to take charge of his own "riches," the *señor barroco* intuits the tension of his objects' opposition: against the false unity of expression, which in a colonial world proclaims the domination of nature, the disappearance of Amerindian religion and custom, and the unmitigated triumph of European styles and symbols, he senses the fragmentation and extension that denies its univocity. Between the "absorption of the forest by the contentious stone" [*absorción del bosque por la contenciosa piedra*]—the transformation of pre-Columbian into colonial landscape—and nature, which "seems to rebel and return to its own jurisdiction" [*parece rebelarse y volver por sus fueros*] the *señor barroco* attempts "to install a little order but without rejection, an impossible victory where all the vanquished could maintain the exigencies of their pride and their squandering" [*poner un poco de orden pero sin rechazo, una imposible victoria donde todos los vencidos pudieran mantener las exigencias de su orgullo y de su despilfarro*] (83). The beauty and the autochthony evident in this dawn of expression is its "impossible victory": Far from any facile sort of "assimilation" or recuperation of subaltern voices, its forms seek to sustain their victims' claims to dignity and "squandering"—something very different, it should be noted, from announcing the satisfaction of those claims. Keeping alive the protest of objectivity, not in a coherent demand but, as with the gifts of Moctezuma and Cortés, through the sparkle of images, expression safeguards the "squandering" of the object's possibilities, all the unpredictable ways it encrypts the final form. One of Lezama's most popular examples of New World baroque included in "La curiosidad barroca," the *indiátide* of the Incan princess carved by the Andean artist José Condori on the door of the Church of San Lorenzo de Potosí, is enlivened by the tension of impossible victory described above. Condori's carvings, for Lezama, owe in particular to the hieratic intimacy of the artist with the stone: under the sculptor's hands, the plastic figure of the princess, "that temerity of the stone obliged to choose symbols, has ignited all the elements so that the Indian princess can parade in the procession of praise and reverence" [*aquella temeridad de la piedra obligada a escoger símbolos, ha hecho arder todos los elementos para que la princesa india pueda desfilar en el cortejo de las alabanzas y las reverencias*] (83–84). It is impossible not to recall in the stone's active resistance the Incan deity's magic transformation of walls into warriors, an image which here seems to animate all the elements of Condori's door, both material and formal, in an invisible battle for the princess's appearance. Put in Adorno's more philosophical terms, this struggle in the image indicates the way "non-identity communicates with that from which it has been separated by the concept": The knowledge and history Lezama calls up from the stone's material in effect "stares at" the colonizing form that envelops it, "it resists the pressure [of identity's claim and] as such it seeks to be audible" (Adorno, *Negative Dialectics* 163).

What these and many other moments of *La expresión americana* reinforce is the status of autochthony as praxis: Identity and legitimacy are never won because their maintenance—which is really only an illusion of constancy—is wrought in tension with *lo difícil,* the dissolution and recomposition of images that I outlined at the beginning of this chapter. None of Lezama's metaphorical subjects, not even the lordly *señor barroco,* attains a definitive comprehension of American place or of America's place in history; the vitality of these qualities depends upon the subject's endless attempt and failure to grasp at once all the vectors tangent to it. In reality the failure of creative expression is just as important as its attempt, since, as we have seen with the images of Cortés and the Indian princess, the experience of resistance floods us with a countercipher of the objective world. By reminding us of the inconclusiveness of history, the negative objections brought forth by the image also assure us that a whole picture is possible, so long as something perceptible still grates against the closure of the imagination in an endless string of identifications, or Benjamin's empty, homogeneous time. For Lezama, as Emilio Bejel has written, "the important objective is not so much to hit the target as to shoot the arrow. One way or another there will be a reward. Thus the spiraling movement of Spanish American baroque never implies the ineptitude of chaos, but on the contrary is the only direction toward hope and progress" (133).

In the small collection of images examined here, I hope to have demonstrated how the tropes of primitive myth and landscape help contour a poetics of place in *La expresión americana* through its relationship to the material objects of history. I have suggested that this relationship is dialectical insofar as it hinges on the protest—or as Lezama likes to say, the *reto*—of an unknown, a non-identity, able to conduct thought toward a singular production of history through the image, and away from the abstract progression of Hegelian logos that traditionally delivered Latin America to the infancy of history. In history America becomes the site of a practice of possibility, composed of a type of time that Lezama, much like Benjamin, does not hesitate to characterize as messianic. The past *is* past in function of its claim to reverse injustice: Its unfulfilled needs constitute the present's relation to the past qua possibility. What the image owes to suffering, then, is also the proof of a fulfillment to come, its "temporal index by which [the past] is referred to redemption" (Benjamin, "Theses on the Philosophy of History" 254). The image of America propelled by myth and landscape remind thought of this final reconciliation as its very condition. *La expresión americana* can be defined, as much as anything else, as the hopeful practice for redemption, for the "day the *gnostic* and *physical* worlds will be univocal" [*día [en que] el mundo de la* gnosis *y el de la* physis *serán unívocos*] (*Obras completas* II: 1219–20).

Chapter 3

Édouard Glissant's Archipelic Thought and Second Nature

There is perhaps no geopoetic figure today with more influence on humanistic approaches to postcolonial cultural politics than the archipelago. Since the first flourishing of the anticolonial archipelic imagination at the Asia-Africa Bandung Conference of 1955, and in Caribbean literature by Aimé Césaire, Derek Walcott, Kamau Brathwaite, and Antonio Benítez-Rojo, aesthetic and political explorations of the archipelago have uncovered and theorized the significant ties among the geographic status of archipelic communities, the vicissitudes of their colonial histories, and the models of self-determination both of these open up[1]; in the increasingly interdisciplinary climate of ethnic and postcolonial studies in Euro-American centers of scholarship, these unique entwinements of the archipelago have made it a major attractor for conversations among black Atlantic, Caribbean, and Oceanic critical concentrations that seek to unearth in the geopolitical vectors of modern colonial experience a trope able to speak to a shared postcolonial condition along the lines of hybridity and fluidity. In their introduction to a special issue of the *International Journal of Francophone Studies* titled, aptly, "Oceanic Dialogues," Pascale de Souza and H. Adlai Murdoch summarize this attraction:

> [T]raditional boundaries of community and binary principles of identity have been subverted and interrogated through [the] discursive and popular frameworks [of Caribbean and Indo-Pacific cultures], extending a hybrid paradigm of identity that mediates both national and transnational articulations of the subject. As

> a result, the discourses that emerge from these sites of affiliation blur the distinction between positionality and place, generating a creative ambivalence from this cultural nomadism that spans the oceans and disturbs the hierarchic assumptions of both centre and periphery (140).

As the authors' panegyric makes clear, the figurative and historic qualities of the archipelago call up all those topics dear to postcolonial studies—diaspora and migration, challenges to binary identity, deconstruction of center and periphery—that tether aesthetic concerns to cultural modes of politics. This alluring consonance with the privileged sites of postcolonial interrogation, in particular the uniquely visual mapping it offers of decentered subjectivity and trans- or post-national movement, has allowed criticism increasingly to consider the usefulness of the archipelago wholly beyond the realm of literary analysis, as a tool of political imagination. Françoise Lionnet, for example, has leveraged the archipelic model of citizenship as a counterpoint to the "continental" orientation of dominant ideas about nationhood, specifically French republican universalism, as a bordered territory that circumscribes a unified, pure, and ultimately abstract body of citizens. Recalling the many ways recent struggles over French identity evidence the inadequacy of universalist notions of national community to address gender and race inequality, Lionnet suggests that the processes of linguistic and political Creolization found in Caribbean and Indo-Pacific archipelagoes may help us to construct a more inclusive and flexible civic paradigm. With the emergence of archipelagic polities, she explains, "it bec[omes] possible to reimagine, in a global context, the twentieth century nation not as a fortress and landmass . . . but as a fluid and open 'one' that is receptive to change and exchange . . . Instead of being kept apart by the waters that surround them the islands form a network of solidarity in which land and sea, the fluid and the solid, are both part of the hybrid legacy of decolonization" ("Continents and Archipelagos" 1508).

It is telling that both these bids to insert the imagination of archipelic and island culture into an idiom of global political relevance lay hand to the theories of Édouard Glissant, both because his oeuvre, perhaps more than that of any other Caribbean intellectual, has become an inexorable body of reference for the geopoetic conceptualization of non-continental societies, and because the trajectory of his career from the 1950s until his death in 2011 is so often analyzed in parallel with the concurrent epistemological drift, from Marxist dialectics to deconstructive and rhizomatic apparatuses, that accompanies a disciplinary shift from regional or national to global scales of study. From the dozens of volumes of poetry, fiction, and essay produced in Glissant's career one would be hard pressed to find a single piece that does not reflect both thematically and formally the entanglement of landscape with culture and politics, an entanglement that Glissant views as the ultimate conduit to a deeper understanding of history and place. From his very first published contemplations on poetic creation in *Soleil de la conscience*, Glissant palpably upholds the experience of landscape as inextricable from the expression of Caribbean reality, and of poetic knowledge in general. Writing of the French countryside during his studies in Paris, he muses:

> I love these fields, their order, their patience; however they are not part of me. Never having had control over my land, I do not experience this reflex of managing the land, of organization. My landscape is still convulsive; the symmetry of planted fields makes me uncomfortable. My time is not a succession of seasonal hopes, but it is still explosive and torn by surging trees [*J'aime ces champs, leur ordre, leur patience; cependant je n'en participe pas. N'ayant jamais disposé de ma terre, je n'ai point cet atavisme d'épargne du sol, d'organisation. Mon paysage est encore emportement; la symétrie du planté me gêne. Mon temps n'est pas une succession d'ésperances saisonnieres, il est encore de jaillissements et de trouées d'arbres*]. (Dash, *Édouard Glissant* 31, 19)

Much more than simple surroundings, landscape for Glissant is an agent of consciousness: it perceptibly shapes patterns of thought and behavior and thereby grounds collective ways of being in a place. More importantly, by observing this structure of place one discovers a more muted index of historical becoming, prying from the physical experience of landscape an embedded sense of the past and of destiny illegible in the historical record. The mainstays of Glissant's geopoetics, which connect Caribbean landscape to archipelic thought, are already apparent in this early text. The difference between France and Martinique registers at once in the visual, emotional, and social economic participation in the environment: the image of the neatly cultivated fields discomforts Glissant, driving him to recognize the ways he, as a tropical colonial subject, is excluded from the fiction of France's telluric symbiosis; Martinique's own fiction, invisible to the universal republican schematics of ownership, production, and seasonal rhythm, is convulsive, unprecedented and as yet inconclusive. His comments conjure a polyvalent juxtaposition between what is already called here "atavistic" cultures—territorial cultures driven by legitimate filiation to a unique root—and composite cultures, which have no fixed origin, generally spring from the promiscuous encounters of colonial expansion, and advance through a movement of errantry rather than linear progression. This codification of the relationship between subject and environment in its historic, social, and aesthetic filaments becomes the foundation of Glissant's theorization of Caribbean writing as a channeling of geographic to literary form, not as description or mimesis but as a platform where submerged intersections of landscape, history, and people can be reactivated to promote the sort of civic self-fashioning Lionnet, de Souza and Murdoch praise. "When I truly possess my land," Glissant continues, referring to both a literary and a political ownership, the prospect of Martinican independence, "I will organize it according to my order of clarity, according to my learned time" [*Quand je posséderai vraiment ma terre, je l'organiserai selon mon ordre de clartés, selon mon temps appris*] (Dash, *Édouard Glissant* 19).

Text and Geography: "Early" and "Late" Glissant

The geopoetic project intuited in the passage just analyzed, which finds an articulation of ever more comprehensive and ambitious scope in Glissant's theories of Creolization, Relation, and Tout-monde, consistently hinges on the brokering between what Antonis Balasopoulos refers to as the "textuality of geography" and the "geography of textuality."[2] While the first "focuses on the semiotic, rhetorical and ideological energies that inform the domain of geographical knowledge and representation," the second "takes stock of the representational and narrative uses of spatial form, or delves into the geographies underlying the distribution, consumption or reception of imaginative texts" (9). The slippage between these two poles, from what we might call, more simply, the text's representation of the "world" to the "world's" inscription of the text, is both compelling and problematic, precisely because, as Balasopoulos points out, "it is the very division between geographical and textual *topoi* that is exposed as epistemologically volatile and unsafe" (9). On one hand, emphasis on this movement can dismantle the complicity between the rhetorical valence of islands and archipelagoes and the ongoing colonial permutations they support, and thus activate contestatory discourses of geographic and historic belonging. The growing popularity of environmental approaches to Caribbean and Oceanic literature attests to the explanatory potential of the contacts among diachronic imaginings of island forms, the spatial dynamics of the "routes and roots," as Elisabeth DeLoughrey terms it, of archipelic settlement, and the ecological and economic determinations of these places under late capitalism.[3] On the other hand, the same fluidity of these connections can easily lull critique into collapsing metaphoric and ideological production in service of the same hegemonic networks it aims to expose. The deleterious effects of such a conflation, according to many critics, correlate closely to the aggrandizement of these regional, sedimented processes as representative models for worldwide phenomena of hybridity, Creolization, and diaspora. When it gets swept up in the theoretical diffusion in which the Caribbean, once a virtual nonentity in intellectual constructions of modernity, as Mimi Sheller phrases it, "has now been voraciously sucked into the vortex of 'global culture'" (188), critical work fails as often as not to undergird the metaphors of waves, currents, shorelines, or insularity with the circumstances of their semiosis, the real historic and social content that geopoetic thinking is designed to highlight. "As poetic as it may seem," DeLoughrey drily notes, "most migrants do not choose to permanently leave their homes because their saline blood flows like the oceans or because they inherited a maritime sensibility through their ancestors. In fact, while this may be an era of the greatest movements of people in global history, it seems that the only migrants who relocate by sea are the elite on luxury vessels . . . or the ultradispossessed on makeshift watercraft" (28). Enthusiasm for the textuality of geography thus all too easily eclipses the geography of textuality, starting of course with the relative geography of the writing and theorizing subject and the places and people that mix, flow, and migrate through her text.

Glissant's work is both reflective of and influential in the trend toward global displacement now associated with Caribbean geopoetics. From the overtly dialectical commentary on Caribbean landscape in *Soleil de la conscience*, which he develops in the novels *La Lézarde*, *La Case du commandeur*, and *Malemort*, and the essays of *L'Intention poétique* and *Discours antillais* into a conceptual armature molded largely around the construction of national and regional consciousness, Glissant's interrogations of place enter a much more global and, by most accounts, abstract terrain starting with the publication of *Poétique de la Relation* in 1990. Drawing on Deleuze and Guattari's theories of the rhizome and on chaos theory, concepts like *Relation*, *Tout-monde*, and *chaos-monde* parlay the natural features of the archipelago (as he affirms in *Poétique*, "the reality of archipelagos in the Caribbean or the Pacific provides a natural illustration of the thought of Relation" [*Poetics of Relation* 34]) into a philosophical stance on history and identity on a planetary level, engendering pronouncements like this one from *Traité du Tout-monde*:

> Archipelic thought suits the allure of our worlds. It borrows from it what is ambiguous, fragile, adrift. It admits the practice of detour . . . We perceive what was continental, thick and which weighed on us in the sumptuous system thinking that until this day has governed the History of the humanities, and which is no longer adequate for our explosions, for our histories nor for our no less sumptuous errantries. The thought of the archipelago, of archipelagoes, opens up these seas to us [*La pensée archipélique convient à l'allure de nos mondes. Elle en emprunte l'ambigu, le*

> *fragile, le dérivé. Elle consent à la pratique du détour . . . Nous nous apercevons de ci qu'il y avait de continental, d'épais et qui pesait sur nous, dans les somptueuses pensées de systeme qui jusqu'à ce jour ont régi l'Histoire des humanités, et qui ni sont plus adéquates à nos éclatements, à nos histoires ni à nos non moins somptueuses errances. La pensée de l'archipel, des archipels, nous ouvres ces mers*]. (31)[4]

One immediately notices, in contrast with the observations from *Soleil de la conscience*, Glissant's confident fortification of geography's textual properties: The thinking of archipelago happens purely in the imagination. Indeed, "we" need not even have lived in an archipelago to reap its rewards; archipelic thought consists of adopting the archipelago's forms as a conceptual instrument for being in the world. This change has provoked a certain anxiety in recent criticism of Glissant to distinguish between pre- and post-Relation thematic orientations, either to recuperate threads of continuity meant, in some sense, to restore the more politically concrete concerns of early works to the increasingly abstruse meanderings of essays like *Traité du Tout-monde*, or to apprehend the ways Glissant's course toward the postmodern and the global echoes the depoliticizing thrust of cultural theory as a whole after the postcolonial turn. Peter Hallward's incisive reading of Glissant in *Absolutely Postcolonial* is an exemplary case of the latter: Hallward counts Glissant among a group of writers who protagonize a definitive movement of postcolonial literature toward singular, rather than specific, articulations of difference. Unlike specific difference, determined vis-à-vis other discrete entities, the singular for Hallward "must preclude the existence of a plurality of individuals, as distinct from the multiplicity of modes of one univocal Individual" (18). This ultimate recurrence to the creative One, which Glissant derives from Deleuze and Guattari's rhizomatics, significantly accompanies the abandonment of a Martinican national project for the immediate global connectivity of Relation, dissolving local specificities "into the univocity of a new world order based on nothing other than constant internal metamorphosis, dislocation and exchange" (68). The subsumption of difference in poetic form, Hallward insists, must needs be complicit with the equality mongering that razes specificity in the world for the benefit of cultural markets, insofar as "the equation of subject and world as a single process of Relation obliterates all 'in-between' space, the space of development and conflict" (124).

Chris Bongie's recent evaluation of the "late" Glissant takes Hallward's seminal insights into more productive territory by training their focus less on archipelic thought's dismissal of the nation state and more squarely on the surreptitious conduits between commercial and aesthetic realms it gives clearance to: The pressing question provoked by the rise of the archipelic and rhizomatic, Bongie maintains, is how literary studies can weigh their "foundational bias toward aesthetic value" against "the increasingly commodified ways in which that value is produced and consumed today" (*Friends and Enemies* 326–27). On this view, the gravest result of Glissant's putative shift after the *Poétique*, even more than the exhaustion of specific national political movements, is its capitulation to cultural politics through a "heightened opposition between culture and politics in which the former is repeatedly privileged over the latter, and indeed assumes its guise" (348). In other words, in Relation, Tout-monde, and other rhizomatic concepts, the power of culture usurps and defuses the tension of social antagonism traditionally addressed by subject-, community- and state-based politics, and in overtaking the platform of political action disguises and abets complacency with the status quo.[5]

The crux of this fraught articulation between literary autonomy and the culture industry is taken up with the opposite objective by critics like Anjali Prabhu and Nick Nesbitt, who identify a continuing adherence to dialectical forms of thought from early Glissant through the period of Relation. The emphasis on poetics that Bongie and Hallward see as a wholesale subscription to cultural politics, for Prabhu can be better explained as a "Marxian attempt to both inscribe a functional-instrumental version of culture as well as fulfill its more utopian ideals," one which "seeks to satisfy the deepest Marxist impulses while fleeing a Marxist idiom" (105). Nesbitt, similarly, counters the perceived break Relation introduces in Glissantian poetics with a reading attuned to the "stealthy, subterranean continuity of a modernist Glissant" (171) from his earliest works through *Traité du Tout-monde*. Both critics signal that the presence of totality, which Relation is careful to retain as an endless and always-changing category of objects' mutual transformation, shares with dialectics the possibility of arriving at a whole through the contradictions that inhere in each particular. Working within a loose Critical Theory framework, Nesbitt locates in the persistence of the modernist in Glissant a special attention to the non-identity of Martinique's society and history, which makes itself felt from under the island's reified production schemes and monumentalized colonial history through the poetic encounter with its frozen surface identities. These encounters form part of a wider structure of Antilleans' critical experience of history, what he labels "aesthetic construction," which "emphasize[s] an uncoerced creativity in which human imagination generates new formal constellations that, as in collage, allow objects to persist in their specificity rather than serving as mere raw material to be transformed into commodities, commodities that only have value in their equivalency with other commodities" (38). Even from my much abridged account of critical attempts to situate the later Glissant within the current series of problems that beset postcolonial inquiry, one can appreciate the wide variation of interpretation his work give rise to, rendering him as culture-industry sellout or lifelong (if "stealthy") Marxist with equal vigor. My own reading inevitably will place yet another version of Glissant on the gamut between these conclusions by following the relationship he cultivates between place and poetics, through its ruptures and continuities, in his oeuvre as a whole. However, I intend to keep the arguments just summarized near the surface of my analysis: My interest, one on hand, is to probe the way landscape and place (*lieu*) drive the sort of aesthetic construction Nesbitt speaks of in what I will call (with Adorno) Glissant's monadic moments, and on the other to assess their role in the intentions and inscriptions of his "singularizing" nomadic moments. Indeed, land, geography, and place seem to me to be pivotal topics for a thorough grasp of the ambivalences between these tendencies. At the current junction of Caribbean and postcolonial critique—as Glissant's popularity ascends in postcolonial academia, as questions of environment and ecology assume the spotlight in current trends of scholarship, and as different actors and institutions busy themselves configuring Glissant's legacy for future theory—the poetics of place presents a nodal point where aesthetic and political circuits and monadic and nomadic spheres all reconcentrate and overlap.[6]

A Poetic Natural History

The poetic act for Glissant is above all a penetration into nature: he declares in *L'Intention poétique*, his first poetic treatise, "The defense of landscape is the first act of the poet. To stand up against its oppression by men: therefore, against the ignorance and the formal exile where men remain" [*La défense du paysage est le premier acte du poète. Se dresser contre son écrasement par les hommes: par conséquent, contre l'ignorance and l'exil formel où les hommes se mantiennent*] (87). In a 2006 interview, he reiterates that "any poetry is linked to nature . . . because poetry is . . . a breath, yes, a breath of the living . . . of all that lives . . . poetry is the breath of life which cannot speak. Which cannot write, which cannot sing . . ." (Dash and Troupe 54). His defense of landscape bears evident parallels with the thought of Lezama examined in the previous chapter, centered on their shared conviction that the natural world delivers an indecipherable meaning to human creation that Lezama himself described as a respiration or "breath." But unlike Lezama's banquets and celebrations of the creative possibilities engendered by the historical image's dialogue with nature, Glissant's landscapes take unapologetic aim at the suffering caught in its physical forms. In a place like Martinique where, as Nesbitt has skillfully documented, the official exercise of history marches irrepressibly from the specious monuments of French republican collaborationism to the commodified spectacles of museums and folklore, recovering a sense of history against the fiction of French (and now global) identity begins where narrative failure meets the unwritten register of events, precisely where humans have crushed (*écrasé*) the land and go on alienated in the "formal exile" of its damaged remains.[7] The hills and fields, dried-up rivers, and abandoned factories of Glissant's writing thus figure as its primary but silent hero, whom the characters are all directed in one way or another to interpellate.

The complexities of these telluric protagonists are on magisterial display in *Discours antillais*, which Glissant begins with a panorama of natural history. From the island's north, "the knotted mass of somber greens which the roads still do not penetrate," where maroons found refuge and Indian coolies were deposited to work the pineapple fields, to the center, where "ruins of factories lurk . . . as a witness to the old order of the plantation" and where "slave prisons still lie hidden underground," to the delta, "chewed up by make-believe enterprises, by an airstrip," and the beaches, where slaves "climbed the coconut trees, once trying to reach out to Toussaint Louverture in the land of Haiti," that are now claimed by tourists: The beaches "are the ultimate frontier, visible evidence of our past wanderings and our present distress" (*Caribbean Discourse* 10–11). "Our landscape," Glissant adds in parentheses, "is its own monument: its meaning can only be traced on the underside. It is all history" (11). Despite this rather grandiose presentation of the island's past, teasing out the history of nature does not entail the erection of new monuments of any sort; certainly Glissant's goal is not to commemorate events by relocating and enshrining their venues. Rather, his poetics brings the edge of incomprehension, the complacent semblance of the status quo, into contact with the palpable imprint of the land's suffering. There is a well-known chapter of *Malemort* in which the three main characters, destitute day laborers (*djobeurs*), travel through nearly two centuries of Martinican history in one rambling sentence, attempting to find a language for the destruction accumulating before them:

> They began to gain consciousness of the time elapsed they saw the land dry up lighten with carved roads with housing tracts with businesses with hotels where the biggest known tractor and the factories one after the other fall along the roads like rusty tin-roofed stores they saw the land deforested disparaged trimmed and overflowing worn down like a man who for four hundred years endeavors to rediscover his image [*Ils commencaient à prendre conscience du temps écoulé ils voyaient la terre tarir s'éclaircir de routes taillées de lotissements d'entreprises d'hotels où s'activait le plus gros tracteur connu et les usines l'une après l'autre tomber au bord des routes comme des bazars de zincs rouillés ils voyaient les*

> *terres déboisées décriées bordées debordées s'user comme un homme qui depuis quatre cents ans s'efforce de retrouver son image*]. (128)

The consciousness of history unfolding in the concatenation of development, decay, and demolition rushing towards the characters is inexpressible. As the breathless sentence impresses upon us, there is no syntax or narrative form adequate to communicate the sense of this suffering: it can only be experienced.

In its ongoing quest for a formal vehicle to serve as the breath of muted natural life, Glissant's geopoetics is coordinated in the ambit of second nature, the reified conventions of society theorized by Critical Theory. Georg Lukács' formulation of second nature in *The Theory of the Novel* referred to the calcification of historical meaning in the modern novel, "a petrified estranged complex of meaning that is no longer able to awaken inwardness . . . a charnel-house of rotted interiorities" (64) conscripted to the stultifying maintenance of bourgeois values.[8] Over against first nature, the silenced, objectified world cut off from subjectivity, second nature draws into itself the static force of nature—much as the Enlightenment usurps the power of myth, according to Horkheimer and Adorno in *Dialectic of Enlightenment*—and thereby expels the historic processes stored in its form: Bourgeois consciousness appears eternal, self-perpetuating, and natural, but inside things are rotting away. This is, of course, what Glissant means when he insists that landscape's meaning must be traced on the "underside": Beneath the unquestioning carapace of Martinique's tourist-covered beaches, parking lots, and shrouded forests lie the effects of colonization, slavery, *departémentalisation*, and dependency partially coded in the land itself, which from the outside projects a smooth narrative of progress. As Glissant would have it, second nature is the central contradiction facing Martinican efforts at historical memory: namely, the contradiction between "a lived experience through which the community instinctively rejects the intrusive exclusiveness of a single History and an official way of thinking through which it passively consents in the ideology 'represented' by its elite" and "a morbidly irrational mechanism, which allows us to accept the implied logic that suggests that from historical evolution to social evolution our community has 'progressed' towards the consumerism that threatens it today" (*Caribbean Discourse* 93).

Recovering the history locked in the land, then, requires one to dispel falsely naturalized accounts of modernization. Yet the need to crack open the shell of second nature cannot be satisfied simply by replacing nature with history, not even an emancipatory or nonlinear history, lest the implicit faith in its final outcome or destiny beget only new mythifications; to avoid yet another monolithic account of the past, we must grasp the ways nature participates in history. As Adorno concludes in his reconfiguration of Lukács' second nature through the idea of "natural history," a critical approach to history must build from its interpenetration with nature, conceiving that even the most "natural" of nature is historic and, conversely, that the most historic of history is natural ("The Idea of Natural History" 117). Against the proven tendency of conceptual thought to divide and hypostatize these two spheres as subjects and objects sealed off from one another, thus cloaking the resistances each offers to the other, the purpose behind the idea of natural history, as Susan Buck-Morss sums it up, is "to destroy the mythical power which both concepts wielded over the present, a power which was the source of a fatalistic and passive acceptance of the status quo" (*The Origin of Negative Dialectics* 49). By reading the gaps that sprout up between nature and history, in which the former interrupts the identity between real history and its concept, and vice versa, natural history pursues an open dialectical movement of historic process and thus a hope, if not a guarantee, for eradicating second nature.

We have so far established that contestation of second nature requires cognition of the history stored in objectified nature as well as of nature's contamination of the subjective claims of history: It should be no surprise, given Glissant's promotion of poetics, that he, like Adorno, considers art to be the privileged site of this contestation. The potential for social critique both thinkers locate in artistic form has to do with its unique situation between autonomous and heteronomous realms of production. For while art is, indeed, a result of social conditions of production, for example of the capitalist division of labor that establishes the non-useful value of art on the crest of bourgeois hegemony in modern society, it carries social antinomies into the hermetic remove of its autonomy, where they are encrypted in the elements of its form. In its internal, immanent problems of form, art relates to the suffering of the objective world, not through imitation but "like a magnet to a field of iron filings" (Adorno, *Aesthetic Theory* 10). Itself an object that "stands opposed to society," art nonetheless contains the subjective fragments of reality—after all, its producers and consumers are social subjects—that stare back at the outside world, protesting in their own antagonisms the identitarian schemes that increasingly reduce everything to eternally fungible particulars (321). Art's relationship to society, Adorno provocatively argues in *Aesthetic Theory*, is that of a monad: Like Leibniz's windowless entities, art is closed off from the world, yet it contains it blindly as its "crystallized, immanent process at rest" (258). As in the monad, the fragments assembled in art do not illuminate the world directly but only through the zones of clarity projected on them through other monads, other artworks and, in Adorno's assessment, philosophical critique. Their reflection on reality obtains in the infinite network of perspectives privy to them, an accumulation of fragments much like Benjamin's constellations. This extreme mediatedness of art's critique of society explains why Adorno, as well as Glissant, refute the notion of its direct social usefulness. Adorno is unequivocal on this point: "What [art] contributes to society is not some directly communicable content but something more mediate, i.e., resistance. Resistance reproduces social development in aesthetic terms without directly imitating it" (321). In a footnote to his discussion of Creole folktales in *Discours antillais*, Glissant clarifies this objective of art in similar terms: "An exploration of the chaos of memory (obscured, alienated, or reduced to a range of natural references) cannot be done in the 'clarity' of a linear narrative. The production of texts must also produce history, not in its capacity to facilitate some happening, but in its ability to raise a concealed world to the level of consciousness. Exploration is not analytical but creative. The exposé is quivering with creativity, obscure because of its incongruous contents whose coming together is not immediately apparent" (*Caribbean Discourse* 107). The consciousness raising Glissant points to in folktales results precisely from their lack of clarity, the fact that they do not present social problems transparently to their audience but rather work to "dismantle the complex mechanism of frustration and the infinite forms of oppression" (107) through the very sort of resistance defended by Adorno. The monotonous uniformity of time in Creole narrative, or the "breathless" quality of the folktale, which passes through a land "that has been suffered [but] is not yet the land that is offered, made accessible" (131), these are the formal features that disentangle the "chaos of memory" through the audience's contemplation of the antagonisms present in their lives.

It is within the slow mediation of the monadic form, its constellated interrogation of deep mechanisms of oppression, that Glissant's geopoetics takes shape. His first novel, *La Lézarde* (translated into English as *The Ripening*), is almost entirely consumed with exploring the domination of nature, seeking to revive in Martinique's landscapes "the content of what the language of nature was trying to say to man in cryptic, almost unintelligible ways" (Adorno, *Aesthetic Theory* 114). As Michael Dash writes in his introduction to the book's English translation, here "[n]atural objects appear as a material representation of an underlying system of meanings, a means of wresting meaning from a flawed world" (Glissant, *The Ripening* 15). The Lézarde river, which gives the novel its title, is in many ways the protagonist of the narrative: from the spring where it first bubbles up deep inside a house in the mountains to the putrid mud of its delta, it guides a group of young political activists toward a foundation of national consciousness in an inexpressible understanding of the land's suffering. The characters' political plot—to assassinate the corrupt government official Garin, a task they delegate to a reclusive mountain shepherd named Thaël—is carried out in palpatory exploration of the land, over which they wander, from mountain to plain to beach, throughout the book. In the Martinique of *La Lézarde*, "the land speaks to everyone, like a pillow speaks to the ear lying on it" (82). A central axis of the plot has Thaël escorting Garin down the river from the mountains to the sea, where he ultimately will drown him: Happening upon the town of Lambrianne, a shabby gathering of houses between the river and a stagnant canal, both men puzzle at its forlornness, the flat and empty quality of its landscape—so empty, they exclaim, that it's not even a town but a hole, a hodge-podge (96)—which nevertheless awakens in them the prescience of its hidden charms. What Thaël discovers, in the pedagogical tone typical of his prophetic character, is that the town's attraction lies in its surroundings, the land, river, and sea that embed it in a spreading composition, negating its identity: "It's full of people who think they are special because they have salons, services and go for a stroll every Sunday afternoon. But this is not the truth of the town! Deep down inside they are aware of the land around them. Beneath the dummy's exterior there is a gleam of light. They cannot live as if this were a real town, they cannot run and shout, because this town is a product of the land, not cut off, there is no wall, it's part of everything, pulling it all together" (97–98). The buried content of the town's alienated forms pushes back against its pretensions of complacent existence, its ersatz town-ness. By thwarting the affirmation of the town's unadulterated identity, landscape supplies its perplexing beauty: "All the meanness of the town calls out to something beyond the horizon, not so? And so the river is what prevents the town from being a town and gives it the chance to be something else, in the heart of the night. That's beauty" (100). The Lézarde curves down to the sea, linking the town with possibilities "beyond the horizon," which here point to the fulfillment of national consciousness: In leading to the sea, the river reawakens the staidness of social forms with openness and futurity ("Because the sea is the future, isn't it? The sea is always open, it allows you to come and go" [100]).

Thaël's epiphany is clearly drawn from second nature and natural history as Adorno defines them. His revelations derive from the observation of the land's suffering, the fact that the land is not worked by the townspeople who prefer to put on airs and suppress their own "natural" history: in this sense the town's beauty partakes of what Adorno calls the beautiful in nature, the "residue of non-identity in things, in an age when they are otherwise spellbound by universal identity" (*Aesthetic Theory* 108). But more important here is the way the dialectic between the novel's social relations and their nonidentity inheres as a matter of artistic form, for *La Lézarde*'s lesson, the "ripening" of a notion of place that it aims for, travels through the experience of landscape dictated by an internal symbolism and antagonism of values much more than through overt denunciations of colonization, slavery, or exploitation. Indeed, the book's denouement reveals that what the whole story has been driving at is an experience of history's muted language through landscape, an experience best induced by writing itself. In a shuffling between second- and first-person narration in the last chapters, "you"—that is, us as readers—are prompted to remember the known events of Martinican history and to grasp their residual diffusion beyond narration in the landscape, in their victims' "supreme effort to identify with the flame tree, the terrible silk cotton tree, the shimmering sand bar" (*The Ripening* 169).[9] A consciousness of history, in other words, is redeemed in the formal meanderings of the characters: "So you realized why neither Mathieu nor Michel nor Thaël sought to enumerate, measure, make sense of this history of suffering in its minutest detail, why it was enough for them for a while to recognize the nature of this suffering, this sombre condition of humiliation" (169). What the novel calls out to in the diegetic movements among river, mountain, and sea is not the documented history of the island but the unknown quality of its suffering, which is at once natural and historical. This formal interpellation is the challenge set to the first-person narrator who appears in the last pages, an "I" suggestive of the young Glissant himself, a firsthand witness to the struggles of Thaël and his friends: Following the instructions of Thaël, "I" must write about their endeavors "like a river. Slow. Like the Lézarde. With rushing water, meanders, sometimes sluggish, sometimes running freely, slowly gathering the earth from either bank. Like that, yes, picking up the earth round it. Little by little. Like a river, murky with secrets that it deposits in the calm sea" (175).

As the fledgling narrator-author of *La Lézarde* learns, a progressive consciousness of place is inextricable from questions of form. And for Glissant, there is no place in which this is more true than the Caribbean, where the island's "dialectic between inside and outside is reflected in the relationship of land and sea" (*Caribbean Discourse* 139). But specifically what sort of service does the monadic quality of art, the mediation of inside and outside, render to Glissant's geopoetics? A brief return to Lezama's thinking of place from the previous chapter can help illuminate this relationship and the way it informs Glissant's archipelic thought. Recall that for Lezama, autochthony also begins with a probe into second nature, what he calls "supranature." According to Lezama, the poetic act captures the tension in supranature between extension, the infinite of sheer possibility, and the vertical penetration of selected particulars—from this metaphorical dyad emerges American expression as a reworking of possibility in the knitting together of far-flung fragments, like a storied tree on a vast plain. In the iconic essay "Preludio a las eras imaginarias," Lezama dissects these two axes further, pondering the duel between the unconditionality of extension and the causality of form: "Form already presupposes second nature, the second birth, the Pascalian 'anything can be nature'" [*La forma . . . presupone ya la segunda naturaleza, el segundo nacimiento, el 'todo puede ser naturaleza' pascaliano*] (*Obras Completas* II 801). Art is predicated on the lost object of first nature, which it defies in the very act of imposing order and causality: its forms cite nature negatively. It is this contradiction, this "challenge to chance" [*reto al azar*] that forms art's link to the absolute of unconditionality—unconditionality that, fully realized, would be a true identity—and not the representation or imitation of the absolute, for "all being is causal, seeks to be causal, to differentiate itself from the succession of infinity" [*todo ser es ser causal, busca ser causal, para diferenciarse de la sucesión en la infinitud*] (797). That is to say, as Adorno also insists, that Being always involves particulars, and that the endeavor to capture an absolute form where the great secrets may be revealed is purely illusionary.[10] For Lezama, "being is being causal, as the tree is forest. Causality is like a forest . . . dominated" [*ser es ser causal, como el árbol es bosque. La causalidad es como un bosque . . . dominado*] (798). The analogy refers to the inherent classifying gesture of causes, which identify and put in motion like elements toward some end, much as the tree is subsumed both symbolically and metonymically to its "kind," the forest. Both of the foregoing relationships dominate the elements involved: being anything at all brings with it an unfreedom that shutters existence off from the infinite. However, Lezama considers the existential burden of this predicament also to be its ethical injunction. One cannot be content merely to "be" in the dictated causality, but must exist against its grain and in blind communication with the extension of inconditionality, germinating a retroactive causality.

Glissant's poetics addresses the same antinomies of identity from a different angle. As he writes with strikingly similar language in *L'Intention poétique*:

> When I say: tree, and when I think of the tree, I never sense the unique, the trunk, the mast of sap that, affixed to others, will form this expanse sliced through with light that is the forest . . . that I should try awkwardly to draw a tree: I end up with a section of vegetation, where only the sky of the page will put an end to the indeterminate growth. The unique is lost in the Whole [*Quand je dis: arbre, et quand je pense à l'arbre, je ne ressens jamais l'unique, le tronc, le mât de sève que apposé à d'autres groupera cette étendue fendue de lumière qu'est la forêt . . . Que j'essaie maladroit de dessiner un arbre: j'aboutirai à un pan de végétation, où seul le ciel de la page mettra un terme à la croissance indéterminée. L'unique se perd dans ce Tout*]. (48)[11]

Attempting to arrive at the particular for itself and wholly identified, we find only the jumbled plane of its interaction—the forest or jungle, an endless chaos only to be challenged, as with Lezama's terrible extension, by the perimeters of art, the "sky" of the page. The snapshot of chaos harnessed by the art form, a section of "ebullient density" [*densité bouillante*] (*L'Intention poétique* 48), imposes the unfreedom of order to release something of the particular hidden in its folds: as a sky, it both contains and opens out endlessly, just as art for Adorno "goes inward in order to go outward and beyond" (*Aesthetic Theory* 368). This is the single point Glissant stresses most about identity and the crucial articulation between textuality and geography he approximates in different ways with the concepts of *retour* and *détour, opacité,* and Relation: place is *incontournable*, inescapable but also uncircumventable—poetry cannot avoid place, nor can it wall it off into a discrete territory. Either way, there is no getting around it. Both Lezama and Glissant view poetry as a repeated situation where the meaning of place emerges processually, as a constellation of pieces rather than in a finalized form. As Glissant goes on to explain in the section of *L'Intention poétique* quoted above, poetry "by stages, by dark, uprooted strata, opens being to its relativities lived, suffered in the world's drama . . . It permits one to anchor the unique, the particular, the dazzling beginning of each community in the patience of its soon to be illuminated connection to the Other" [*par paliers, par strates obscures et arrachées, ouvre l'être sur ses relativités vécues, souffertes au drame du monde . . . Elle permet d'ancrer l'unique, le particulier, le fulgurant principe de chaque communauté dans la patience de son rapport bientôt éclairé à l'Autre*] (47–48). The monadic form of Glissant's geopoetics helps clear up some of the ways place is to figure in archipelic thought: namely, it shows that poetry provides no essential link to identity—for Glissant there is nothing ontological about place—but only a bit of order, form, or causality without which being at all would be impossible. Through the accumulation of experiences and representations that give place its form, what Jacques Coursil calls a "topic of narratives" [*topique de récits*]—poetics brings forth place's nonidentity, the content of chaos that roils its hardened conceptual boundaries. It is in this sense that, as Coursil states, "the world is in a place" [*le monde est dans un lieu*] (90). As Coursil's overview of Relation details, place (not coincidentally conceived, for Glissant as for Lezama, as an expanse, an *étendue*) is not spatial but a site of repeated and remembered meaning: "Thus, the world is a physical reality that contains humans who in turn contain representations of this world, but it is in the representations that they live. In the folds of the world, there is a multiplicity of unknown expanses. Each expanse is a space of life" [*Ainsi, le monde est une réalité physique qui contient des humains qui à leur tour contiennent des représentations de ce monde, mais c'est dans ces représentations qu'ils vivent. Dans les plis du monde, il y a une multiplicité d'étendues insues. Chaque étendue est un espace de vie*] (Coursil 90).

From Monad to Nomad: Relation and Tout-Monde

In fleshing out the monadic relation that mediates social and aesthetic values in some of Glissant's early works, I have been concerned to outline a central apparatus of his geopoetics, many of whose most important insights and assumptions persist in the evolving renderings of Relation and Tout-monde he offers, starting with *Poétique de la Relation*. Reading his more "global" theories with a focus on the place of poetics makes apparent the ways they actually deepen and extend some of these monadic traits: Relation and Tout-monde start out from the conclusions of a work like *La Lézarde*, its confidence in the sylleptic force of place—and more and more, the place they recur to is the archipelago—also with an eye to combatting embedded mechanisms of oppression. Both Relation and Tout-monde are, simply put, ways of describing a totality in flux that nonetheless refuses the generalization of a universal view (the "totalitarian," as Glissant terms it) and moves toward a sense of the Whole as it obtains in endless particularities.[12] Insofar as Glissant considers these concepts to be views wrought from the experience of modernity—the suffering caused by conquest, colonization, the territorialization of the earth and its people, and other projects of "root" thinking—their primary goal is, in fact, to discredit and replace universality, as the *Traité* announces:

> The pretention to abstract a universal from a particular no longer sways us. It is the very matter of all places, their meticulous or infinite detail and the glorious unity of their particularities, that are to be placed in collusion with those of all places . . . The idea of the world is legitimated by the imaginary of the world, interwoven poetics that allow me to guess the way my place conjoins with others, how without moving it adventures abroad, and how it carries me along in this immobile movement [*La prétention d'abstraire un universel à partir d'un particulier ne nous émeut plus. C'est la matière même de tous les lieux, leur minutieux ou infini détail et l'ensemble exaltant de leurs particularités, qui sont à poser en connivence avec ceux de tous les lieux . . . L'idée du monde s'autorise de l'imaginaire du monde, des poétiques entremélées qui me permettent de deviner en quoi mon lieu conjoint à d'autres, en quoi sans bouger il s'aventure ailleurs, et comment il m'emporte dans ce mouvement immobile*]. (*Traité du Tout-monde* 120)

Conceived as a type of immobile voyage, Relation and Tout-monde pick up on Glissant's geopoetic probing of nonidentity—a formal survey of landscape that gleans a sense of land's suffering in second nature—and relay it to a global nexus modeled on the geographic, historic, and cultural features of the Caribbean: a natural passageway, a sea that "explodes" and "diffracts" (*Poetics of Relation* 33), and a site of Creolization, "a new and original dimension allowing each person to be there and elsewhere" (34), the Caribbean is emphasized as a place that indeed goes inward in order to go outward, a place that has always already been infused with its Others. The landscape of the Caribbean is thus elevated from a place for thought to a thought of place, a veritable mapping of a new imaginary of the earth. The second nature Relation and Tout-monde target is not so much the obstacles that stand in the way of the autonomy of Martinicans and other (de)colonized populations, the alienation that has to be overcome to make the land "ours"; rather, they rally against all territorialization, orienting our perceptions of a given place to all its Others, in a process that ideally works like Lezama's countercipher. In Lezama's phrasing, what Glissant would like us to realize is that place is really an answer to a question that cannot be formulated. Those Caribbean landscapes most closely associated with openness, instability, and exchange—the mangrove, the beach, the Rocher du Diamant—are offered as touchstones for the becoming-archipelago of the world, voicing the non-identity that everywhere rises up against the partitioning of the earth into bordered, policed territories.[13] For Glissant, it is precisely in the measure that this voice becomes audible, that "the regions of the world become islands, isthmuses, peninsulas, promontories, lands of mixture and crossing, and which nonetheless persist" [*les régions du monde deviennent des îles, des isthmes, des presqu'îles, des avancées, terres de melange et de passage, et qui pourtant demeurent*] (*Traité du Tout-monde* 181).

It is well known that the shift in scale from regional or national consciousness-building to a worldwide becoming, showcased in assertions like the one just quoted, owes heavily to the rhizomatic theories of Deleuze and Guattari, an epistemological universe composed of the continuous regroupment of unstable, centerless assemblages that conduct unprecedented flows of change and creation. The influence of the rhizome thus largely accounts for what we may characterize as a reorientation from monadic to nomadic art in Glissant's geopoetics, insofar as it seeks to acknowledge, as Tom Conley states in his introduction to Deleuze's own most monadic work, *The Fold*, how "[o]ur experience of a shrinking globe inflects the vision of the monad, since compressions of time and space modify 'the difference of inside and outside and public and private' . . . , [leading] contemporary artists and musicians [to] transform monadology into nomadology" (xv).[14] It is significant, for example, that Glissant's overture to rhizomatic thought in the *Poétique* begins with a defense of errantry, a "circular nomadism" distinguishable from the "arrow-like" trajectory of epic and conquest in that it "gives-on-and-with the negation of every pole and every metropolis" (*Poetics of Relation* 19)—in other words, a nomadism that neither originates from nor travels toward a consolidated identity. Yet the ease with which the general notion of nomadism translates to motifs of movement, flight, and indeterminacy distracts from the way place remains indispensable to it, the way the nomad clings to locality. Deleuze and Guattari are careful to correct these commonplace associations in their introduction to nomadology in *A Thousand Plateaus*, insisting that "it is . . . false to define the nomad by movement" (381): They explain that the nomad does not have movement—a relative, extensive displacement of some unified body along discrete points—but speed, which is an intensive occupation, "the absolute character of a body whose irreducible parts . . . fill a smooth space in the manner of a vortex" (381). Rather than carry some entity through space for resettlement like migration, which necessarily recurs to an atomized vision of the whole—what Deleuze and Guattari refer to as a relativized global or universal—nomadism relates to space as a matter of qualitative change, "the spot where the forest recedes, or where the steppe and the desert advance" (381–82). Change and variation are the territory of the nomad: He "reterritorializes on deterritorialization itself" (381), occupying an absolute and unlimited locality. "[T]he absolute, then, does not appear at a particular place but becomes a nonlimited locality; the coupling of the place and the absolute is achieved not in a centered, oriented globalization or universalization but in an infinite succession of local operations" (383).

One need not be a particularly dedicated reader of Glissant to recognize the echoes of Deleuze and Guattari's nomadology in Relation: The plantation, the archipelago, and Creolization all constitute absolute localities in the sense they describe. Of course, the turn to the nomadic requires a concomitant abandonment of relatively defined places—namely, the nation-to-come of Martinique—that goes far to explain the discomfort of critics like Hallward, who is absolutely right to pinpoint Relation as a moment of singularization in Glissantian poetics. However, taking the preference for singular understandings of difference as sufficient evidence that Relation effectively erases the space of development and conflict or, according to Bongie's calculations, that it supplants politics with culture, in my view dispenses too hastily with the nuanced understanding of locality wrought in Glissant's nomadism. In this the thrust of their critiques, though on the whole well warranted, is inexact in two important regards: First because the relationship of place to poetics in these concepts, as I want to show, retains the monadic nature of art's link to society—that is, as a matter of form—and second because the political intervention Glissant claims for them, at least in his most viable articulations of monadic and nomadic optics, likewise corresponds to the limits of art, subordinating the infinite movement of Relation to the necessary frame of order so that it becomes an immanent expression of poetics. This minimum order required for chaos, I believe, is key to understanding how the archipelic thought of Glissant's later work calls back to, and may even be able to address, his earlier concerns with second nature.

How do we arrive at the social mediation proper to the artwork from the absolute localities that proliferate in the pages of *Poétique de la Relation* and *Traité du Tout-monde?* The possibility of such localities is predicated, first of all, in globalization, not against it but inexorably within it. The difficulty of accepting Relation and Tout-monde comes from the often maddening vagueness of the hair's breadth distance they open up between globalization and its alternatives, the almost imperceptible space between totalization and totality or between commonplaces and common places in which Glissant mobilizes them, and which for their detractors too seamlessly cedes to the stream of commodified indifference.[15] Glissant is by no means unaware of this difficulty: indeed, however idealist and triumphalist Relation may seem at times, it departs from a perspective of extreme cynicism. From the current state of dependency in Martinique, the "privileged disquiet" (*Poetics of Relation* 145) of citizens who trade a subsidized improductivity for the right to partake of imported luxuries and enjoy the veneer of artificial comfort, or from the less dissimulated regimes of oppression shouldered by small countries and marginalized populations everywhere, there is no telling where the ideological reach of standardization is exhausted, if at all. On one hand this is true, Glissant avers, because as the track record of countless movements of resistance has proven, every opposition is prone to buckle under one or another variety of atavism[16]; on the other hand, turning away from identity to brave the vagaries of globalized commerce is also not an option: both rooted place and the negation of place ultimately reinsert us in the cogs of market capitalism because they provide no method for cognizing the relation of particular situations beyond the spectacularized movements that history, fashion, media networks, and other ideological vehicles present as the facts of reality.

The data of globalization, which Glissant dubs "active relays"—"the intervention of one State on the territory of another, genocide, the universal triumph of a way of life, generalization of a standardized product, humanitarian aid" (*Poetics of Relation* 177), and so on—truly do induct the violences that make up the changing face of domination in the world, but only by veiling their real effects in the dazzle of their consumption: they are "flash agents" that "literally reflect th[e] matter [of Relation], their reflections manifesting its violence without shedding any light on it or shifting it or changing it" (178). The decision to take a stand with or against any visible line of force misses the real problem, that a given force's manifest links to the suffering it creates or attempts to combat is always caught between the "active relays" of reported events and the "neutral relays" that play out in experiences on the ground. "Anyone who wishes to intervene in modes of Relation . . . will find his action on unsure footing because of this indeterminacy between active and neutral relays. This is why such an intervention 'in Relation' can only really happen 'in a place,' one simultaneously closed in on its components and open to its returning echoes" (178). Of course, the "place" where interventions are possible is not a physical location in the usual sense, but the intensive occupation of change in the manner of absolute locality. Place, here, has no center and no borders, so although recounting its particularities approximates us asymptotically to its definition, what comes closest to the mark in such an exercise is the share of Relation in each example, the Others running through each "here," relating it through a line of demarcation with the same incalculability as the shoreline often invoked by chaos theory: a solid line that is actually immeasurable, dissolving under magnification into endlessly shifting grains of sand.[17] It is in this sense that place, for Relation, is both "distancing" and "determinant," approaching through specificity the infinite and always changing connections of Relation, and vice versa (169–74).[18]

It is with the possibility of acting on Relation in a place that the absolute locality proper to nomadism can be said to reassert certain monadic principles of art and its specific mode of intervention in society. For it is precisely the indeterminacy between active and neutral relays, the difficulty of limning a secure border between the dazzling spectacle that announces a worldwide connectivity and its unpronounced effects on the practices of life in a place, that recommends the viability of Relation as poetics. The proposals tentatively set forth in the *Poétique*, and more forcefully in the *Traité*, are accordingly poetic projects, new ways of "relating to the earth" directed at this indeterminacy, not as a foregone element of meaning but as a fluctuation captured and released over and over in creative thought, so that "at every moment Relation becomes complete but also is destroyed in its generality by exactly what we put into action in a particular time and place" (*Poetics of Relation* 203). Glissant's notion of "aesthetics of the earth" homes in on this fluctuation, claiming it as the site of an imaginary of land to be wielded both against the blanket imposition of standardized, "denaturized" networks of consumption and anachronistic solutions of a "return to the land" in tokenistic production. In a place like Martinique, for example, steering local tastes away from Coca-Cola and caviar cannot be achieved through promotion of homegrown foods alone, lest local production become another taste manufactured by the market's seduction, a folkloric niche managed by the same whims that make Martinican children dream of dried sausage (148). "No matter where you are," Glissant insists, "the forces of this market will find you. If there is a profit to be made, they will deal with you" (152). The obvious alternative—and today the option explored in the overwhelming majority of the Caribbean—of making the land a respite of Nature cleared entirely of the production that elsewhere artificially sustains it, the "air-conditioned nightmare" of "Museums of Natural Non-History" (150), is clearly no better. What poetics offers to this impasse is an imaginary of totality enacted from the difficult, even abominable circumstances of one's surroundings, an imaginary Glissant pointedly terms an ecology.

Aesthetics of the Earth and Eco Art

The type of ecology favored in "aesthetics of the earth" figures with some frequency in the *Poétique* and in later works as a register of thought labile enough to mobilize the aesthetic as well as the pragmatic transformation of Martinique's import-export economy through activity envisioned primarily as poetic: as Glissant suggests in *Introduction à une poétique du divers*, poetics takes on the role of guiding ecologists in their anxious search for a "return to more evident, more simple things" [*retour à des choses plus évidentes, plus simples*] (135). It is in this capacity, however implicitly, that poetics enters into Glissant's most sustained ecological initiative to promote specialized organic crops for export, a program he supported along with Patrick Chamoiseau, Gérard Delver, and Bertène Juminer in the 2000 "Manifeste pour refonder les DOM," and whose basic thrust is outlined in a section titled "Martinique" in the *Traité*. Following the lines of a "utopian" project of making the Caribbean an exemplary common place, he urges,

> Let us clean up our world, and let Martinique, for example, proclaim and maintain itself, as a single entity, a pristine ecological land . . . Let us seek in the elsewhere of the world the places where products that we will have desired, planned, and realized through a common will might be offered and accepted. In the world there is a place (of buyers, of determined amateurs, of those with a passion for exchanges) for all that might arise from a space of light, for all that might appear from a will to clean the waters and clouds, the Gardens and Sands [*Commençons de nettoyer autour, et que la Martinique par exemple se proclame et se mantienne, d'un seul tenant, terre biologique et de clarté . . . Cherchons dans l'ailleurs du monde les endroits où des produits que nous aurons voulus, aménagés, réalisés selon notre commune détermination, pourraient être proposés et acceptés. Dans le monde il est une place*

> (*des acheteurs, des amateurs convaincus, des passionnés d'échange*) *pour tout ce qui surgirait d'un espace de lumière, pour tout ce qui procéderait d'une volonté de nettoyer les eaux et les nuages, les Jardins et les Sables*]. (Nesbitt 185, 227)

The manifesto-like quality of the imperative verbs and the talk of markets and buyers make the passage stand out in the *Traité*, a treatise so exclusively focused on the poetic that it appears, as Bongie notes, to reject outright any recourse to "principled politics." Here we are exhorted to act, and yet the oddly romantic phrasing of the work to be done as the assertion of a "pristine" land, a "space of light," remains wedded to a resolutely poetic sphere of action, for the proposal to create a Martinican "ecological land," Delphine Perret reminds us (93), refers above all to the creation of a place (*lieu*) in the world, a task whose efforts and effects are guaranteed first in the imagination. As such it maintains the extremely mediated social impact proper to poetics which, as Glissant pronounces less exuberantly elsewhere in the *Traité*, "today have no effect, absolutely no effect against the concrete oppressions that stupefy the world" [*ne sont aujourd'hui d'une aucune efficacité, absolument d'aucune efficacité contre les oppressions concrètes qui stupéfient le monde*] (*Traité du Tout-monde* 18). Glissant's ecology is thus pulled in two apparently irreconcilable directions: on the one hand, it appeals to an action as immediate as a matter of thought, as though rhetorically willing an "organic" Martinique into being should make it appear[19]; on the other hand, it remains couched in the skeptical caveats attendant on the autonomous function of poetics. At the heart of this tension, of course, is the question of the status of poetics, arguably the central point of contention in discussions of archipelic thought in general: simply put, exactly where and how does poetics act on the world? Between nomadic and monadic impulses—that is, between the self-generation of the global archipelago and the perhaps more old-fashioned adage of aesthetics that art influences society, in Adorno's words, "by changing consciousness in ways that are ever so difficult to pin down" (*Aesthetic Theory* 344)—what hope does poetics have of addressing material suffering? A further probe into the movements captured in Glissant's self-described ecological stance, particularly in the way it shifts between monadic and nomadic perspectives on art, society, and politics, can afford us a more precise evaluation of the stakes of archipelic thought for his geopoetics.

Both Nesbitt and Bongie have taken up the topic of poetics as it crystallizes in the ecological project of an organic Martinique, each discovering in it a fulcrum from which to read the investments of Glissant's oeuvre as a whole. For Nesbitt, the proposal of the *Traité* "brilliantly unites a putatively *dépassé* modernism and a global consciousness of relation" (171):

Although it "recovers a political and ethical dimension seemingly lost in his later thought" (184), in positing a poetic ecology it opens the subject/object dynamics of modernist strains of poetics toward "interpenetrating and interdependent subjectivities" (187), toward the possibilities assemblage and becoming extend to the passive suffering of ecological objects. For Bongie, the project galvanizes quite a different assessment of Glissant's poetic trajectory, one that forces our attention to the slippery transvaluations the defense of "autonomous" poetics can make available to cultural politics in the heyday of postcolonial academic markets. The rise of Glissant's own star in global theory, Bongie argues, must not be viewed separately from his decision in the mid-1990s to reissue many of his previous works with the Parisian publishing house Gallimard as a series of "*Poétiques*," a series that would later add the "hyper-aestheticizing" (*Friends and Enemies* 341) *Traité* and *La Cohée du Lamentin* as part of a retroactive uniformization of his career in the mold of a great modernist writer, an author in the "bastion of pure literature" (342–43). From the capital accrued to the disinterested activity of the "mature" artist, as Bourdieu has it, the market is free to pursue its own interests. This helps to explain, for Bongie, the sudden economic tenor of Glissant's ecological posturing, which clinches the transferral of cultural to political value in what he calls the "scribal politics" of postcoloniality.

There is much merit in both Nesbitt and Bongie's appraisals of the poetic in Glissant's later work in that they manage to alert us to the risks inherent to its conflation of autonomous and heteronomous spheres of cultural production without discarding out of hand the liberationist potential in negotiating the two. Although Nesbitt, for example, generally holds that the introduction of rhizomatic schematics vitiates Glissant's dialectical tendencies, dismissing such "postmodern" concerns as "in some sense superficial and in any case not [his] most interesting theoretical dimension" (171), he nonetheless welcomes the prospect that a decentering of subjectivity through the lens of ecology may in fact "exten[d] the work of enlightenment" (186). Similarly, for all Bongie's wariness of the magical properties of the poetic that seem to sweep under the rug Glissant's very interested positioning in the theoretical marketplace, he stops short of disparaging the real value a principled separation of literature and politics may yet reserve against the juggernaut of cultural politics, reasoning that "the drawing of this line [between politics and poetics] has the signal value of forcing us to question the legitimacy of conflating any cultural theory, such as that of creolization, with the exigencies of politics" (*Friends and Enemies* 350). The concessions each critic makes to what they otherwise see only as an unscrupulous mixing of opposed aesthetic frameworks infuses their conclusions with a strambotic sensibility, one which I think can be traced to the lack of mediation between monadic and nomadic understandings of poetics.[20]

The status of poetics remains a problem with important consequences for archipelic thought because it throws into relief the set of social processes intervening in the distance between imagining a more egalitarian, archipelic existence and actually living one. For a poetics that claims aesthetically to expunge the extant divisions of society, the dangers are as old as those articulated around the avant-garde's pretended sublation of art and life, the risk, as Adorno had it, that "art speak directly to people, as though the mediate could realize itself immediately in a world of universal mediation" (quoted in Jameson 188). We can see how this risk informs Glissant's poetics of place in some of his last writerly interventions in the public sphere, particularly in the "Manifeste pour les 'produits' de haute nécessité," a piece in which he, along with eight other signatories, proclaims support for the 2009 Lyannaj. Lyannaj, Creole for *liennage* or alliance, became the name for the explosion of strikes and protests in Guadeloupe—and subsequently in Martinique, Guyane, and Réunion—against the economic straitjacket of imported French products whose inflated prices impose a de facto regime of "*la vie chère*" on local economies. In solidarity with the movement, the signatories propose a reconceptualization of the standards of economic well-being—such as the measures of "purchasing power" or the rhetorical "market basket" of the consumer price index—as a matter of poetics: "When the 'prosaic' does not open up to the elevations of 'poetics,'" the writers submit, "when it becomes its own finality and is consumed as such, we have the tendency to believe that the aspirations of our life, and its need of meaning, can be found in the barcodes of 'purchasing power' or the 'market basket'" [*quand le 'prosaïque' n'ouvre pas aux élévations du 'poétique,' quand il devient sa propre finalité et se consume ainsi, nous avons tendance à croire que les aspirations de notre vie, et son besoin de sens, peuvent se loger dans ces codes-barres que sont le 'pouvoir d'achat' ou 'le panier de la ménagère'*] (Bréleur et al. 4). By "reinserting work into poetics" [*réinstaller le travail au sein du poétique*] (9), the manifesto claims, the DOM-TOMs stand to remake their economies into operations of "autoproduction," which would seek out opportunities of social engagement and ecological revitalization rather than obeying the "prosaic" prison of capitalist accumulation. Their alternative basket of essential "products" comprises the indices of emotional and social quality of life, such as "an amplification of the imaginary, a stimulation of cognitive faculties, an ignition of everyone's creativity" [*une amplification de l'imaginaire, une stimulation des facultés cognitives, une mise en créativité de tous*] (10).

Although it was written collectively, the manifesto bears some of the prominent features of the work of Glissant's interlocutors Deleuze and Guattari, particularly Guattari's ecological theories in *The Three Ecologies* and *Chaosmosis:* For Guattari's own triplex of mental, social, and environmental ecology, it is similarly poetics that can make the biggest strides toward a reconceptualization of society. Over against capitalist regimes of value, Guattari promotes the superimposition of "instruments of valorization founded on existential productions that cannot be determined simply in terms of abstract labor-time or by an expected capitalist profit" (*The Three Ecologies* 65), what amounts to a "new stock-exchange of value" centered on a production of subjectivity unbeholden to the market's flattened scale of value (43). Thus the pathway out of the reified social forms that I have described here as second nature, begins for Guattari with the insertion of production in poetic logic: it involves a poeticization of economics, a "new art of living in society" (*Chaosmosis* 20). The utopian bent of Guattari's mental ecology, echoed in the "Manifeste," easily substantiates Bongie's complaints about the eclipse of "principled" politics in favor of an overriding toothless cultural politics: like the more frustrating moments of Relation and Tout-monde, a poetic ecology along these lines appears to smooth out the antagonisms between capitalist equivalency and non-identity in a wider, all-inclusive equation of "poetics" that pretends to win the struggle against identity and imperialism through a simple shift in aesthetic optic. Certainly, this is one possible outcome of archipelic thought, a hapless conflation of aesthetics and politics that so rankles critics of Glissant and Deleuze and Guattari alike. Yet I think in the urge to jettison the ideas of "late Glissant" in view of this eventuality, we may foreclose some of their promising concessions to his earlier monadic principles of art, as well as the partial capitulation of these to nomadic notions of poetics: what I will argue in the remainder of this chapter, in short, is that the rapprochement between the two may well provide a more viable poetic ecology, one simultaneously able, as Nesbitt has it, to "exten[d] the work of enlightenment" (186) through decentered subjectivity and, in Bongie's words, to "forc[e] us to question the legitimacy of conflating . . . cultural theory . . . with the exigencies of politics" (*Friends and Enemies* 350).

The proximity of monadic and nomadic art has to do, at bottom, with art's (in)finite existence. We have seen how Adorno praises art's ability to reflect the world darkly in the folds of its forms, at once closed in on themselves and open to infinity. From within its enclosure, art challenges the reigning contradictions of society: The non-identity it captures stands opposed to the status quo with a "hidden 'it should be otherwise'" (Adorno, "Commitment" 89). Guattari's ecology, and indeed Deleuze and Guattari's ideas about art in general, posit a similar connection between aesthetic forms and life. "At the heart of all ecological praxes," writes Guattari, "there is an a-signifying rupture, in which the catalysts of existential change are close at hand, but lack expressive support from the assemblage of enunciation" (*The Three Ecologies* 30). The creative forces of deterritorialization, the very catalysts of Guattari's prophesied poetic subjectivation, act everywhere imperfectly voiced by the dominant refrains of meaning, what he calls "Integrated World Capitalism." They await only a new plane of consistency, a singular terrain also open to the chaos of infinity, to give full-throated protest to existing oppression. This is the essence of "eco-art" for Guattari, an existential terrain that is "precarious, finite, finitized, singular, singularized, capable of . . . opening up processually from a praxis that enables it to be made 'habitable' by a human project" (35). In other words, the test for art is to express a consistency of meaning for the investment of new ways of being, without falling prey to the many clichés already equalized by the market, or dissolving back into the chaos of endless deterritorialization. Thus, although Deleuze and Guattari stringently reject the autonomy of art and of subjects, they apprehend art largely as a matter of finite compositions, acknowledging that "we require just a little order to protect us from chaos," as they stipulate in their discussion of art in *What Is Philosophy?* (201). The order of form, of line and of color, though unattached to any of the social autonomy of Adornian aesthetics, is yet essential to make apparent the heterogeneous claims of becoming within the "stratification" of existence. Stephen Zepke outlines this process as an "immanence of the abstract machine" in stratification, "an articulation of [painting's] finite and infinite dimensions, an art of creation that in its finite processes of construction absolutely deterritorialises the world" (118). Balanced between the chaos it has "taken into a frame" and the stratification that partially determines it as art, art wields the former as a weapon against the latter, hoping to bring into view a missing people to come. In this way, Deleuze and Guattari muse, art holds the peculiarity of "pass[ing] through the finite in order to rediscover, to restore the infinite" (*What Is Philosophy?* 197).

Without overestimating the affinities between certain elements of Deleuze and Guattari's philosophy of art that I have very briefly sketched here and Adorno's aesthetic theory, we can still appreciate their concession to art's monadic relationship to society, its (in)finity.[21] The same precept has been present throughout Glissant's work—quite pointedly in novels like *La Lézarde*, as we have seen, but also in later treatises—as the defining relation between Mesure and Démesure. While Mesure, in a first instance, is the order of form plied to probe the deeper meaning of things, a "tutelary obstacle" [*obstacle tutélaire*] "given in advance [and which] makes surge forth and expresses mystery, or depth" [*donné d'avance [et qui] fait surgir et éxprime le mystère, ou la profondeur*] it also serves as "the echo of human breath . . . no longer the probing of depth but the inspiration of extension" [*l'echo du souffle humain . . . [n]on plus la recherche de la profondeur mais l'inspiration de l'étendue*] (*Traité du Tout-monde* 91). The meanings brought to the surface of art by the "tutelary obstacles" of language, meter, or color, relay in the final instance to the infinite of its outside, much as the Lézarde River at the end of Glissant's early novel opens to the horizon of the sea. The ideal meeting of the two, for Glissant, is the instrumentalization of order, rhythm, and particularity towards the sentient accumulation of Démesure, the share of Others that, as in Relation, allows for the composition of *lieu:* In other words, one thinks through and against Mesure to apprehend the Tout-monde, the archipelago, and the missing people poetics promises to deliver.

Conclusion: An American Archipelago

This ideal meeting, what one might call a negative dialectical relation of Mesure and Démesure, is explicitly pursued in one of Glissant's last poetic treatises, *La Cohée du Lamentin*. The volume, structured like most of his later works by the fluid alternation among literary and artistic exegeses, musings on globalization and empire, and autobiographical fragments, is nonetheless overwhelmingly focused on a formal comparative examination of poetry and plastic arts. His ruminations profess at the outset a continuing resonance with Deleuze and Guattari's ideas about art—the book opens, for example, expressing agreement with their conviction that "the function of literature as well as art is first to invent a missing people" [*la fonction de la littérature comme de l'art est d'abord d'inventer un peuple qui manque*] (*La Cohée du Lamentin* 16)—yet the analyses themselves attempt to recapture the fundamental gestures of art as a monadic activity, a mediated intervention in life through form. Glissant's treatment of the oeuvres analyzed—from a group including familiar references like Wilfredo Lam and Roberto Matta, but also contemporary artists like Antonio Seguí, Gerardo Chávez, and Gabriela Morawitz—pivots on the qualities of line, style, color, and composition, with the ultimate aim of surprising something of their Relation, of opening up each work through its others [*de les ouvrir les unes par les autres*] (225).

It is the evidence of this formal capacity to Relation that Glissant most wishes to highlight here: thus, he detects in the imposing houses of Argentine painter Mario Gurfein "a play of reflexivities between the raw grasp of what brutalizes our world and the slow, differed ascent of what could bring it luck" [*un jeu de reflexivités entre la saisie brute de ce qui ensauvage notre monde et la montée lente, différée, de ce qui pourrait lui porter chance*] (*La Cohée du Lamentin* 64); in Italian artist Valerio Adami's sharp, vibrant images he signals a "cutting" [*coupure*] able to deflect and relay each work's contents so that they "switch universes even as they remain in the obliqueness of their movement, [and] refract their nature in an elsewhere that does not stop being here" [*changent d'univers tout en perdurant dans l'oblique de leur mouvement, [et] refractent leur nature dans un ailleurs qui ne cesse pas d'être ici*] (208); and Wilfredo Lam's landscapes, as he has described elsewhere, "amas[s] elements, forms, sovereign germinations, on his island and in his memory, . . . distribut[ing] them in movements that soon will orient illumination and the fiesta, the encounter with the other" [*amas[se] d'éléments, de formes, de germinations souveraines, dans son île et dans sa mémoire, il les distribue en mouvements qui bientôt dirigeront l'enluminure et la fiesta, la rencontre avec l'autre*] (190). The juxtaposition of the dozens of writers and painters featured in *La Cohée* provides an exercise in relational thought, meant to train us to contemplate in the fixed order of Mesure a constellational movement towards a complete picture of things: "Each one of these drawings and paintings, through its very fixity, trains us to view the spectacle of the world and to evaluate its severe detail, but their ensemble introduces us to the sparkle of Diversity. The painting fixes and reveals structures and projections, but when one joins it to other paintings, when the panorama of these clichés unfolds, then we conceive the trembling cinema of these universes" [*Chacun de ces dessins et de ces tableaux, par sa fixité même, nous exerce à regarder le spectacle du monde et à en évaluer le sévère détail, mais leur ensemble nous introduit à la chatoyance du Divers. Le tableau fixe et révèle des structures et des prévisions, mais quand on le joint à d'autres tableaux, quand le panorama de ces clichés se déroule, alors nous concevons le frémissant cinéma de ces univers*] (216).

As Glissant reveals near the end of *La Cohée*, these quasi-pedagogical arguments also serve as a critical prelude to one of the numerous civic projects begun in the last years of his life, the Musée Martiniquais des Arts des Amériques. Although the planning of the museum never proceeded beyond an initial traveling exposition of the works of many of the artists discussed in *La Cohée*, Glissant envisioned it as a meeting place for artists of the American continents, where an aesthetic comparison of their various experiences of historical space-time might be initiated. All peoples of the Americas, Glissant contends, work through a "lost" or "stolen" time ("The peoples of Brazil, of the Caribbean, of the islands, and even Latin American peoples, their time has been stolen" [*Les peuples du Brésil, de la Caraïbe, des îles, et même les peuples latino-américains, on leur a volé leur temps*] [Obrist 34]); they reconstruct history forcibly through the "chaotic" lens of slavery and colonization rather than through linear progression. The goal of the Museum, he explains, is to "make, not equivalences, but a putting-in-relation of all these different times to try to see what pulses and what bubbles up in the American environment" [*faire, non pas des équivalences, mais des mises en rapport de tous ces temps différents pour essayer de voir ce qui palpite et ce qui bouillonne dans l'environnement américain*] (Obrist 35). This vision of the museum—it remains, of course, only a vision—encapsulates what I think must be the most productive negotiation of the monadic and nomadic threads of Glissant's geopoetics: it points to an archipelic thought (indeed, Glissant imagines the museum itself as an archipelago) without effacing the space of mediation between imagining an archipelic world and actually living in one. The necessary distance is assured in the works of art themselves, which in their enclosure reflect society as a "variable daily dazzled by the world" [*une variable quotidiennement éblouie du monde*] (*La Cohée du Lamentin* 218). Despite Bongie's accusations against *La Cohée*, which he singles out as an example of Glissant's "hyper-aestheticizing" turn, I do not believe its proposals constitute the sort of cultural politics that the conflation of monadic and nomadic sensibilities normally delivers. That is, there is here no direct poeticization of life. Rather, the decentering processes detected by a globalized, Relational view of cultural subjectivity are immanent in the intact forms of art: They become, to follow Zepke's characterization, an "immanence of the abstract machine" in stratification, a promise of deterritorialization incipiently voiced by finite compositions. Articulated as such, Glissant's geopoetics may have its best chance to direct archipelic thought toward the second nature that preoccupied him the whole of his career. Although the specific encodings imposed by art curtail nomadism's blind faith in deterritorialization, they may properly strive to be an "eco-art" as Guattari imagines it, precisely by approximating in their concatenated opposition to stratification—the "stolen" time of American histories that Glissant refers to, as well as the globalized economies that make them possible as art—an art of living in society that is still unimaginable. This is also the concession monadic thought makes to nomadism, the mere recognition that thought as it exists today, no matter how critical, yearns for a new world with which it would be incompatible, that "every citizen of the wrong world would find the right one unbearable": "Even if [we] could imagine all things radically altered," Adorno admits "[our] imagination would remained chained to [us] and to [our] present time as static points of reference, and everything would be askew" (*Negative Dialectics* 352). In this sense, Glissant's last mediations between second nature and archipelic thought, between the old world and a new one, may yet reveal hidden insights to a poetic projection of a people to come.

Excursus

Poetics and Place from Autochthony to Globality

The rise of the postcolonial critical idiom has bifurcated the paths available for the management of Latin Americanist and francophonist intellectual objects: Beyond the timeworn frameworks of the regionally, linguistically, and historically determined discipline, there now exists a series of apparatuses ready to unleash the heterogeneities suppressed by the commonplaces of locationist thought, and to recode and reabsorb them as a strain of globalized cultural politics. Weighing the risks and opportunities involved in talking about Latin American and Francophone cultures and literatures as postcolonial thus means also deliberating on their inescapable global inscription, insofar as university discourses of postcolonialism and globalization share a set of tenets about the politics of culture: Following Timothy Brennan's summary, these include "the striving for ambivalence as a matter of principle; the ardent belief that answering a question 'forecloses' it; the elision of meaning in pursuit of epistemological doubt; and, most of all, the deployment of a variety of tropes such as 'migrancy,' 'nomadism,' 'hybridity,' and 'decentering,' which are marshaled in order to make the case that mobility and cultural mixing—not as contingent historical experiences but as modes of being—are states of virtue" (46). The thrust behind the common convictions of theorizations of globalization and the postcolonial, Brennan emphasizes, is that of an ethical imperative: They advertise themselves not just as one of many lenses through which to take stock of specific cultural experiences today, nor—as Brennan conceives them—as a newcomer to earlier and deeper debates about hegemony and imperialism, which trades its intellectual antecedents for a terminology more in tune with current academic priorities. They are rather perceived as the ethically superior option, the only option for a cultural theory committed to dismantling once and for all the lingering residues of imperialism, the "West," nationalist chauvinisms, and other impediments to the full realization of pluri-, multi-, and trans-cultural circuits of signification.

As far as the gatekeeping of the disciplinary object is concerned, the choice between regional-historic identities and postcolonial decenterings is on this view largely a false choice. Moreiras, supplementing his main points in *The Exhaustion of Difference,* observes this impasse as a patent feature of theories of transculturation and hybridity: Whether or not these maintain the singularity of a Latin American colonial legacy, "[i]dentity is now difference, and it is no longer major and national, but minor and fragmented: translation is self-translation, and subjectivity is now transcultural and hybrid. Its stasis, the point of closure of this ideological formation, is now the essence without essence of the local in resistance, that is, the merely representational against other representations, where representation represents nothing but the representational struggle itself, brings nothing new to presence, only re-presents (itself) against. Let us call this the moment of globalization, or the moment of cultural studies" ("Mules and Snakes" 207). He is signaling the inevitable outcome of remedial attempts to shore up the Latin Americanist object either with or against postcolonial theory, the ideological closure preordained in the very aperture announced by the postcolonial, in Brennan's formulation, as an ethical imperative. This is as true for retrenchment in local theories of Latin American heterogeneity as it is for interdisciplinary adaptations of the postcolonial optic, in that it merely mimics in reverse the postcolonial's gesture of appropriation, "turn[ing] expropriation into property, and turn[ing] property into the ultimate horizon of thinking." In this sense localized postcolonialism "fails to the precise extent that it succeeds" ("Mules and Snakes" 219) in resisting appropriation, for it is no less a function of neoliberalism in answering to a final translation of thought into capital as the underlying social bond of any community.

The entanglements of globalization with the preferential option for the postcolonial are even more visible from the perspective of Francophone Studies, particularly since its adoption of the postcolonial label has replaced hexagonal mappings of Francophonie with the *monde,* as recent debates over the *littérature-monde en français* attest. Several commentators have noted the way the prophetic language of the *littérature-monde* manifesto itself describes francophone literature's accession to a world scale as a matter of historical destiny, a "Copernican revolution" in literature.[1] The manifesto retroactively relates how, from the restraints of Francophonie—"the light of a dying star" (Le Bris et al. 299)—writers long anticipated an entrance on the global stage, on a par with anglophone postcolonial writers: "How many writers in the French language, themselves caught between two or several cultures, mulled this strange disparity that relegated them to the margins, themselves 'francophones,' an exotic hybrid barely tolerated, while the children of the former British empire were, with complete legitimacy, taking possession of English letters?" (298). In the rhetoric of the *littérature-monde*, the *mondialisation* of French-language letters is not only a concomitant postcolonialization in the mold of Commonwealth writers; it is also the irrepressible future of writing in French as a whole, the definitive end of colonialism, nation, and exclusionisms of all kinds. The concluding flourish of the signatories affirms "the birth of a new constellation, in which language freed from its exclusive pact with the nation, free from every other power hereafter but the powers of poetry and the imaginary, will have no other frontiers but those of the spirit" (300).

What critical onlookers less confident in this cosmic future point out, along with several other shortcomings of the *littérature-monde* program, is how slender the proper terrain of the "world" really is within its specifications, a category just as restricted as the outmoded "francophone" appellation, if perhaps more celebratory.[2] The French-speaking author of the *monde*, in Lydie Moudileno's characterization, is a "Francosmopolitan": a figure "whose personal and professional itineraries and migrations have him/her evolve in the centrifugal, nomadic, ever-changing and endlessly hybridized modes of transnational circulation, but whose miles accumulate on Air France (rather than, say, British Airways), and whose privileged linguistic affiliation and creative home remain (in) French" ("Francophonie" 119). Far from the freewheeling movement suggested by the manifesto, the trajectory described by *the littérature-monde* is thus, in reality, supremely targeted and centripetal, to the detriment of all those real peripheries, or "ultraperipheries" in Moudileno's terms, deemed not worldly enough.[3] Even for those who appreciate the democratizing value of the *littérature-monde* aegis, writes Haitian poet Gary Victor, the question remains "How to overcome a globalization which is in fact nothing but one center's seizure of the world, thus the marginalization of authenticities, if not their destruction" [*Comment dépasser la mondialisation qui n'est dans les faits que la mainmise d'un centre sur le monde, donc la marginalisation des authenticités, si ce n'est leur destruction*] (318). He regrets the way so many authors now packaged as "global" "sometimes resemble creators who accept to play the game of power . . . to be formatted" [*ressemblent parfois à des créateurs qui acceptent de jouer le jeu des pouvoirs . . . d'être formatés*] (318). Such complaints revive the objections to postcolonial and global designations already aired by Latin Americanist critics over the past few decades, and by anglophone specialists before them. It is the central dilemma confronted, from opposite directions, by

Latin Americanism and Francophone Studies faced with the referendum of postcolonial and global literary models, namely, the fact that no guarantee exists within any possible response to their centrifugal force that opening up regional-historic disciplines provides respite from the strictures of identity, that de-centralizing thought is not a leap from the frying pan of disciplinary canons and hierarchies to the fire of consumption.

To my mind, the status of aesthetics is not insignificant for this juncture of critique. It has been my contention thus far that an apperception of aesthetic experience, something like an experience of the undeconstructible, can offer traction against the twin undertows of identity—regional-historic locationism and the global selfsame—by drawing us closer to the antagonisms that spring up between thought as appropriation and any conceivable Latin Americanist or francophonist postcolonial object. Granting the priority of the object through the accumulative account of conceptual thought's discrete inadequacies, this experience mobilizes both its skeptical and utopian faculties—on one hand the fact that concepts cannot achieve a "true" identity with their objects in any foreseeable program of thought, and on the other the persistent realization that concepts would not be possible at all without a minimum correspondence with the reality of the world's suffering, that hope for unity is the very condition for thought's endeavor. To think thus from the "need in thought," following Adorno—"wishful thinking" in the vocabulary I have opted for—acknowledges that the ineffable of its object is already present and active in the concept, in indecipherable but determinate ways. Braced between these limits and possibilities, a wishful thinking of the postcolonial in Latin Americanism and Francophone Studies can stand firm against the stasis of heterogeneity as ontopology, as a commodified state of virtue: It seeks, not to outline an adequate representation of difference, nor to avoid representation altogether, but to bring about a society where subject and object, difference and identity, would be one.

The geopoetics of José Lezama Lima and Édouard Glissant lay out viable models for such a wishful thinking. For Lezama's American expression or Glissant's monadic and nomadic explorations of second nature, isolating the unique forms of suffering and joy in the regional-historic assemblages of the Americas or the Caribbean requires the spiraling effort of poetics, which advances a wager about its object's relationship to the world while retracting the impulse to adduce this relationship to a structure of reproduction or a progression of causes and effects. This is, of course, the way Lezama reads American history contra Hegel with the tandem operations of metaphor and image, according the magical right of analogy to name and describe the qualities of an American being but only in light of identity's dissolution in the image, the experience of a lost nature that floods us with a sense of non-identity and resists classification in narration or nomenclature. So too

Glissant's theorizations of Caribbean history and nature attempt to flesh out their differential locations, not by recuperating a definitive idea of its historical memory but through a collection of impressions of its relations to others, the foreign or unknown that pushes back against the frame placed over chaos. In both cases identity is approximated as a constellation, something that, as Adorno wrote, "circles the concept it would like to unseal, hoping that it may fly open like the lock of a well-guarded safe-deposit box: in response, not to a single key or a single number, but to a combination of numbers" (*Negative Dialectics* 163). Pursuing a concept of the postcolonial as a matter of geopoetics along these lines would forbid any contemplation of the virtues of cultural mixing, of transculturation or métissage; indeed recounting the states of heterogeneity, seeking to name them with a postcolonial concept, even strategically, is for Lezama or Glissant beside the point. Their interest is rather to trail thought to the non-identity that repeatedly and actively renews cognition of a regional-historic particularity. The conceptual site of the postcolonial that Latin Americanism and Francophone Studies could best make use of would thus relate to the identities of those disciplines as a need, or a stain, one that upsets their identitarian closure in its unpredictable negative protest.

A stain is exactly what Moreiras perceives at the heart of a de-localizing option for Latin Americanism—against the disciplinary entropy I have been referencing, which he calls "sad passion"—in the *paso* of the Lezamian neo-baroque, the same *paso* toward the abyss taken by the mule of Lezama's famous poem "Rapsodia para el mulo." There is, as he points out, a degree of de-localization proper to the historical progression of the baroque in its American environment, as an aesthetic seat for the installation of imperial power in the colonies, which nonetheless spawns new loci of authorization in *criollo, mestizo,* Afro, Indian, and other modalities of the baroque arts. Insofar as it captures both of these movements, the baroque subject comes to consciousness through an awareness of power as well as of the limits of power (Beverley, *Una modernidad obsoleta* 24, quoted in Moreiras, "Mules and Snakes" 203): It is an "imperial subject in withdrawal" (205). In this elliptical constitution of the baroque, at once an occupation of hegemony and a confident flight toward its exterior and excess, the *paso* has "hardly an untainted word, but where the taint is the name of the very possibility of thought" (218).

The difficulty in de-localizing thought would be activating it in the excess that strays from our ideological inscription, but without allowing its refortification in a new essence, either as a savoring of regional-historic localism—the sort of autochthony that Lezama's American expression can easily conjure—or, what for Moreiras is the same, as a freedom from localism in globality, which is a plausible result of Glissant's archipelic thought or the *littérature-monde*. Identity and freedom from identity, articulated in these alternatives, segue into one same relation to capital in which criticism authorizes itself as the mouthpiece of a specific geopolitical object, tendering it as a content uniformized for exchange. If the problematic here boils down to a question of aesthetics and politics, literature as an instrument of the state in the canonical tradition of Latin American letters, or literature against the empire-state in Francophone Studies' break from the institutional domain of the hexagon, we may do well to interrogate more closely the profile of these objects' aesthetic and political interventions.

The Politics of Aesthetics and the Aesthetics of Politics

Latin Americanism and Francophone Studies can be said to pertain to aesthetic projects inasmuch as they provide, in Jacques Rancière's language, "a specific sensory experience that holds the promise of both a new world of Art and a new life for individuals and the community" (*Dissensus* 115). The realm of experience associated with them is structured by a fiction: Working from either viewpoint means contending with the fact that no historically adequate referent exists for the objects they invoke, and that wielding these referents indeed amounts to the projection of an experience that, under the right circumstances, promises a new Art and a new life. To the extent that the study of these fields is an aesthetic experience driven by various scholarly, pedagogical, or institutional interests, it will also be constrained to the scope of the aesthetic Rancière limns in his abundant meditations on art and politics: In short, it requires a minimum distance between the art and the life it bridges, an active conjunction "and" to prevent the radical closure of aesthetics in pure art (total autonomy) or pure life (limitless heteronomy). Only the flexible maneuver of the conjunction guarantees the political efficacy of art, the "politics of aesthetics," which Rancière defines, in what is also an acceptable thesis of Latin Americanist and Francophonist enterprises, as the reframing of the world that "help[s] create the fabric of a common experience in which new modes of constructing common objects and new possibilities of subjective enunciation may be developed" (141–42). The sticking point of the politics of aesthetics for Rancière is that its reconfiguration of experience bears no cause-effect relationship with the compass and gradation of political expression, but "impl[ies] a move from one given world to another in which capacities and incapacities, forms of tolerance and intolerance, are differently defined" (143). This may be an obvious caveat for self-styled heteronomous constructs like the *littérature-monde* or Glissant's "poetic" market basket of goods that claim to reflect transparently the needs and possibilities of the community, inventing upon impact a Deleuzian people-to-come. But it applies equally to the pretended autonomy of certain critical fictions of Latin America, its matchless ways of being, sui generis dynamics of oppression and heterogeneity, and singular postcoloniality. The critical conceit of Latin Americanist autonomy is no more able to predict its repercussions on a given political landscape than the *littérature-monde*'s appeal to a clamor of pure spirit. In each case, the eclipse of the "and" cancels out the properly aesthetic office, whose divagation into politics becomes the mask of a mere thing.

Indeed, Rancière's objective in elucidating the path of aesthetics between autonomy and heteronomy is to foreground its capacity to affect the distribution of sensible forms as a function precisely of the life that creates a space and a will for art from its exterior. Only the Hegelian "heterogeneous sensible" (Rancière, *Dissensus* 127), the energies foreign to art itself, which interject in its creation as well as its contemplation and consumption, ensures its dissensual faculty. The dissensus opened by the aesthetic revolution is the fracture "between sense and sense," "a rupture in the specific configuration that allows us to stay in 'our' assigned places in a given state of things" (143), made possible by the play between the disinterested territory of art and the interests that both circumscribe and penetrate it. Just as the most rarefied statue incorporates in its forms an intention and vision that are necessarily heteronomous, the approximation of art practices to consumerist spectacle or quotidian events yet retains a margin of sensibility extraneous to life itself. The collapse of the heterogeneous sensible—an art transparent to itself, or conversely an art that is just life—means the end of aesthetics and the universal agreement of sense about " 'our' assigned places" in the world. The parallels between Rancière's insights and the lessons of Glissantian and Lezamian geopoetics should be clear: The superposition of metaphor and image, the looming tree of the landscape that accommodates the eternal expanse of nature, the Mesure that grips chaos within the confines of the page, the absolute localities of Relation, all of these hold forth on Rancière's "and" as the condition of localized—and, in their optimum scenarios, de-localized—thought.

Rancière's terminology allows us to appraise the courses of action these geopoetics may be able to arbitrate in the face of the globality/postcoloniality mandate I have been discussing. It leads Brett Levinson, in an analysis of Latin Americanism, to posit the historic emergence of Latin America as a phenomenon of globality. After commenting at length on the obstacles that prevent criticism from securing the distinctive space and time of the agency of subaltern contingencies—from precolonial subjectivities to contemporary indigenous and peasants' movements—Levinson recalls Rancière's stipulation that within modern political intelligibility, any agency on the grid of representation is ultimately a question of aesthetics, of visibility. The "aesthetics of politics" he employs is a mirror image of the politics of aesthetics: The political framing of sensibility requires first an aesthetic manifestation of peoples, causes, or entities that surface as such only by rendering others invisible. Movements like the Zapatistas, or the life stories of *testimonio*, Levinson avers, rely on a scene of political redress which "renders an emergent field visible through a frame, a border, which serves also to exclude, push out, other emergencies," and without which politics would be impossible: "Without borders, without an exclusionary violence against *one oppressed peoples* by *other oppressed peoples*, there is no politics, no traversing or intervention, no more emergences or emergencies, only bad infinities, only the endless fulfillment of history in neoliberalism" ("Globalizing Paradigms" 77). From aesthetics' complementary political pole, he probes how the same "and" separating art and politics mediates the disciplinary object's insurmountable relationship to globalization. If the politics of aesthetics refers to art's digestion of non-art as the only possible grounding of its autonomy (Rancière, *Dissensus* 116), the aesthetics of politics refers to the emergence of political voices as a scene of enunciation carved on the backs, so to speak, of other voices these bury from politics' sensible range. Levinson's point is that no Latin America would exist at all without the others made invisible in the staging of its own scene. In his account, Latin America thus amounts to a "political aesthetics" ("Globalizing Paradigms" 80) whose relation to the globe is constitutive in this regard. More important, given the coextension of modern politics with global capitalism, is that this constitutive relationship makes "a market stand and a stand in the market" the trade-off for political contestation, so that "an affirmation of, and a certain complicity with, the very neoliberalism that the interventions combat, is a vital requirement for any countermarket politics" (78).

No counteridentity without a stake in identity: The aesthetics of politics cedes a share of its visibility to what is opposed to aesthetics, the infinite leveling force of market logic. Inverting Levinson's conclusions, we can say that Latin Americanism or Francophone Studies as a politics of aesthetics or wishful thinking also inheres partially in what it is opposed to, the commodification of its fictional framing of a new life. Whether the channels of induction for the disciplinary object's prefiguring of a changed reality are broached from the political or the aesthetic front—two planes of its meaning that are relayed but, according to Rancière, nontransferable—it is incumbent to adjudicate its measure of identity as the very motor of critique, lest Latin America or the *littérature-monde* become another voice of consensus, the agreement between sense and sense that says "it is perfectly fine for people to have different interests, values, and aspirations, nevertheless there is one unique reality to which everything must be related," and whose dominant contemporary terrain, as Rancière concurs, is economic globalization (*Dissensus* 144).

I think Levinson seconds Rancière's conviction when he asserts the essentially global inception of Latin America. His arguments are echoed in recent comments by Alain Mabanckou on the bogus claim to some entity "Africa" foisted on African writers living abroad. Following V. Y. Mudimbe's famous formulation, he reasons,

> Africa—or at any rate *that* [invented] Africa—does not exist, nor does a literature orchestrating such a way of thinking. The problem for African authors is not their relationship with the Dark Continent. The problem is first and foremost a literary one, as for any writer. Could the Africa they describe or sketch be an empty shell, a prefabricated object? . . . Perhaps we should reconcile ourselves to the idea of redefining the very notion of Africa and stop picturing the continent as a circumscribed geographical entity. For Africa is no longer solely in Africa. By dispersing all over the globe Africans create *other Africas*, embarking on ventures perfectly liable to enhance and promote African cultures. . . . We need confrontation, in the sense of face-to-face interaction between cultures, and where these take place is of no consequence. True reciprocity stems from spaces of creativity, not from geographical locations. ("Immigration" 86–87)

Mabanckou defends diasporic writing against the insistence, from certain literary and critical communities, that he speak from Africa: For him, as for Levinson, the key question is ultimately one of making visible, of creating a scene where a claim for the object may be staked. Levinson and Mabanckou's support for global political aesthetics aims to disband the fetishistic pursuit of a regional material anterior to its conceptual figuration and capable of mustering a pure retort to "Latin America's" or "Africa's" global face. They remind us that the fetish, a subsumption of social relationality to a relationship between things, just as easily becomes a consensual stand-in for the autonomous regional object as for its interdisciplinary or postcolonial avatars. The only viable alternative they see to the roundabout consensus to globality garnered through the protected, pure object, is the trade-off of commodification, the portion of identity that Levinson sees as the price of political existence.

Yet what a generous reading of Levinson and Mabanckou will accept as a savvy bid to brave market schemes on their own terms, against the impending ossification of any hermetic understanding of Latin American or African cultural production, still makes no headway toward a systematic vigilance of the integrity of the places they speak for: No guarantee exists here that Africa does not dissolve in the variegated simulacra of its diasporic representatives, that Mabanckou himself is not one of the global writers "who accepts to play the game of power," in Victor's terms, and to be formatted. This is not a risk to be taken lightly: Indeed, if the cost of emergence on the globe is not yet widely acknowledged in the privileged venues where Latin Americanist metaphors of difference continue to circulate, the fortunes of the *littérature-monde* amply demonstrate its effects. Jean-Marc Moura, expounding on today's Francophone literary system, notes with more than a hint of resignation that the texts it puts on the market on multiple continents "are no longer considered as representative of preexisting, real cultures (or 'natures') but as spaces of invention and playfulness based on available codes." Their legitimacy for the transnational readership—without a doubt the same readership claimed by the *littérature-monde*—demands that "the works provide what the reading public expects from them: a hint of difference that is not too disorienting" (34). Levinson's own final postulation that a Latin America created from globality necessarily exists only "in theory" similarly invites speculation on the radicalization of the North-South stratification of Latin Americanism that has already launched so many Jeremiads against postcolonial and globalized reading paradigms. The proper rebuttal one can formulate on behalf of the stance of Levinson and Mabanckou, and perhaps the best available rebuttal within the current state of critique, is that no systematic vigilance exists for these constructs that is not itself finally a ruse of equalization: There is no "protecting" the heterogeneity of Africa or Latin America through the aesthetic or political means of representation simply because, as Levinson theorizes, its only protection is invisibility, nonexistence.

Applying here the rigor of Rancière's position on aesthetics and politics obliges us to tighten even further the strategic range of the regional-historic discipline in the global era, shuttering it as well to the aesthetic shortcut of hybrid or transculturated troping that pronounces on the *fait accompli* of postcoloniality and globality as the "state of virtue" Brennan spoke of. The degree of commodification inextricable from the aesthetic regime is itself sufficient admonition against the leap from the metaphoric appearance of difference to the fortification of a political program. Glissant and Lezama's poetics are well aware of the issue of that leap into the "horrible vanity of reproducing" exerted by the unchecked force of poetic metaphor, before which Lezama shudders (*Obras Completas* II 156). The concept metaphors of hybridity, transculturation, and other lexemes of the postcolonial arsenal do nothing to protect the heterogeneous material of the Latin Americanist or francophonist referent the moment they step in to negotiate a scene of visibility, to speak politically for a new frame of the sensible as a matter of ethical imperative. The confluence of aesthetics and politics navigated by the disciplinary object at every turn offers no shelter from the requisite codes of the marketplace, and in the end no shelter from the globe. Critique must rather think from its globality, from and against its commodified scene of enunciation.

If aesthetics is to have any say in its trajectory, it may best be described by the *paso* of the neobaroque vision espoused by Glissant's geopoetics as much as Lezama's: an exodus from the location of thought and the exercise of conjuring new frames of communal experience that political forms, at the right historical junction, might adopt. Indeed, despite the rumored modeling of the *littérature-monde* on Glissant's Tout-monde, more than one critic has puzzled at his contribution to the signatories' volume of essays: a reprint of an earlier interview, "Solitaire et solidaire," which covers a number of his familiar refrains about the monadic properties of poetics.[4] Here, he repeats his initial understanding of the relationship between poetry and politics, "that poetry was not political, that no political poetry existed, but that great poetry was not conceived without this underlying relationship, subterranean and at the same time explosive, which was the link to the situation of the cultures of the world in their interrelationship. In other words, that there was no poetry which is not political and that there is no poetry that is in itself political" [*la poésie n'était pas politique, qu'il n'existait pas de poésie politique, mais que la grande poésie ne se concevait pas sans cette relation sous-jacente, souterraine en même temps qu'éclatante, qu'était le lien à la situation des cultures du monde en relation les unes aux autres. Autrement dit, qu'il n'y avait pas de poésie qui ne soit pas politique et qu'il n'existe pas de poésie politique en soi*] (Artières 78). For this reason, Glissant asserts in his closing comments, "*Paradiso,* the absolutely subversive novel of Lezama Lima, is the best thing that has happened to the Cuban Revolution. Lima used to say 'If the revolution is strong enough, it will be able to digest *Paradiso*' " [Paradiso, *le livre absolument subversif de Lezama Lima, est ce qui est arrivé de mieux à la révolution cubaine. Lima disait: 'Si la révolution est suffisament forte, elle pourra digérer* Paradiso] (Artières 86).

Chapter 4

Mikilistes and *Modernistas* in Paris

Consuming Modernity's Capital

Thanks to Benjamin, the rise of commoditization as the hallmark of capitalist modernity is perhaps most vividly plotted in the scenes and trends of nineteenth-century Paris. Digging through the city's remnants and archives, he reconstructed the myths of progress and history animated in the ephemeral shells of fashion and arcades, the monumentalized technology of the World Expositions, and the panoramic vistas of Haussmannized urban space. Through all these forms the city itself emerges as a fetish object, as David Harvey has argued, absorbing as natural features the social relations that construct and reconstruct its surfaces and fueling its dominance as the century's world capital of culture.[1]

This effect is nowhere more palpable than at the remove of France's imperial satellites, where the mythic object of Paris brims with its own metaphysical subtleties and theological quibbles. *Modernista* poet Rubén Darío, as he recalls in his autobiography, prayed as a child in Nicaragua not to die before seeing Paris: "Paris was for me like a paradise where one breathed the essence of happiness on earth. It was the city of Art, of Beauty and Glory; and, above all, it was the capital of Love, the kingdom of dreams" [*París era para mí como un paraíso en donde se respiraba la esencia de la felicidad sobre la tierra. Era la ciudad el Arte, de la Belleza y de la Gloria; y, sobre todo, era la capital del Amor, el reino del ensueño*] (Darío, *Obras Completas* I 102). Darío would serve as an icon for, and the most inveterate victim of, the terrible "Paris complex" of the Spanish American *fin de siglo:* For his generation of literary aesthetes, gaining Paris both discursively and physically meant accession to modern letters, together with the fields of symbolic and economic exchange these gave currency to.[2] At roughly the same time of Darío's adolescent prayers, French officer Savorgnan de Brazza was moving furiously along the western shores of the Congo River establishing treaties with local leaders to justify France's colonial entrance into Equatorial Africa. East of the river, his Belgian competitor King Leopold prepared to build a fortune off a genocidal rubber industry under which the severed hands of noncompliant villagers came themselves to constitute a form of currency.[3] Riding the tails of the Congo's violent insertion into capitalist modernity, the myth of Paris would be disseminated over the next century through the circulation of clothing, literature, and goods brought with the colonial administration.[4] In the postcolonial capitals of Brazzaville and Kinshasa, Paris became the storied destination for young, usually disenfranchised men seeking to capture social prestige through a successful migration to, and return from, Europe.[5] As the center of high fashion and luxury, Paris confers on the *mikiliste* (in one possible translation from Lingala, a "man of the world")[6] the reputation of sartorial virtuosity—reinforced by the designer wardrobe he goes there to acquire—which can open new channels of social mobility for him and his family upon his triumphant homecoming. In historian Didier Gondola's characterization, the *mikilistes* "envision Europe as an immaculate, immense city of light, where magical, mechanical passageways carry people along, where fortunes are easily made, and the climate is healthy. In short, a place where the living is easy" ("Dream and Drama" 28).

For *mikilistes* and *modernistas*, formal and informal peripheral subjects of the capital of modernity, movement to and from Paris is indeed a journey of commodities, an importation of the fetish object of the city for maneuver in local economies. But this fact does not in itself clarify the much more complex and volatile regimes of value the commoditization of Paris is made to cathect in Spanish American and Congolese societies. If, as Benjamin illustrated, the outward signs of Parisian modernity served to cloak the process of reification and stagnation under the endless litany of "newness" that is meant to some extent to be representative of a worldwide progressive commoditization of social life, they nonetheless enter a more heterogeneous register in turn of the century Spanish America and in urban Congo. Extrapolating from these contexts to narrate a full "cultural biography" of Paris as an object for global consumption, one would inevitably retrace some of the pathways Igor Kopytoff lays out in highlighting the non-economic life of commodities: in short, a life of periodic diversion to a "black market" of nonexchangeability, where "[the object's] status is inevitably ambiguous and open to the push and pull of events and desires, as it is shuffled about in the flux of social life." "Thus," writes Kopytoff, "even things that unambiguously carry an exchange value—formally speaking, therefore, commodities—do absorb the other kind of worth, one that is nonmonetary and goes beyond exchange worth" (83). In its real passage through social life, the commodity undergoes numerous and competing conversions to different singularized fields of value that extract it partially from the chain of equivalence under which it is normally exchanged.[7]

My interest in focusing this chapter on the niceties of *mikilistes'* and *modernistas'* consumption of Paris is to follow the push and pull of its valorization in their societies, the "drama," in Kopytoff's word, of its shuttling between raw consumerism and an array of impulses of singularization. In doing so, I hope to alter the way scholarship considers these phenomena relevant to the postcolonial concept, and not simply by demonstrating the similarities between appropriations of Paris from very different geographical, historical, and demographic contexts; rather, by pointing out the variable relationship between these actors' adherence to the commodity fiction of Paris and their retraction from exchange, I want to signal how their discourses turn back the identitarian claims of modern capital, summoning their non-identity. Unlike previous readers of both *modernismo* and *mikilistes*, I do not see the operative connection to the postcolonial as a matter of resistance or ambivalence.[8] Putting into play once again some proposals of earlier chapters, we can rather see the manipulation of Parisian capital as a wish from within capital, which envisions in determinate but indecipherable ways a freedom from or control over its equalizing compulsions. The point of reading *modernista* and *mikiliste* narratives this way is to apprehend how their invocation of Paris, the identity imposed on them through the attempt to lay hold of its aura of modernity, contains a hope for its alternative, a transformed society. The assertion of this hope, however illegible, is the measure of their link to the postcolonial.

The *Modernista* Stylization of Paris

A summary introduction to *modernista* and *mikiliste* discourses makes readily apparent just how dramatic the impulses of its singularization can be. In *modernismo*, Paris provided a key bargaining chip through which writers could stake out a new, heterogeneous literary authority, opposed both to the conventions of bureaucratic "civic" literature sanctioned by the fusion of political, literary, and educational purposes during the decades of Spanish American nation-building, and to the unskilled "reporting" in demand after transatlantic telegraph cables and other advances in communication converted newspapers and periodical literature into transmitters of ever greater amounts of unfiltered information. Therefore, when Darío prefaces his fantastical *Prosas profanas* (1896) by mocking his society's academicians, poets, professionals and functionaries as *Celui-qui-ne-comprend-pas*, professing to counter their priggish literary sensibilities with cosmopolitan references—

"Shakespeare! Dante! Hugo . . . ! (And to myself: Verlaine!)" ["*¡Shakespeare! ¡Dante! ¡Hugo . . . ! (Y en mi interior: ¡Verlaine!)*"]—Paris signals the final break with otiose Hispanic letters: To his imaginary Spanish grandfather, Darío admits "my wife is from my land; my sweetheart, from Paris" [*mi esposa es de mi tierra; mi querida, de París*] (Darío, *Obras Completas* V 763). The Parisian intertext not only secures his rupture with provincial institutions, it equally liberates him from the mercantilization of literature that increasingly abets them. The prerogative of *l'art pour l'art*, strenuously defended by Symbolist art and poetry and embodied in iconoclast figures of the *poète maudit* (such as Verlaine, mentioned above), inspired the most definitive *modernista* tie with Paris, in that these poets' myriad designs on the city aimed to leverage an aura of disinterested creation, studied elegance, and incorruptible beauty against the restraints of their social and economic reality.

Because they were generally products of Spanish America's new middle classes, hence raised without the social capital and leisure time necessary for a true life of unfettered literary contemplation, *modernistas* entered the region's cultural markets as salaried authors of newspaper chronicles: Commenting on events and everyday scenes of Buenos Aires or Mexico City (or for those lucky enough to work as foreign correspondents, New York or Paris), the *cronista* wrote as an informed guide to modern urban life. Discursively, the chronicle takes the form of a narrated stroll among the products and people on display in the city. As such, it is inextricable from capitalist pursuits, insofar as the *cronista*, like the *flâneur*, mediates between the offer of the marketplace and the demand of readers to master new modes of consumption patterned after foreign metropolises. The cachet of the salaried writer thus resides in his ability to stylize and domesticate the city, to distill its poetic charms from the meaner commercialized aspects of modern life and thereby aestheticize his own product, differentiating it from the news items and raw data printed alongside it. The contradictions inherent to this authority of stylization, as Julio Ramos has demonstrated, are essential for understanding *modernismo* as a whole and, by extension, the larger edifice of twentieth-century Spanish American literary institutions: Stylization, he writes, "is a heterogeneous yet not heteronomous discursive site: [it] presupposes a literary subject, a literary authority, a highly specific gaze. The chronicle assumed this specified gaze, yet it is a gaze without a proper space; a gaze that is subordinated, limited, by other authorities that converge . . . in the chronicle. Thus, from a formal perspective, the chronicle may represent and even thematize the work of a literary subject (stylization) as well as the limits of his autonomy (information)" (107). The aesthetic niche of the *modernista* chronicle strains against its utilitarian purpose to prove its distinction from mass-produced information; its failure finally to break free of its conditions of production imbues its stylized narrations with a sparkling tension that contains the dialectic of *modernismo*'s commoditization. Ramos articulates the two main sites of this dialectic: Not only does the frustrated autonomy of chronicle writing actually facilitate the development of the *modernistas*' lofty poetics, precisely as a foil to the less heroic discourse of journalism (87), it also lodges an anxiety at the heart of their treatments of capitalist modernity, so that the more their language attempts to purify and ornamentalize it, the more it reveals its own commodity status. "Stylization, in the optics of excess and luxury, rejects the use value of the word in the deployment of its will to autonomy; and yet, in doing so, it remains inscribed as a most elevated form of fetishization where the word is a strict exchange value" (116).

Paris is a prime conductor for the fluctuation between commoditization and autonomy, not least because an intimate knowledge of the city guarantees the *modernista* writer's symbolic access to the realm of pure art at the same time that it enhances his marketability in newspapers back home. The Parisian chronicle is in every way, as Ramos phrased it, an import journey (86).[9] Drawing on a series of highly codified topoi of the city, its most iconic monuments, neighborhoods, and streetscapes, it sets the stage for the dance of the word's exchange value. Here, the real itinerary of the foreign visitor parades as literary adventure; the tourist's paths of discovery are extended before the reader in glittering phantasmagoria. In "París nocturno," Darío embarks on an excursion through the city's nightlife, tracing successively the variety of trajectories to follow according to budget and taste. Departing from Nôtre Dame, passing through the bohemian cafés of the Left Bank and the more grandiose establishments of the Right Bank, he ascends to the Moulin-Rouge:

> When one arrives beneath the lights of the Moulin-Rouge, if one has experience of Paris, accompanied with a little knowledge, one enters in an artistic cabaret; if one is the foreigner recently arrived with checks or gold coins in his pocket, one enters those establishments full of smoking jackets, resplendent with silverwork, adorned with slender backs and red gypsy costumes, and where the obligatory bottle of champagne flaunts itself in the ice bucket. These are the houses with names of Rabelaisian abbeys and dead scoundrels. There, the indispensable violinists begin the dance of the hetaeras, or Hittites, who convert into seduction the *louis* of certain or doubtful gentlemen [*Cuando se llega ya bajo la iluminación del Molino-Rojo, si se tiene la experiencia de París, acompañada de un poco de razonamiento, entra uno a un cabaret artístico; si se es el extranjero recién llegado con cheques u oros en el bolsillo, entra a esos establecimientos llenos de smokings,*

> *relucientes de orfebrerías, adornados de espaldas esbeltas y por el rojo de los tziganes, y en donde la botella de champaña obligatoria se ostenta en la heladera. Estas son las casas con nombres de abadía rabelesiana o de roedor difunto. Allí, los indispensables violinistas hacen bailar a las hetairas, o heteas, que convierten en campaña los luises de los gentlemen ciertos o dudosos*] (Darío, *Obras Completas* IV 1054–55).

Darío showcases what was for many travelers the real destination of Paris—a night of reckless spending and debauchery with one of the city's many classes of prostitute—as a procession of fairylike tableaus. The titillating exoticism of the scenes, the ludic euphemisms for procurement and transaction, and the profiling of clientele by status and preference all literally advertise a certain experience of Paris; they sell it precisely through the stylized narration, which envelops the city's various tourist circuits in literary myth.[10]

The dialectical shimmer of passages like this one is intensified by their attempt to smooth over the collision between the literary commonplaces of the *modernistas*' city of dreams and the increasingly contrived landscape they were charged with delivering to readers. Retreating from the visible encroachment of mass culture, from the throngs overrun with the very sensation seekers portrayed in Darío's night jaunt—Latin American *rastacueros* and gaudy Americans and Englishmen—fervent adherents to literary Paris build up their fetish object around a select composition of mythologized elements, rarefying its immutable—and thus all the more consumable—qualities.[11] The Paris of Enrique Gómez Carrillo, as Cristóbal Pera observes, reinhabits the spaces of the bohemian mid-century Latin Quarter that had disappeared decades before his arrival: "the same neighborhoods, the same characters and identical images and hyperboles gradually cement this myth which, packaged and distributed by way of the chronicle, becomes a commodity appreciated in all Spanish America" [*los mismos barrios, los mismos personajes e idénticas imágenes e hipérboles van fijando ese mito que, empaquetado y distribuido a través de la crónica, se llega a convertir en una mercancía apreciada en toda Hispanoamérica*] (92). David Viñas, similarly, recounts how the Argentine gentleman pilgrim, horrified by the "smell of the bourgeoisie" on Paris's streets, flees to a city constructed of museums and opulent interiors.[12] This retrenchment in a mythical Paris, an artifice opposed to the real artifice of the city's commercialized march toward progress, precipitates the discursive reversal of early twentieth-century Spanish America towards cultural models of autochthony and nostalgia for a return to national roots.[13]

In a chronicle written on the occasion of the 1901 new year, Darío himself notes a certain decadence in the raffish histrionics and celebrity culture that increasingly eclipse the moral and literary virtues eulogized during Paris's golden age: "Today everything is ruled by farce and affectation. Woman is a decoration and a sex . . . The Americans have wedged their way in with the blows of golden mallets. Obsession with money has penetrated to the heart of France and especially of Paris" [*Hoy reina la pose y la farsa en todo . . . La mujer es una decoración y un sexo . . . Los norteamericanos han metido sus cuños a golpe de mazos de oro. La enfermedad del dinero ha invadido hasta el corazón de la Francia y sobre todo de París*] (Darío, *Obras Completas* III 500). Paris's decline, like the mythic object of its Spanish American admirers, owes to an irresistible dream, which feverishly "spirals into [the] abyss of pleasure, beauty, and madness" [*se gira en [el] abismo de gozo, de belleza y de locura*] (501). "Paris," Darío muses, "gives the sensation of a city that was dreaming, and looked at itself in dreams, or that of a city mad with a universal and collective madness" [*París da la sensación de una ciudad que estuviese soñando, y que se mirase en sueños, o la de una ciudad loca de una locura universal y colectiva*] (501–2). A universal and collective madness: His comments echo Benjamin's angel of history, watching the unstoppable storm of Paradise sweep him backward into the future. In the Parisian paradise too, Darío suggests, progress is a delirium. Like a runaway train, it rushes "with the fury of a thousand demons to explode against I don't know what wall of history, to fall into I don't know what abyss of eternity" [*con una presión de todos los diablos a estrellarse en no sé qué paredón de la historia y a caer en no sé qué abismo de la eternidad*] (502). As we will see, the double-faced discourse of *modernismo*, the aesthetic exchange value of its own words, also contains a ruin of the unfulfilled need it attempts to respond to.

La Sape and the Adventure of Paris

Paris's entry in the Congolese economy of *mikilisme*, as into the heterogeneous discourse of *modernismo*, similarly answers a multifaceted set of needs, demands, and values, each satisfied in different ways by the acquisition and display of designer clothing. The figure of the *mikiliste* is above all that of a *bon vivant*, one who has conquered "worlds" (*mikili*)—namely, Paris—and re-enters local society to capitalize on the social prestige accorded his persona by his exploits, all amply publicized from abroad through photographs, letters, word of mouth, and even popular songs and national television.[14] He presides at the pinnacle of a vast hierarchical cult of fashion, spectacle, and personal charisma, where *la gamme*—a wardrobe of authentic designer labels, bought in Paris—serves as currency, exchanged through a web of uneven secondary economies of popular music and illicit trade that relay his feats along a transnational grapevine of fame and reputation.[15]

Mikilistes are practitioners of *la sape*, a widespread, mostly male pursuit of the art of dressing well and being seen. Clubs dedicated to S.A.P.E

(Société des Ambianceurs et Personnes Élégantes) appeared in the 1970s in Brazzaville and Kinshasa, although these drew on trends of sartorial display stretching back at least to the early twentieth century.[16] The phenomenon of *la sape* hinges on the convincing performance of wealth and elegance: It does not reflect so much an effective class discourse as its simulation which, for its most foremost adepts, ultimately has the power to achieve a social mobility otherwise unavailable to non-elites of Congolese society. This explains the popularity of *sape* practices among young men left (by economic crisis, political corruption, and other travails of the postcolonial Congolese nation states) with no viable educational or professional paths to financial independence. For them, *sape* is about supplementing and supplanting reality with appearance: As Justin Daniel Gandoulou explains, it "deals with harnessing the exterior signs of success, echoing them for one's own satisfaction and for the approval and reinforcement of the group of reference: *sapeurs* dedicate themselves to imitating the exterior appearance of those who attain the summit of social elevation in Brazzaville, without of course possessing the instruments of objective success" [*s'agit de capter les signes extérieurs de la réussite, de les répercuter pour sa propre satisfaction et pour l'approbation et le renforcement du groupe de référence; les sapeurs s'evertuent à imiter l'aspect extérieur des gens arrivés au sommet de l'échelle sociale à Brazzaville, sans bien sûr detenir les instruments de la réussite objective*] (*Au Coeur* 19).

The process of becoming a *mikiliste* (a term interchangeable in most contexts with *Parisien* or *Aventurier*) begins with adherence to a local *sape* club: Members gather to show off brand-name ensembles, which they can either rent or buy from returning migrants. Frequenting bars, private parties, and public parades, initiates make themselves visible to prominent members of the group; during the summer months, they flock to hear the paeans and anecdotes of experienced *grands* who come from Paris to spend their vacation. *La sape* is thus characterized by an ongoing cycle of performance and adulation, through which novices reinforce received narratives of success from those who have proven themselves abroad. By practicing the simulacra of a cosmopolitan lifestyle they accrue the social standing that prepares them for an eventual pilgrimage, the true test of their image. Advancement depends on overall elegance but also on knowledge of Paris, from its topography, landmarks, and metro system, to the latest styles being worn. The most fortunate *sapeurs* migrate illegally to Paris with the aid of established acquaintances, where they usually work in an underground trade and cohabit with several compatriots in cramped apartments of abandoned or condemned buildings. The purposefully marginal existence of the *sapeur* in Paris, apart from his illegal status, owes to his ultimately local consecration: He forgoes precisely those amenities and comforts associated with metropolitan life in order to afford the extravagant goods that will clinch his social elevation back home.

In Alain Mabanckou's novel *Bleu blanc rouge* (1998), one of the most complete literary explorations of *sape* migration, the adventures of the protagonist follow precisely the trajectory outlined above. Massala-Massala, an unemployed youth from a town near the Congolese coast, has grown up with a dream of Paris as conduit to affluence and elegance. He participates in the community's adulation of Moki, the most prominent neighborhood *Parisien* who returns each dry season to administer an "annual mass" (86) of his own legacy to local believers. Inspired by Moki, Massala-Massala strives for and finally embarks on his voyage to Paris, convinced he is following a path of personal achievement and family honor. Crushed by the discovery of the squalid existence that awaits him in the metropolis, he nevertheless agrees to join the illicit business of a fellow *mikiliste* as part of his indenture to the network of compatriots who sponsored him. His very first sale of stolen metro cards among the street vendors of Château Rouge ends in arrest by French authorities, then in eighteen months of imprisonment before he is forcibly repatriated on a charter flight. As the dark ending of the novel attests, Mabanckou offers in *Bleu blanc rouge* a demythologization of the pilgrimage to Paris. In fact, the novel is structured around the gaping difference between the dream and the reality of migration, rendered more shocking as the reader follows the protagonist's firsthand disillusionment. In the solitude of prison, Massala-Massala reflects on his impending return home as a "*Parisien refoulé*," or failed Parisian, noting that those who will ridicule him "*ne savent pas que notre monde à nous est un autre monde*" [do not know that our world is another world] (215). The ambiguity of his phrase, signaling on the one hand the incompatibility of the *mikiliste*'s dream with the true experience of Paris, and on the other the self-containment of his social imaginary, highlights the hybrid value coding of phenomena like *la sape* vis-à-vis the transnational matrices with which they interact. That is to say, the *mikiliste*'s world is a different world, but it is also an autonomous world. The ambivalent tone of Massala-Massala's remarks is redoubled when, as he boards the charter flight home, he considers a second effort at migration. Mabanckou, after deconstructing his character's fantasy of Paris, ultimately leaves it intact.

The overwhelming disparity between the vision of Paris promoted by the *mikiliste* and the real experience of the city he submits to is cortical to Paris's articulation as fetish object on his own social horizons. Within the ritualized pathways of *sape* migration, the exchange value of designer labels—and more broadly, the sumptuous lifestyle associated with Paris—must be diverted at several points to a locally coded economic index if it is to yield the type of gains this circuit is designed to realize. These gains are not inherently capitalistic but in fact respond to the absence of capitalist practices of accumulation and investment, the failure to "develop" in line with neoliberal principles: The commodities prized by *mikilistes* are made to communicate the prestige of Parisian upper classes in a context where the infrastructure of their symbolic value—a class hierarchy buttressed in a universal model of accumulation and growth—is nonexistent. The circulation of luxury products in Kinshasa and Brazzaville thus bears the central features of postcolonial societies unevenly inserted in global capitalism, where, as Joseph Trapido enumerates, "local forms of social distinction rely on exogenously sourced prestige goods and so necessitate a connection with capitalist modes of production[,] [y]et those who effect this articulation use their 'wealth' within a set of political-economic arrangements which are not themselves capitalist" (206). This transnational importation of prestige is economically hybrid, "at once post-traditional and at the same time non-capitalist" (207).

It is in the gaps opened up by the post-traditional and non-capitalist logic of *sape* and *mikiliste* cults of fashion that one detects resistance to the encroachment to identity, to the all-pervasive exchange value of globalized capitalism. Herein lies the primary, fascinating drama of Paris as import commodity in the Congo: The antinomies attendant on the *mikiliste*'s economic improvement are not coincidental to this commodity's exchangeability, nor do they detract from its value; on the contrary, the adversity and risk of humiliation represented by the life of a migrant in Paris impute to the image of the *mikiliste* its particular distinction. In place of the usual chain of fungibility one attaches to the symbolic value of prestige goods—all the financial trappings of a capitalist, class-based infrastructure, which are expected to ground the elite habitus in concrete growth—the *mikiliste*'s conspicuous consumption is backed by, and retroactively proves, his personal worth. Thus, Trapido argues, in the economy of *mikiliste* migration "the considerable wealth in things appears, in the final analysis, as a kind of prop—essential but nonetheless an adjunct—to performances designed to establish the rank and value of persons, and it is persons who act as the primary 'asset' " (206). Adventure and risk, rather than comfort and leisure, are the premium of Paris's symbolic luxury. Because capturing the exterior signs of prosperity requires penury, marginality, and often criminal activity, the accoutrements of the well-appointed *mikiliste* reflect his persona, the body that has been subjected to the challenges of immigration and has prevailed: His wealth in things, as Trapido has it, is a mere testament to his wealth in person. Sociologists Janet MacGaffey and Rémy Bazenguissa-Ganga similarly describe the path of the *mikiliste* as a test of oneself, "trying one's body," according to one popular phrase:[17] "Clandestine immigration is an experience of self-fulfillment in which the actor is constantly evaluating himself. '*L'aventure*' entails the use of physical and mental skills, and even sometimes putting one's life in danger. In '*l'aventure*,' migrants do not stake assets which are exterior to them . . . Rather, they put their own potential and power, their very selves, on the line" ("Vivre et briller à Paris" 55).

The fundamental difference between the *mikiliste*'s passage through Paris and an economic migration aimed at financial security in the metropolis allows us to appreciate the ways his possessions are made to express a series of values that exploit but also interrupt their commodity status. Primary among these is his eschewal of "honest" work in favor of employment in one of the many rackets developed by the Congolese community in Paris, as well as Brussels and London, during the 1980s and 1990s: Check fraud, black market sale of designer clothing or metro passes, management of squats in abandoned buildings, forged identity cards, and other kinds of *bizness* provide many times more payment than the minimum-wage jobs the *mikiliste*—as an unskilled, uneducated, and illegal worker—would be forced to take in the regular economy[18]; the hustler who is wily enough to carry out his activities undiscovered by authorities in this sense wears the proof of his cunning, his personal value, in his clothes. What is more, his prowess has the bonus value of successfully outwitting the system of mainstream metropolitan society. The illegal endeavors of migrants serve as a kind of payback for colonization and its aftermath, a "colonial debt," as Gondola terms it, which justifies and enhances their infractions.[19] The presence of all these values, indiscriminately mingled in the figure of the dandified *Parisien*, indeed throws a dramatic twist into the commodity narrative they intersect. The tantalizing lie of *la griffe* signifies quite differently on the celebrated *mikiliste* than in a strictly capitalist sphere of exchange. To read its biography we must ply the artifice of the *mikiliste* against the standard bearer of commodity fiction, by following the various detours Paris and its products take in his journey toward distinction.

The Parisian Ideology of the Second Degree

In this superficial review of *modernista* and *mikiliste* cults of Paris, it becomes clear that no systematic logic is sufficient to organize the uses and limits of exchange value levied therein into a coherent story of capitalism's exportation to peripheral society. It is clear, for example, that although the manipulations of Paris outlined here are, on the whole, designed to parlay its prestige into material advantage, they cannot be defined adequately by Bourdieusian symbolic capital; that is, they do not simply build upon and disguise as disinterest the relative autonomy granted by economic structures.[20] The transvaluations *modernistas* and *mikilistes* exercise upon the fetish object of Paris and its commodities are rather of the kind anthropologist Roberto Schwarz described as "second degree." His argument, centered on the contradictions intrinsic to the evolution of political and literary modernity in Brazil, is instructive for the cases at hand because it calls attention to the tergiversations and reversals necessary to make modern ideas stick in societies where their very appearance seems absurd. For nineteenth-century Brazilian slaveholders, Schwarz reasons, the ideals of European liberalism could not be given a straightforward interpretation; but dispensing with the ideas of free labor, order, and universal rights excluded them altogether from the club of modernity. A creative compromise was therefore in order: By deploying liberal rhetoric to authorize practices of a much more arbitrary and erratic system of favor, Brazilian society gave the veneer of modernity to its principal actors without disturbing the sleeping beast of their dependence on slavery. Thanks to this adequation, Schwarz writes, "the antagonism vanished into thin air, and the opposing positions walked hand in hand" (23). Unlike the first-degree lie of ideologies that spread a false conception of a real situation, ideologies of the second degree "do not describe reality, not even falsely, and they do not move according to a law of their own; . . . Their law of movement is a different one, not the one they name; it honours prestige, rather than a desire for system and objectivity" (23). In other words, second-degree ideologies have the capacity to unveil the false semblance of modern ideas simply by taking them beyond the limits of plausibility, for if it is true that through the wedding of favor and liberalism "one could methodically call dependence independence, capriciousness utility, exceptions universality," and so on, it is also true that "inasmuch as they became preposterous, these ideas also ceased to mislead" (24).

Ideologies of the second degree, then, do not simply allow us to comment on the fraudulence of ideology in general, but also harbor in the dissonances they create a chance to decipher some of the contradictions through which alienation and injustice are perpetuated in the first place. This is why, as Schwarz stipulates, "it does not help to insist on their obvious falsehood. We should rather observe their dynamics, of which this falsehood is a true component" (28). Within the fiction of the commodity object appropriated by *mikiliste* and *modernista* discourses of Paris, we can use Schwarz's conclusions to advance an initial characterization of the way their ideas also cease to mislead. In order to capitalize on the value of the modern built up in the image of Paris, each discourse must tear it from its context of exchange. *Modernistas*, as we have seen, attempt to dress up the raging mercantilization of the city in a language of aesthetic purity, the grounds for their own refuge from the whims of the market. *Mikilistes* fashion Paris as a narrative and physical site of social metamorphosis, where both the means and ends of accumulation effectively reinvent the lie of the commodity fetish.

Neither manages to uphold the fiction of the commodity object's natural qualities of social relation. On the contrary, the further afield they take the symbolic value of Paris and its immutable modernity, the more they reveal the swindle at the core of its claims to infinite exchange as an inevitable expression of human life. The more ethereal and mythological *modernistas'* stylization of Paris becomes, the more plainly their discourse betrays itself and its objects as products for sale. The more fervently *mikilistes* promote the transformative power of accumulation and migration, the starker the contrast between the economic realities of impoverished neighborhoods of Kinshasa and Brazzaville and their spectacle of easy living.

Both groups use the fetish of Parisian modernity to erase antagonisms, to make opposites walk hand in hand. But if their adaptations of this modernity can usefully be described as postcolonial, it is not (or not simply) because of the aberrant forms commoditization assumes on the margins of global capitalism. The task is not, as Schwarz says, to insist on the falsehood of these ideologies but to dissect the dynamics of which their falsehood is a true component. By mobilizing the pressure the second-order fictions of *modernistas* and *mikilistes* place on the primary fiction of Paris's magical modernity, this sort of reading will uncover the ways their lies are a true condition of thought: In other words, it aims to recognize their aberrations not as a state identified with postcoloniality, but as a protest of non-identity against the relentless identification that the importation of foreign modernity, as a rule, pursues. The very falsehood of these discourses thus recommends them as objects for the wishful thinking of the postcolonial concept I have been exploring in previous chapters.

Falsehood is in fact the first priority of these groups, starting with their stringent control over the image of Paris consumed by their followers. The training of the *mikiliste* involves the cultivation of a mental map of the city, which serves the future pilgrim as a surrogate possession of his Mecca: As Massala-Massala recalls in *Bleu blanc rouge*, certain adoring fans of the *Parisien* Moki "would describe with an unbeatable talent the metro lines, station by station, making believe they had traveled to Paris" [*décrivaient avec un talent inégalable les lignes du métro, station par station, à croire qu'ils avaient séjourné à Paris*]; some even assumed the names of metro stations as their own pseudonyms, calling themselves "Monsieur Saint-Placide, Monsieur Strasbourg-Saint-Denis, Monsieur Colonel Fabien," and so on (Mabanckou, *Bleu blanc rouge* 62). The mental appropriation of the city is the initial step of the *mikiliste* in developing a convincing performance of the *Parisien:* "One must first convince at home," Moki explains to his pupils, "and then attain the City of Light" [*on doit d'abord convaincre ici au pays et ensuite gagner la Ville Lumière*] (75). Once disembarked in Paris, the evolved *mikiliste* easily confirms the virtuosity of his performance; his seamless movement through the metropolis only proves the fiction he has already spun before leaving the Congo. Boasts Moki to his audience: "I knew Paris even before taking the plane for the first time in Luanda . . . As soon as I got off the plane, I confidently took a taxi and I indicated to the driver the route to take . . . To him, I was not a foreigner. I was at home" [*Je connaissais Paris avant même de prendre l'avion pour la première fois à Luanda . . . Dès que je suis sorti de l'avion, j'ai pris avec assurance un taxi et j'ai indiqué au chauffeur l'itinéraire à suivre . . . Pour lui, je n'étais pas un étranger. J'étais chez moi*] (85).

The *mikiliste*'s fiction of Parisianness, of course, is elaborated for exclusively local consumption. It matters little whether the *mikiliste* really blends in, because the tale of his achievement is directed at those back home. His account tailors the value of Paris to the specific desires of the local community through what Lydie Moudileno has called the "fiction of migration," a rigorously controlled narrative of transformative voyage and return built around "the representation of an imaginary universe, the invention of a hero, a series of 'laws of narrative' to follow and, above all, the presence of a narrative authority that regulates accounts and images" [*la représentation d'un univers imaginaire, l'invention d'un héros, une série de 'lois des récit' à suivre et, surtout, la présence d'une autorité narrative qui régule récits et images*] ("La fiction de la migration" 183). Moudileno's definition of the term stresses the way regulated fiction organizes and sanctions the experience of travel to Paris, so much so, we could add, that the management of the discourse of migration is itself an indispensable good in the wealth to be gained by the *mikiliste*'s journey. The uniform tale the *mikiliste* spreads about the way migration should happen acts as insurance: It primes the environment of his *descente* from Paris in which to realize the maximum returns from the final performance of his storied metamorphosis. In the *descente*, the star moment of the returning *mikiliste*, the discursive and material goods collected along the way achieve their mutually affirming apotheosis, as Moki's dramatic arrival in his old neighborhood shows us:

> As soon as he was out of the car, noticing that all looks were fixed on him, he began a demonstration close to a fashion catwalk, to the great joy of the fans that besieged the bar. He unbuttoned his jacket, handed it to one of his brothers behind him. Under the transparent shirt, the lightened skin, almost pale, without the irritations or allergies that plagued local imitators. This metamorphosis stunned the crowd. The Parisian adjusted his trousers to the level of his belly button. The gesture was affected, measured and studied for the purpose of showing off his socks, which matched his tie. One of his brothers handed him a pair of Emmanuelle Khanh sunglasses, not to wear but

> to place gently above his forehead. A torrent of bravos ensued [*Aussitôt qu'il était hors du véhicule, s'avisant que les regards étaient braqués sur lui, il se livrait à une démonstration proche d'un défilé de mode, au grand bonheur des fanatiques qui assiégeaient la buvette. Il déboutonnait sa veste, la remettait à l'un de ses frères derrière lui. Sous la chemise transparente, la peau éclaircie, presque pâle, sans irritations et autre allergies sévissant sur les imitateurs locaux. Cette métamorphose stupéfiait la foule. Le Parisien rajustait son pantalon jusqu'au nombril. Le geste était gourmé, compassé et étudié en vue de mettre en valeur ses chaussettes qui s'assortissaient à sa cravate. Un de ses frères lui tendait des lunettes de soleil Emmanuelle Khanh, non pour les porter, mais pour les poser légèrement au-dessus du front. Un torrent de bravos s'ensuivait*]. (Mabanckou, *Bleu blanc rouge* 70)

Moki's poses, his expensive outfit, the delicate pallor his skin has acquired under the winter sky (in reality, the effect of skin-lightening creams), his retinue of assistants, and the effusive applause of his audience all complete the tale of his cycle through Paris with a victorious finale.[21] Thus solidly affirmed, the fiction of migration supports the endeavors of fledgling *mikilistes* (as will be the case with Moki's acolyte, Massala-Massala) to repeat his success.

Part of the labor of the maintenance of the *mikiliste* myth of Paris is to discredit alternative versions of the capital that focus on the difficulty of survival and unsavory conditions facing clandestine migrants. In *Bleu blanc rouge*, the accounts of life in Paris brought back by non-*mikiliste* migrants, called *Paysans*, are dismissed out of hand as vulgar and necessarily false, not only because they fail to corroborate the image reproduced by *Parisiens*, but more importantly because their appearance and behavior reflect none of the transformative magic travel to Europe is supposed to effect: The *Paysan* returns home with a few t-shirts and jeans in his suitcase; he eats sitting on the floor with his family and takes public transportation; his arrival occasions no fanfare, no festivities; he doesn't understand grandeur or elegance. Indeed, a simple comparison of the common *Paysan* with the celebrated *Parisien* gives ample evidence of his lies: "One hears him lament that life is difficult in France. Liar! Always lies. He lies like he breathes. And vice versa. He's just bitter and incompetent. He is not listened to . . . He won't change. His frustration is the same. He takes the easy way out" [*On l'entend se lamenter que la vie est difficile en France. Menteur! Toujours des mensonges. Il ment comme il respire. Et vice versa. Ce n'est qu'un aigri, un incapable. Il n'est pas écouté . . . Il ne changera pas. Sa frustration est la même. Il aime la facilité*] (90). The same matrix of discursive, material, and performative values overlaid in the *mikiliste*'s importation of Paris serves as the criterion for disproving the *Paysan:* His narrative, quite simply, has no purchase in the *mikiliste* economy because it offers none of those holders of social value through which Paris is made exchangeable in local society. The uselessness of the *Paysan* goes much deeper than failing to acquire *la griffe* or affect the proper behavior of a man of leisure. What his lack of elegance ultimately reveals is a lack of adventure and self-fulfillment. In ceding to the difficulties of reality and wallowing in frustration, the *Paysan* forfeits all the wealth to be captured through the trip to Europe, most pointedly the "wealth in person" the physical adventure in Paris awards the *mikiliste*. For the *Paysan*, adversity remains just that; it yields no transmutation. His Paris is quite rightly a false Paris: Indifferent to the desires migration is meant to address, it is justly deemed worthless.

These failings of the *Paysan* throw into relief the full range of capital exploited by the *mikiliste*. The realities of migration that his stories of Paris leave unaltered—the precarious living arrangements, marginalization, and material scarcity—are also enfolded into the *mikiliste*'s achievement. The hardships he has overcome attest negatively to his singular talents; their dissimulation is the measure of his personal wealth. The more smoothly the *mikiliste*'s simulacra covers over the *Paysan*'s ugly truth, the more resoundingly he proves its falsehood, asserting his own glittering lie in its place. This conversion is his unique capital. Moki hints at this secret truth of the Parisian adventure: "But there is a whole story behind us. You only see the sunny side of the mountain, what in good French is called *l'adret*. Is it pretentious of me to say that we are almost heroes?" [*Mais il y a toute une histoire derrière nous. Vous ne voyez que le versant éclairé de la montagne, ce qu'on appelle en bon français,* l'adret. *Est-ce prétentieux de ma part que de dire que nous sommes presque des héros?*] (83). The second-order lie of Moki's Paris wields miraculous properties of exchange: Its heroism denies the commodity form its usual necromancy, insofar as the fetish of Paris here consists of rejecting labor, consumption, and accumulation even as it favors their representation in things. This rejection peeks out from behind the *mikiliste*'s simulacrum, like the dark side of a mountain, throwing the commodity from its usual path of valorization.

The *modernista*'s miraculous falsehood, like Moki's fiction of migration, asserts control of a uniquely valid version of Paris. He administers an authorized experience of the city for the cultured reader, molding the new Spanish American consumer classes' desire for Paris into a proper social distinction. By the turn of the century, the Atlantic crossing constituted a rite of initiation for debutants of the moneyed families of the region's capitals, establishing the practice of the "boomerang voyage," by which Paris, as David Viñas explains, becomes an obligatory stop on the institutionalized path of social ascent: The boomerang voyage is "neither [for] pioneers, nor precursors, nor adventurers; those who celebrate it adopt more and more the air of officiants and the itinerary becomes a rite. One travels to Europe in order to be sanctified there and return consecrated" [*ni [para] pioneros, ni precursores, ni aventureros, quienes lo celebran adoptan cada vez más el aire de oficiantes y el itinerario se convierte en rito. Se viaja a Europa para santificarse allá y regresar consagrado*] (39). The chronicle funnels the base demand for foreign modernity into a tutorial in good taste, training it in the *modernista*'s special aura of disinterest. In doing so, it repeats many of the commonplaces of the phantasmagoria cited by Benjamin's Arcades Project; but by taking them to extremes, as we will see, it can also give a glimpse of the undoing of the commodity's original deceit.

Darío's coverage of the 1900 World Exhibition is exemplary in this regard. Benjamin envisioned world exhibitions as "places of pilgrimage to the commodity fetish," "a school in which the masses . . . are imbued with the exchange value of commodities to the point of identifying with it" (*The Arcades Project* 18–19). The world exhibition's panoramic views and breathtaking displays provide a picture window on a new universe of consumerism, through which the masses are invited to absorb the objects on the other side as a real social medium, training themselves in the art of desire. The chronicle takes this further: Recreating the exhibition's showcase—Ramos rightly notes that "the shop window [becomes] a metaphor for the chronicle itself as a mediation between the private subject and the city" (128)—it brokers a remote possession of Paris, starting with the same structured vision that guides the savvy shopper. Darío introduces the exhibition with a sweeping glance from the Eiffel Tower: "Seeing the magnificent spectacle as an eagle would see it, that is, from the heights of the Eiffel Tower, the city appears so fabulous that it is difficult to convince oneself they are not witnessing the realization of a dream. The eyes tire, but even more the spirit, before the overwhelming, monumental perspective . . . In the clear sunlight with which the beginnings of spring gratify the heavens and earth of Paris, the panorama, from its eminence, dazzles you" [*Visto el magnífico espectáculo como lo vería un águila, es decir, desde las alturas de la torre Eiffel, aparece la ciudad fabulosa de manera que cuesta convencerse de que no se asiste a la realización de un ensueño. La mirada se fatiga, pero aun más el espíritu ante la perspectiva abrumadora monumental . . . A la clara luz solar con que la entrada de la primavera gratifica al cielo y suelo de París, os deslumbra, desde la eminencia, el panorama*] (Darío, *Obras Completas* III 380). By first commanding an aerial view of the fair, Darío organizes it as an object for consumption; his encomium recalls the panoramic sights used in many of the brochures that advertised the exhibition, visually mapping it out as a series of landmarks to be taken in at once.[22] Placing the reader in the eye of his description through the passive voice and the direct invocation of "*os*," Darío solicits his active participation in the discoveries and evaluations of Paris's display.

Beginning with this initial possession of the city from above, the reader thus appraises its many exhibits along Darío's tour of informed opinion: Moving between impressionist scenes of the passers-by and summary reviews of art, architecture, and fashion, Darío simultaneously dictates and affirms his reader's aesthetic discernment. He pauses before the Porte Monumentale, the fair's main entrance, to instruct the reader in the proper appreciation of its design: "Behold the great entrance through which we will penetrate, reader, the magnificent door which, surrounded by banners and between elegant posts that hold big electric lamps, is in its architectural novelty deserving of contemplation; admire the vast cupola, the superb arcade, the openwork, and the decoration, and avoid the sin of Moreau-Vauthier, the dressed-up damsel balancing on her billiard ball" [*He aquí la gran entrada por donde penetraremos, lector, la puerta magnífica que rodeada de banderas y entre astas elegantes que sostienen grandes lámparas eléctricas, es en su novedad arquitectural digna de ser contemplada; admírese la vasta cúpula, la arcada soberbia, la labor de calado, y la decoración, y evítese el pecado de Moreau-Vauthier, la señorita peripuesta que hace equilibrio sobre su bola de billar*] (Darío, *Obras Completas* III 384). Darío first explicitly renders the reader's presence, as that of a pupil, by his side; he next draws his attention to its salient details, informing him of what is and is not deserving of the viewer's praise. His conceit as *cronista*, as I have explained, is to disguise the exchange value of his office, to dress up the city in phantasmagoric garb. In this way, chronicles (and *modernista* literature in general) contain a sparkling struggle in their very language, which is visible both as eternal aura and specialized product—in Ramos's words, both as autonomy and information. The insistence with which the former is asserted over the latter becomes the chronicle's index of commoditization. We see how these two functions coalesce in Darío's disdain for the Moreau-Vauthier statue of a *grisette* at the top of the Porte Monumentale. The offending maiden, represented as a contemporary young woman of the working class, destroys the fair's—and Paris's—timeless illusion. Explains Darío:

> That is not art, or symbol, or anything more than a wax figure for a dressmaker's shop window. The marvelous nudity of goddesses is the only one that, kissed by the air and bathed in light, can stand at the coronation of a monument of beauty. . . . [T]hose who praise this statue for its realism and currency, should understand that the city of Paris cannot be symbolized in a figure akin to that of Yvette Guilbert or Mademoiselle de Pougy. . . . Parisian fashion is charming: but the modern mundane cannot substitute

> the glory of the allegory or the symbol of what was consecrated by Rome and Greece [*Eso no es arte, ni símbolo, ni nada más que una figura de cera para vitrina de confecciones. La maravillosa desnudez de las diosas, es la única que, besada por el aire y bañada de luz, puede erguirse en la coronación de un monumento de belleza . . . [L]os que alaban esta estatua por lo que tiene de realismo y actualidad, deberían comprender que la ciudad de París, no puede simbolizarse en una figura igual a la de Yvette Guilbert o mademoiselle de Pougy . . . La moda parisiense es encantadora: pero todavía lo mundano moderno no puede sustituir a la gloria de la alegoría o del símbolo a lo consagrado por Roma y Grecia*]. (Darío, *Obras Completas* III 385)[23]

The banality of the statue interrupts the façade which elsewhere drapes the exhibition's attractions in spellbinding spectacle. It cites directly the underlying relation of capital that draws crowds to the fair: As such, Darío observes, it belongs in a dressmaker's shop window, not atop the crowning jewel of the hypostatic vision of modern progress. By inserting a mimesis of labor—the *modiste*, a member of the urban, female workforce—directly into the context of labor's disavowment, Moreau-Vauthier reverses and violates the fundamental operation of phantasmagoria, to cloak relations of capitalist production. For Darío, the statue thus "sins" by elevating mundane signs of production to the level of their own reproduction in images, a realm that the *cronista*'s claims to autonomy lead him to reserve exclusively for himself. This explains why the same figure of the *grisette*, in all her mundanity, can masquerade as a goddess in many of Darío's chronicles—indeed, in "París nocturno" the Parisian is an "exquisite priestess" [*exquisita sacerdotisa*] for the many foreigners who dream of her from afar, enslaved by "her way of walking, her way of talking, her way of gathering her skirt, eating a fruit" [*su manera de andar, de su manera hablar, de su manera de recogerse la falda, de comer una fruta*] (Darío, *Obras Completas* III 1056)—while her literal representation in the place of a goddess can only be construed as a bad joke. At the level of art, the *grisette* announces what Paris really is: a courtesan. In doing so, she rends the veil from around the commodity form of Darío's own stylization. He directs the reader away from her folly and thereby reasserts control over his Paris, allegorized and symbolized in the forms of ancient glories. The example of the *grisette* affirms that, for Darío's purposes, the phantasmagoria of Paris must be taken further than it can take itself. All semblance between reality and representation must be revoked to maintain the very currency of Paris as import fiction: Through the second-order ideology of Paris, the *modernista* carves out his own space of singularization, within which he also inevitably promotes its exchange.

Wish Images: The Utopia of Production

The foregoing examples initiate a rough sketch of the central mechanisms of *mikiliste* and *modernista* ideologies of Paris as a fiction of the second degree. Through the narrative control of the importation of Paris as fetish object, they plant its commodity forms in a reality that does not support them. Rather than suppressing the exploitation and alienation that invisibly fuel the commodity's exchange value, they suppress the very absence of these dynamics: Paris covers over the fact that *modernismo* has no proper space from which to speak, no complete (if false) autonomy where its phantasmagoria could masquerade seamlessly as reality, just as it disguises the *mikiliste*'s marginalization from the metropolis's mainstream economy. Paris's prestige is false, but differently false from the comedy played out in the myths of fashion, history, and progress that weave its original aura of modernity. In a way, creating this disjuncture is the whole point, for by importing "misplaced" ideas to paper over local reality, *mikilistes* and *modernistas* attempt to transform reality for the better. Their chance depends on the channels of singularization to which they manage to submit Paris's charms. It is thus not coincidental that both groups are often characterized as dandies: Like the dandy, as Baudelaire first portrayed him, they embody the blasé elegance of men of the leisure classes while dispelling from the aureola of their persona the crass means of its construction. Class, for the dandy, is a matter of character: He "does not aspire to money as to something essential; this crude passion he leaves to vulgar mortals; he would be perfectly content with a limitless credit at the bank" (27). More important, the singular simulacrum of the dandy plays upon the unruly transitions between old and new codes of social stratification in recently bourgeoisified European societies: "In the disorder of these times, certain men who are socially, politically, and financially ill at ease, but are rich in native energy, may conceive the idea of establishing a new kind of aristocracy, all the more difficult to shatter as it will be based on the most precious, the most enduring faculties, and on the divine gifts which work and money are unable to bestow" (28). The dandy, of course, is a product of a class system and has no real escape from capital; but the protest of his uneasiness with the "disorder" of the times—a disorder, it should be noted, that also plagues postcolonial Congolese society and urbanizing Spanish American capitals of the late nineteenth century—manifests in a utopian vision of distinction, where not capital but divinity and nature, gifts from heaven and earth, ensure his well-being.

While Baudelaire's dandy may repeat some common motifs of phantasmagoria, he directs them against the rampant law of exchange value taking root around him. In him, the spectacle of capitalism is routed towards its opposite, a classless society.[24] His utopian gesture expresses the same desires

Benjamin found latent in the "wish images" of modernity, the designs and forms that decorate new technologies in mythic "ur-history" and nature. Dressing the uncertainties of new products of nature—technologies "come too soon"—in archaic images of an unfulfilled utopia, wish images project on the new, as Susan Buck-Morss's authoritative gloss asserts, "an ur-image of the desired social *ends* of their development" (*The Dialectics of Seeing* 117). In doing so they break with the recent past and "attemp[t] to transcend as well as to illumine the incompletedness of the social order of production" (quoted in Buck-Morss, *The Dialectics of Seeing* 114).[25] Wish images should not be read in themselves as a revolutionary consciousness, just as the dandy's dream of a divine aristocracy does not in itself break from dominant class ideology; rather, these represent unconscious collective impulses of singularization, the desire to capture and train the forces of production still in flux toward their wildest dream of what the future may hold. It is in this sense that I want to bring the example of the dandy and the ur-forms of wish images to bear on my final examinations of *modernista* and *mikiliste* uses of capitalist modernity.

It requires no stretch of the imagination to assert that Darío, among the *modernistas*, was the master manipulator of wish images of ur-history in his contemplations of the poet's modern-day predicament. *Azul*, written before Darío had ever visited Paris, presents a series of fables that narrate in fairy-tale settings his confrontation with the forces of commoditization, where cupidinous figures of petty-bourgeois authority are bested, often bitterly, by mythical standards of production. Among these parables, "El rubí" offers the most direct commentary on the commodity: It situates the struggle of the *modernista* poet among a clan of gnomes who work in an underground grotto harvesting jewels, and who discover with horror a new, synthetic ruby brought straight from Paris. Meditating on the impostor, which has been presented to them by a visiting sprite, the gnomes hear him report: "Those rubies! In the great city of Paris, flying invisible, I saw them everywhere. They sparkle in the courtesans' necklaces, in the *rastacueros*' medals, in the rings of Italian princes and in the prima donnas' bracelets" [*Esos rubíes! En la gran ciudad de París, volando invisible, los vi por todas partes. Brillaban en los collares de las cortesanas, en las condecoraciones exóticas de los rastacueros, en los anillos de los príncipes italianos y en los brazaletes de las primadonas*] (Darío, *Obras Completas* V 666).

The focus on jewels here is significant: As a product they incarnate the precious, natural, and authentic value of resources uncommonly resistant to uniform capitalist production schemes. For Marx, diamonds represented a limit-case of the commodity form. Unlike corn or wood, whose harvest and processing easily commutes their exchange value to a quantifiable rate of labor expenditure, diamonds are sourced from a highly unpredictable, often inefficient harvest procedure.[26] The undisciplined nature of the labor that brings them to market adds to their extravagance, redoubled—though this goes unremarked by Marx—by the aura of nobility, a redolence of ostentatious ornament that attached to precious stones well after they became widely available to bourgeois customers in the nineteenth century. In jewels, then, the commodity fetish is skewed, both because the relations of labor it expresses as natural qualities are highly variable and involve extremes that are obscured by their reduction to a medium of exchange, and because the use value the fetish form is said to conceal never properly exists: The jewel's use value, after all, is its very uselessness as lavish adornment.[27] These paradoxes no doubt explain a large part of the appeal of precious gems for *modernista* writers, who used them widely as symbols in poetic and journalistic work alike.[28] In "El rubí," the jewel clearly stands in for literature. The juxtaposition of the factory-made Parisian stone with the artisanal hammers of the underground creatures, who chip away at the glittering walls of their cave, all too obviously recalls the affront posed to *modernista* literary sensibilities by factory-like newspapers and periodicals, where prose was often churned out at a set rate per page and displayed haphazardly alongside advertisements and other miscellanea of daily life.

Giving an incredulous account of the ruby's new mechanical production, the elder gnome thus actually seizes upon the same vagaries travelled by the commodity form in mass-produced literature: "Behold, without studying aristotelic formulas, without knowing kabbala and necromancy, a man of the nineteenth century manages to create by light of day what we manufacture underground. What witchcraft! Twenty days of fusion of a mixture of silica and lead aluminate. Coloration with potassium bichromate or with cobalt oxide. Words that truly appear to be a diabolical language" [*He aquí que sin estudiar las fórmulas aristotélicas, sin saber cábala y nigromancia, llega un hombre del siglo decimonono a formar a la luz del día lo que nosotros fabricamos en nuestros subterráneos. ¡Pues el conjuro! Fusión por veinte días de una mezcla de sílice y de aluminato de plomo; coloración con bicromato de potasa o con óxido de cobalto. Palabras en verdad que parecen lengua diabólica*] (Darío, *Obras Completas* V 663–64). The passage turns on an encoding of the commodity form. The utilitarian mode of production at first seems all too trivial, unworthy of a jewel, but if we are to be dismayed that the work of ancient magic is now achieved in the daylight of a modern laboratory, it is only to discover the false ruby's own necromancy, the theological pretensions of its formulaic birth. Through it the scientific combination of chemicals becomes a spell of incantation with its own diabolical language, which multiplies as if by magic the minerals lining the buried grotto of the gnomes. Underneath the more apparent allegory about the commercialization of literature and gems, the fable's concern with manipulating the language of production stages a deeper struggle over the representation of production, in short, the type of phantasmagoria best authorized to enshrine mass-produced literature.

Through this struggle, the second half of "El rubí" responds to the first: The gnomes contest the synthetic stone with a competing narrative of production, not a diabolical language of chemicals and machines, but an origin myth of romance and tragedy. True rubies, the elder gnome recounts to his audience, are born from the blood of a virgin kept prisoner in his cave: Responding to the calls of her lover from above, the captive attempts to flee and tears her flesh on the sharp diamonds scattered along the floor, infusing them with the blood of her dying body. The gnomes, after hearing the elder's story, enthusiastically smash the Parisian ruby, hailing the fecundity of their own producer, mother nature: "You, oh Mother Earth! . . . from your tawny womb spring the sap of robust trunks, gold and diamantine water, and the chaste fleur-de-lis. All that is pure, strong, incorruptible!" [*tú, o madre Tierra! . . . de tu vientre moreno brota la savia de los troncos robustos, y el oro y el agua diamantina, y la casta flor de lis. ¡Lo puro, lo fuerte, lo infalsificable!*] (Darío, *Obras Completas* V 671). Their magical cave, against the witchcraft of the laboratory, promises a mythic nature in which gems (and literature) fall like manna from the ur-form of mother earth. Thus, the competing tales of production offer a deeper insight into the duplicity of phantasmagoria in *modernista* discourse. Darío makes the two paths of commoditization cite each other mutually, in that the exchange value denounced in the false ruby is mirrored in the gnome's fairy tale of production, in a language so ornamental that it betrays, in reality, the same sorcery the gnomes decry in the fictional synthetic gem. The mask of the commodity is traded for Benjamin's dream image: For if "El rubí" recognizes in itself a diamond of the mass-produced variety—like most of Darío's creative work, it was written for a newspaper before appearing in book form—it nevertheless dons the robe of myth to insist, however precariously, on the singularities of labor and value uneasily represented by its commodity status. The Paris of fake jewels, of courtesans and *rastacueros*, is unavoidably Darío's Paris as well, a frantic headlong rush conducted by the commodity fetish toward an abyss of modernity; the ur-forms of his escapism, even as they serve to brand his market niche, nonetheless have the redeeming quality of desiring a better set of social ends for mass culture. Darío dreams an alternative to the commercialization of the literary market, where the singularity of his labor, like the divine gifts of Baudelaire's dandy, might be preserved. His dream images in this sense look forward by looking back, "to transcend as well as to illumine the incompletedness of the social order of production" (Buck-Morss, *The Dialectics of Seeing* 114).

For *mikilistes*, the language of diamonds has served as an even more authoritative interface for the mediation of foreign capital, thanks to the role of the violent parallel economy of diamond trading in southern Democratic Republic of the Congo (Zaire) starting in the 1960s. Indeed, the ethos of adventure and self-making embraced by *mikiliste* rituals of migration responds to a much broader civic discourse of *débrouillardise*, literally self-starting or "making do with nothing," which originated in the liberalization of the diamond industry after Zaire's independence. MacGaffey and Bazenguissa-Ganga locate the beginnings of *débrouillardise* in the declaration of president Albert Kalonji to his constituency of the then-rebel state South Kasai, to "fend for yourself" (*débrouillez-vous*), which effectively sanctioned the illegal mining and trade of diamonds in lieu of a publicly managed budget (*Congo-Paris* 54).[29] The metaphorization of diamond mining to refer to enterprises of commerce, exchange, and survival in general is evinced in the term *kobeta libanga*, "breaking stones," a euphemism for illicit trade but also for the forms of patronage and clientelism, particularly *mabanga* or music dedication, that help many *mikilistes* expand their social recognition.[30] The underlying logic of social and capital exchange that *mikilistes* thus share with the informal diamond industry elucidates a set of significant parallels between their adventure of self-making to the north and the migration many other inhabitants of Kinshasa undertake south to the Lunda province of Angola to try their luck at diamond mining. These migrants, called the *bana Lunda* or "the children of Lunda," set out for the UNITA-controlled diamond mines across the border guided by a similar hope of achieving social mobility through the capture of wealth and distinction, though the risks and hardships they face are considerably more formidable. Filip De Boeck's authoritative study of the diamond economy of Lunda from the mid-1990s documents the many dangers facing *bana Lunda* from the 1980s on: Besides pay-offs to border patrols and the possibility of robbery during the treacherous trip on foot to Angola and back north to the Congo, they face forced labor and often torture at the hands of the UNITA forces that manage the mines, as well as land mines scattered through the territory from Angola's civil war. Even the treasure that has enticed them abroad harbors hidden perils, for the dollarization of the diamond economy in the 1990s brought hyperinflation that rose at times upwards of 5,000%: The thousands of dollars brought in by a lucky diamond hunter could, at times, buy barely enough food for a day (De Boeck, "Domesticating Diamonds" 786–87).[31]

The extreme stakes attending the venture of the *bana Lunda* on the outskirts of the global diamond economy make palpable the commodity's magical powers. Dollars and diamonds, explains De Boeck, often represent to migrants the qualities of living objects, "that behave in irrational and even 'demonic' or 'satanic' ways" ("Domesticating Diamonds" 787). Around the diamond mines, sources of wealth become unpredictable and sinister: "Like wild and dangerous animals[,] they need to be captured, trapped, snared, tamed" (786). Volatile and fraught with hazards, the channels of capital growth available to the diamond hunter thus necessarily direct him away from practices of accumulation and investment. Diamonds and dollars are unreliable as repositories of value, and useless in themselves for social advancement: They must be treated as animals to be hunted, domesticated through capture and incorporated to the self through ostentatious distribution.[32] This is why extravagant spending is the *bana Lunda*'s main conduit of social success. As one of De Boeck's informants explains: "To make oneself known, one has to distribute money. Everybody has to know that you have money, the women, the friends. If you have US $40,000, it is very easy to spend $3,000 or even $4,000 on a woman in one night. And you are not going to court just one woman. The women have to be numerous so that everybody will know you. Your friends have to know that they are dealing with a real *patron*" (793). The diamond migrant's circuit of self-enrichment echoes the transvaluated triumph signified through the *mikiliste's griffés:* Like the *mikiliste* who proves his conquest of Paris in his clothes, the *bana Lunda* spreads word of his exploits with wild expenditure. The returns in social prestige are similarly anchored in a combination of the economic value of the diamonds and dollars he has managed to hunt and release in the service of his self-promotion and the valor, intelligence, and luck represented by his defeat of the many dangers waiting in the Lunda: in short, his success in adventure.

I have taken a detour through the example of diamond migration because it fleshes out visually how the acquisition of wealth in people integral to *débrouillardise* involves entries and exits from a properly capitalist field of commodities. The outrageous spending of the *bana Lunda* partakes of western-style conspicuous consumption at the same time that it draws on precolonial discourses of clientelism and prestation, a potlatch uniquely characterized, as Trapido describes it, by "recklessness and public drama" (207). *Mikilistes* are prominent participants of this potlatch. Trapido, for example, remarks on the common practice among well-known *Parisiens* of throwing armfuls of dollars at children in the street, or discarding designer jackets to be trampled on the dance floor. Various famous *mikilistes* have brought expensive cars home to Kinshasa to put them in service as taxis. The transaction embedded in such gestures of destruction, notes Trapido, pivots on the transferral of value from the lost item to the individual who disposes of them: "The reasoning here, recounted to me on several occasions, is that [the item] is *eloko pamba*—a worthless thing—to 'one such as myself'" (208). MacGaffey and Bazenguissa-Ganga identify a similar logic in the extravagant spending they witnessed in *ngandas* (small underground bars) in Paris, what informants called "living": Not only were menu items substantially more expensive in *nganda* than in legal establishments, patrons commonly bought several times as much as they and their guests could consume. Such behavior, the authors reason, "shows that the actors do not follow a logic of the management of everyday life characteristic of retention, or a logic of survival . . . Spending like that is to fulfill one's social being within the small, closed-off environment of young Congolese-Zairean traders in Paris" [*montre que les acteurs ne sont ni dans une logique de gestion de la vie quotidienne caractéristique de la rétention, ni dans une logique de survie . . . Dépenser ainsi, c'est réaliser son être social dans ce petit milieu fermé de jeunes comerçants Congolo-Zaïrois à Paris*] ("Vivre et briller à Paris" 132).

What one could demonstrate with a more extensive investigation than I am able to undertake here is that the wealth in people accrued by the *mikiliste* through his collection of clothing, social exhibition, and other practices of consumption responds to a network of flexible strategies for negotiating the strictures of capitalist circulation implanted by colonial-era ideas and infrastructures with the deep-seated collective understandings of social ranking and personal worth that guide local networks of patronage. Jane Guyer, studying the phenomenon of commoditization in nineteenth-century trading between European travelers and missionaries and different groups of the Congo River Basin, dubs these networks "continuous value registers" to distinguish them both from gift economies and free market commodity economies: Judging from the patterns of sale and preservation among Congo River groups confronted by foreign buyers, a continuous value register "reflect[s] neither intricately indexed hierarchies nor the freedom of the market, but a multiplicity of control and access mechanisms, at many levels, that makes definitive order—of either the goods, or the people, or the principle of operation—virtually impossible" (252). In other words, under the fiat of wealth in people, commodities enter an unregulated adventure of valorization, indeed a *débrouillardise*, where the standard measure of worth remains the person's capacity to access and control untapped or undedicated resources. The individual of this social regime is the master locus of its singularizing impulses: The agility with which he manages to insert and remove commodity forms from the value register on which the game of self-worth is played determines his singularity; "the 'assets,' the pools of wealth, in such systems were ultimately the extraordinary people . . . whose self-realisation careers skipped around the value register and then moved beyond its range into the domain of total singularity that, when it applies to people rather than goods, one could term *charisma*" (253). Insofar as the *mikiliste*'s control and capture of Paris subjects it to the sort of continuous value register analyzed by Guyer, we can say he recreates the credo of divine gifts espoused by Baudelaire's dandy. Wrangling the symbolic value of Paris to a position in Congolese society of his own determination, the *mikiliste* stands to reinvent himself as the singular value of the local economy, implementing just the kind of "aristocracy" of charisma the dandy dreamed of.

Mikilistes and *modernistas* offer an object lesson in the adventure of foreign capital in its peripheries, a singular drama through which the commodity as the very medium of identity ends up expressing the most remarkable heterogeneity of interests. Above all, this drama makes visible Paris's endurance as an index of hope that the uniformization of life announced by peripheral capitalism may yet be transformed. Paris, in this sense, is the famous "last illusion" beheld by Julián del Casal's tragic hero, which "sweetens the evil of life" [*endulze el mal de la vida*], and which "is always found, like a fine pearl in a dusty coffer, in the saddest hearts, that illusion which is never lost, perhaps" [*algo que constituye mi última ilusión, la que se encuentra siempre, como perla fina en cofre empolvado, dentro de los corazones más tristes, aquella ilusión que nunca se pierde, quizás*] (283). The young Congolese photographer Baudouin Mouanda, commenting on a recent series he dedicated to *sapeurs*, relates a more cheerful illusion of the city: The delight of seeing how the gaily dressed *sapeurs* brightened the Paris metro, he recalls, helped him realize the importance of *sape* for the emotional recovery of Brazzaville after the first Congolese civil war. "There wasn't anything left to do in town; everything was shut down. The *sapeurs* recreated the atmosphere that is part of Congolese day-to-day life. For the traumatized population, the attraction of the *sapeurs* was to show that you had to have hope. Their message was 'We didn't get dressed up to stay at home! We have been spared by the hostilities and we are lucky to be alive. There's no point in fighting; we can talk and take each other by the hand.' The *sapeurs* often advocate this peaceful message. That's why I, as a photographer, wanted to follow them. Images travel and spread messages. I want to show that a joyful Africa exists" (Goni par. 3). An illusion of joy that, for all its falseness, submits a model for experience independent of its commodity fiction: Paris, as Adorno would say, thus becomes "a concept of the thing itself, [rather than] a poor projection from things" (*Negative Dialectics* 373). Is this not the wish attached to its purchase on the margins of the capital of modernity?

Chapter 5

Minor Truths

Menchú and Ouologuem in the Multicultural Metropolis

The main concern of the studies of this book has been to explore the possibilities of an object-oriented analysis of the postcolonial in Latin American and Francophone literature wrought through something like an experience of the undeconstructible. Such an analytics, I have tried to show, could better manage the anxiety of identity that characterizes Latin Americanist and Francophonist engagement with postcolonial theories and issues by reintroducing the object's resistance to identification into its own hermeneutics. This closing chapter will bring my proposals to bear on the realm of literary identity politics, in particular what we might call the economy of minority literature.[1] I will deliberately maintain a broad interpretation of "minority" here in order to remain mindful of the way hyphenated or immigrant identities of the multicultural first world increasingly enter into the same circuits of marketing and recognition as non-Western writing under the inflated labels of global or postcolonial literature.[2] As Shu-mei Shih's work in Asian American cultures has labored to demonstrate, the flexibility of the routes of minoritization is a main channel through which late capitalist logic streamlines the symbolic economy of ethno-racial value coding in globalized literature, producing " 'the West' as the agent of recognition and 'the rest' as the object of recognition, in representation" (17). Under the apparatuses of this economy, what Shih calls technologies of recognition, "what is national in the Third World is turned into ethnic culture during minoritization after immigration, and, similarly, even those who are outside Western metropoles are metaphorically and oftentimes practically minoritized" (23). Beneath this equalizing aegis of the minor is made visible a series of mechanisms of transvaluation designed to orchestrate across various fields—including the culture of prizes and literary prestige, international book markets, and the epistemological safeguards of the modern authorial institution—a unified structure for the commission and reception of minority representation as a verifiable portrait of otherness.

My first objective is to pinpoint some of the ways these mechanisms have overdetermined readings of the *testimonio* of Rigoberta Menchú and Yambo Ouologuem's novel *Le Devoir de violence* (translated into English as *Bound to Violence*), two of the most polemical works of Latin American and Francophone "minority" writing to date. Menchú and Ouologuem were each the subject of historic scandals that helped lay bare the contradictions between political and literary representation inherent to non-Western and/or postcolonial authorship. If the circumstances of the initial reception of *Me llamo Rigoberta Menchú* and *Le Devoir de violence* partake of Shih's technologies of recognition—most saliently, Ouologuem's winning of the Prix Renaudot for his authentically "African" novel, and Menchú's Nobel Peace laureate—the scandals that follow Western audiences' early effusions offer an ideal lens through which to dissect those technologies. Minority scandals document the failure of recognition: They magnify the investments that appoint texts of difference as a commodity by interrupting what appears on the surface to be a smooth process of transvaluation. Many critical commentators on these and other literary scandals of the last half century have set about unearthing the various ways writing deemed minority troubles accepted modern Western norms of authority, precisely because it attempts to ratify new premiums of authenticity through the legal and discursive networks established to conserve notions of authority, originality, and ownership.[3] Of course, the chauvinisms that become evident in controversies like those surrounding Menchú and Ouologuem are not limited to minority writing but rather reveal the contingent and circular nature of the rigor of truth in discourse as such. After decolonization and the dawn of multiculturalism, under the regime of authenticity, the whole edifice of literary propriety dissolves into simulacrum, prompting us to conclude with Henry Louis Gates, Jr. in his observations of one iconic literary hoax that "like it or not, all writers are 'cultural impersonators'" (1). What is at stake in scandal, on this view, is not truth but truth effect, a "causing-to-appear-to-be-true," in Algirdas Julien Greimas's terminology.

My second objective will be to question the preeminence of truth effect in strategies for reading minority literature. In view of the minority label's exponential powers of identification and exchange, any successful probe into minority literature's mechanism of truth must confidently attend to the way its adventure of identification—both its capture and release from technologies of recognition—inheres in historical contingencies shared by form and institution, object and subject alike. Truth effect is reliable against epistemological collusion between modern standards of subjectivity and authorship and the imperial hierarchies they authorize in the multicultural arena, but is of little recourse against the relationship to capital which underwrites the minority category's functional principle of flexibility, and which on that principle draws infinite partners into its sphere, including university discourse's own defense of minority literature. I find Adorno's proposals in *Aesthetic Theory*, specifically his understanding of the truth content of art, to be useful for putting pressure on the premises of existing interpretive paradigms for the two texts examined here. Like truth effect, truth content denies the appeal to any transcendent truth: It does not pertain to some "real" recuperable from discrete representations. But rather than find in the untruth of the content of art an occasion for postulation on the end of truth as such as a new, positive term of critique, truth content refers art's falsehood to the historical contradictions that, embedded in it, prevent its disillusionment: The truth content of art works, ironically, is "the negation of their being," an index of the antagonisms that block their eventual deciphering. Thus it "is posited not simply by them alone but, indirectly, also by their participation in, and determinate critique of, history" (*Aesthetic Theory* 193). Truth content sets its sights directly on art's relation to capital, the spellbound schema that makes voices of difference recognizable to the minority label, but its view of commodification is wielded against the historical configuration that binds art's content as illusion, against which the content of art also lodges a negative protest. The truth of minority works like *Me llamo Rigoberta Menchú* and *Le Devoir de violence*, while it remains illegible on this reading, nonetheless signals from its commodified state the historical transformations under which a real truth-telling might unfold. This is their minor truth, which I will argue here is essential for a reconstruction of their link to university discourse and to the postcolonial concept.

Lies and Plagiarism: The Menchú and Ouologuem Scandals

Menchú's *testimonio*, a firsthand description of the repression of Maya-Quiché indigenous communities during Guatemala's bloody civil conflict recounted to (and later transcribed and edited by) Venezuelan ethnologist Elisabeth Burgos, was received enthusiastically by academic and educational audiences in the United States during the 1980s and 1990s. Owing largely to the unique generic parameters of *testimonio*, *Me llamo Rigoberta Menchú* had the special draw of providing a verisimilar voice of cultural and political difference at the exact moment the first generation of U.S. scholars concerned with issues of gender, ethnicity, race, and colonialism began to seek out non-Western texts able to contest the Eurocentric moorings of the traditional liberal education. Menchú's text became required undergraduate reading during the curricular reforms of Stanford University in the 1980s and served as a prominent pawn of the so-called culture wars between the U.S. left and right in academia and media, a phenomenon Mary Louise Pratt characterizes as "a fatal collision between two historical processes: on the one hand, the arrival on university faculties of the 'children of the 60's,' and on the other, the arrival at the White House of Ronald Reagan along with a dogmatic political right hungry for power" (30). On a global scale, Menchú's work for Amerindian rights made her story a poignant response to colonial legacies on the 500th anniversary of Columbus's landing in the New World, leading to her being awarded the Nobel Prize for Peace in 1992.

The political embroilment of *Me llamo Rigoberta Menchú* intensified in 1998 when North American anthropologist David Stoll published *Rigoberta Menchú and the Story of All Poor Guatemalans*, an analysis of the Guatemalan civil war aimed at correcting what he viewed as Menchú's unilateral depiction of the socialist *guerrillero* movement. After spending several months in Guatemala investigating the details surrounding the disappearance, torture and death of Menchú's brother, father, and mother—without a doubt the most gripping events of her narrative—Stoll questions key representations of Menchú's family and personal background. According to Stoll's sources, Menchú was not illiterate or uneducated, as her book claimed, but had received several years of instruction with a group of Belgian nuns; the bitter dispute over her father's rights to the land the family cultivated for subsistence was not waged against rich landowners, as the book claims, but against a group of in-laws; and the gruesome scene in which Menchú describes watching soldiers torture and burn alive several political prisoners, including her own brother, never happened.

Although, as numerous critics have pointed out, the real political target of Stoll's claims was the U.S. academy—an institution that Stoll and many conservatives of the culture wars accused of praising like-minded ideologies to the detriment of "truth"—ostensible proof of Menchú's "lies" took center stage in public discussions on the subject. The fact that Bill Clinton was undergoing investigation for lying about his involvement with Monica Lewinsky at roughly the same time undoubtedly gave Menchú's story more play. The wider media scandal began with a front-page *New York Times* article in December 1998, followed by editorials in *U.S. News and World Report* and *Time*.

The reversal of fortune accompanying the plagiarism scandal of Ouologuem, much as Menchú's case, reflects a negotiation of Western reading institutions with the demands of a growing market niche for minority representation, in this context the novels and poetry of the *evolués* of former and remaining French colonies, whose successes flattered waning French imperialism that its *mission civilatrice* had ultimately paid off. When Ouologuem published *Le Devoir de violence* in 1968, he had earned a degree in English at the École Normale Supérieure in Paris and had spent six years living and working in France. Indeed, Ouologuem refers to himself as a "black pearl" of colonialism, a subject groomed from Malian and French schooling alike to deliver the long-awaited "evolution" of post-independence African writing.[4] His book narrates the history of the fictional Nakem empire from the thirteenth to twentieth centuries as a tyrannical dynasty beset by endless corruption and slavery, abetted first by Arab invaders and then by French colonization. It appealed to critics who sought an authentically "African" novel: on a basic level, because it reproduced the images of violence and sexual perversion that had fueled European clichés about Africa for centuries, but more important, because it combined a novelistic structure that was accessible to Western readers (and implicitly considered a more sophisticated genre than the episodic literature descended from oral sources), with elements borrowed from oral tradition, Koranic verse, and Islamic histories of Africa.[5] Thus did *Le Monde* hail it as "the first truly African novel," and Ouologuem himself in an interview claim to have drawn from historic maps and documents as well as recordings of African music to give his novel "a vision arising authentically from black roots" (Watkins 34). This same display of authenticity led critics to award *Le Devoir de violence* the 1968 Prix Renaudot.

The very trappings of success seem to have fomented the infamy that befell the author when, starting in 1971, several articles appeared attacking Ouologuem's originality. Eric Sellin, an American professor, first raised suspicion by juxtaposing the opening passage from *Le Devoir de violence* with parts of André Schwarz-Bart's 1959 novel *Le Dernier des justes*. A string of defamatory articles followed in *Le Figaro* and *The Times Literary Supplement* identifying similarities to works by Graham Greene and Guy de Maupassant. Ouologuem countered these accusations by explaining in one exchange that his original manuscript signaled his borrowings with quotation marks, but that his publisher, Editions du Seuil, ignored these and never consulted him with the proofs before printing the book. Following a complaint by Graham Greene, Editions du Seuil pulled *Le Devoir de violence* from bookstore shelves and from further publication.

The framing of the Ouologuem and Menchú scandals around the perceived betrayal of audience expectations, a betrayal for many commentators exacerbated by their marginal status, provided a forum for debates over the intersections and interdependencies between the Western ideological grid of truth and authority and colonial, neocolonial, and racist dynamics of power. In short, exactly what kind of truth or originality was violated in Menchú's "lies" or in Ouologuem's "copying," and how did their perceived otherness condition this transgression? While their accusers attacked a climate of academic political activism seen to condone minority misrepresentation, fashioning Menchú, for example, into a "sacred idol of the left" (Patai 272) and a "semireligious political icon" (Leo 17), rebuttals in their defense were quick to highlight the residues of (neo)colonial discourse latent in the rhetoric of the controversy. One editorial on the Menchú scandal in *El País* points out that other Nobel Peace Prize winners (e.g., "the opaque Arafat" and "the very disgusting Henry Kissinger") escaped questioning of their own dishonesty by virtue of their status: "But, of course, all of those are men, powerful men, and Rigoberta is nothing but a poor Indian woman in her forties with braids" (Montero 77). Similarly, Christopher Wise describes the double standard under which critics praise the primitivism modernist art borrowed from African sources but attack Ouologuem's work as plagiarism, noting that "few art historians speak of 'plagiarism' or 'theft' when discussing the paintings of Pablo Picasso, Georges Braque, or Amadeo Modigliani" (9). The point of contention for both sides, for different reasons, is the way political representation muddies the supposedly colorless offices of the authorial contract, where they carry the additional burden of multicultural agendas of social justice and the commercial interests that co-opt them.

To arrive at something like an anatomy of the Ouologuem and Menchú scandals, and through them to apprehend some of the ways truth functions as a nodal point in the management of minority textuality as a whole, we should begin with an enumeration of the overlapping networks of economic, political, and cultural valuation that coalesce around the inscription of the minor as a discrete category of consumption. This tangle of concerns is perhaps best described by the relation that connects multiculturalism to capital, in Slavoj Žižek's prominent characterization, as its symptom. Žižek details the defining operation through which the political sanctioning of principles of cultural tolerance and diversity fortifies global capitalism as the naturalized site of social life: by recuperating a certain form of ethnic plurality for public maintenance—one which "'respects' the Other's identity, conceiving the Other as a self-enclosed 'authentic' community" (44)—multiculturalism drives overt racism underground, releasing from the political stage the evermore-effective forms of exclusion guaranteed by multinational capital and, in fact, strengthening them with its dissimulating screen of tolerance. Issuing in these guises a new "racism with a distance" (44), multiculturalism is thus, for Žižek, "the form of appearance of its opposite, of the massive presence of capitalism as universal world system. . . . It is effectively as if, since the horizon of social imagination no longer allows us to entertain the idea of an eventual demise of capitalism . . . critical energy has found a substitute outlet in fighting for cultural differences which leave the basic homogeneity of the capitalist world-system intact" (46).

It is not difficult to locate the symptomatology provided by Žižek in the initial reception of Menchú and Ouologuem's texts: The active mobilization of *Me llamo Rigoberta Menchú* as the cornerstone of the intent to decolonize university curricula during the heyday of U.S. multiculturalism and the acclaim of *Le Devoir de violence* as an achievement of the spirit of French-African *coopération* among the first generation of post-independence writers both stake a claim for the assimilation of "the Other as a self-enclosed 'authentic' community" into established spheres of cultural consumption without questioning the underlying relations of capital that uphold them. The final consecration of these texts through the prizes awarded Menchú and Ouologuem is only the most visible vehicle of their assimilation, cueing in what James English calls the "economy of prestige" the supple intraconversion among symbolic, political, and economic capital, at the same time that it facilitates the seamless transfer of minority culture from local or national to global scenes according to the interests of different actors in this economy.[6] The radical flexibilization in the various codings applied to minority culture recalls the point most stressed in Žižek's reading of multiculturalism: The affirmation of particular, "authentic" differences, which attempts through the very recognition of difference to preserve a superior, omniscient perspective—the disavowed Eurocentrism of the autonomous, rational subject—in actuality disguises the fact that self-determining "rooted" cultures no longer exist, that all subjects and nations, even disavowedly Eurocentric ones, are already self-colonized by global capitalism. "[T]he stain of particular roots is the phantasmatic screen which conceals the fact that the subject is already thoroughly 'rootless,' that his true position is the void of universality" (44). This paradoxical clash between, on one hand, the elastic forms of exchange that secure the homogenization of capital as the reigning precondition of an increasingly broad set of lifeworlds, and on the other, the "old" autonomous subject that ensures exchange as the basis of modern life, to my mind gives an adequate description of the dynamic of minority scandals insofar as these are also arbitrated as a failed attempt to preserve a universal model of subjectivity. In scandal it becomes clear how minority literature partakes of multiculturalism's feckless protest against global capital, precisely by anchoring the perpetually diversified mode of cultural exchange of the minor, in the final analysis, in the mainstays of the modern institution of authorship.

Ownness and Ownership: The Antinomies of Authorship

From its beginnings, of course, the modern author has been defined as a function of capital. In its original articulation, authorship is embedded in the dual agency of the self-owning individual which, turning on the two meanings of "property" as ownness and as ownership, establishes the rational autonomous subject as the linchpin of modern liberal regimes. This dyad is first definitively phrased in John Locke's assertion in *Two Treatises of Government* that "every man has a property in his own person. . . . The 'labour' of his body and the 'work' of his hands, we may say, are properly his" (305–6). Locke's principle of property in the person hinges on the union of two different orders—persons and things, the alienable and the inalienable—without clearly privileging one over the other as the keeper of the subject. The interdependence of the two categories, as Etienne Balibar has noted, leaves us to construe subjectivity as inseparable from the act of ownership, through which "the individual subject practically identifies himself with that property from which he forms his essence, [and] recognizes his identity in the actual process of appropriation and acquisition" (303). In these terms, people are, in a sense, what they have; their insertion in the community, as well as the existence of the community itself, comes from the contract of their labor or goods, which also represent their person. At the same time self-ownership extends the operative claims of libertarian variants of democratic thought, it informs the foundations of modern authorship. Mark Rose explains that, in the Lockean rhetoric used to legitimize the first copyright laws of early eighteenth-century Britain, intellectual property becomes a measure of ownness and ownership alike: "A work was also the objectification of a writer's self, and the commodity that changed hands when a bookseller purchased a manuscript or when a reader purchased a book was as much personality as ink and paper" (121). In other words, the authority of the modern professional writer stems both from his right to hold goods individually and from his personhood. By lending out the alienable qualities of selfhood in the objectified "good" represented by the book, the author imbues his product with the inalienable rights of the individual, which are themselves proven through the labor of creation.

Insofar as the legitimacy of the modern author is shored up in his proprietorship, it feeds the reading institution with a clear fungibility from economic to cultural capital: a writer is proven trustworthy by virtue of his participation in the market. Within this general system, however, the recognition of minority authors stands out in that it translates capital more easily in the opposite direction. One could say the marketability of minority authors, and indeed the ownership of their labor, is posited on the identity represented by the products they create. Central to this reversal in the order of transactions undergirding authorship is the priority of commodification: minority literature is premised in the exchangeability of a certain good of life—namely, an identity registered as Other by multicultural discourse—which, by virtue of this fungibility, attaches the thing exchanged to the inalienable qualities of the self-owning individual. A curious matrix of value-coding thus inheres along the trajectory of minority literature, one which confounds the late capitalist impetus of multiculturalism as described by Žižek with the property-personhood dyad of self-ownership. For if the first expresses a predilection for what is different and exotic, qualities to be ensured primarily by the person of the author, the second remains the bulwark of institutional authorship, which it verifies through the same dialectic of identity (I own, therefore I am/I am what I own) that grounds contractual liberal society. Without appealing to its circularity, one could describe this matrix as follows: The value of minority literature depends upon its representation of a culturally different, oppressed and/or exotic life, which is only valid if it can be attributed to the real life of a free, inalienable subject, who is free and inalienable because he or she made and sold the story.

The anomalies inherent in this logic, if they serve to reveal the tenuous grounds of the entire enterprise of minority literature, also help explain the causes of minority scandals: these result from a lack of self-ownership and hence a lack of personhood on the part of the author, as well as from a disappointing investment on the part of the reader, who was not able to enjoy the thing he or she purchased. Both of these failures are scandalous in that they violate the norms of moral and economic contract that adjudicate public discourse in the modern liberal world. In her thoroughgoing examination of plagiarism, Marilyn Randall signals its inscription precisely as a transgression of one or both of these contracts: "Primarily, plagiarism is unethical because it contravenes the fundamental right to the exclusive enjoyment of and control over one's property, either real or symbolic—that is, it is a form of *theft*—and, second, it is a misrepresentation of one's self in situations where the justified expectations of others entail honesty and authenticity; in other words, it is a form of *fraud*" (15). The legal gravitas of the vocabulary used to evaluate cases of scandal—for fraud and theft, like truth and lies, belong to the language of crime and punishment—clues us in on the ways the properties of the inalienable subject are reasserted over the alienated products of his or her labor as the ultimate safeguard of the authenticity exchanged in minority literature. It is reasonable to assert with Foucault that the authorship of Menchú and Ouologuem obtains "only when [they] bec[o]me subject to punishment" ("What Is an Author?" 124), insofar as they can be made responsible for the transgressions of their texts. The fastidious need so often expressed through scandal to verify the identity behind the text, to speculate on the intentions and character of the author, indicates that the authenticity readers and critics expect to consume in minority literature is always already conditioned on the presence of the self-owning individual that buttresses the Western literary edifice. Not just any representation of an Other kind of life or experience will do; an authentic representation of Otherness is necessarily *a certain kind of representation,* one that abides by the premises of property in the person, that is attributable to a subject who is determined through concession to the market and thus already slightly less Other. The controversies surrounding Menchú and Ouologuem bear out this point: Their texts do not lose authenticity because in the light of scandal they seem to deal less with questions of poverty, war, and colonialism, or because the authors themselves suddenly become less marginalized, but as a direct result of their violation of the proprieties attending authorship, their failure as trustworthy autonomous subjects.

The irrepressible resurgence of this phantasmatic autonomous subject is the operative site for rehearsals of the latent colonial and racist anxieties that, as Žižek noted, preserve the exclusion of minority cultures by keeping them at a distance. Faltering in their embodiment as self-owning individuals, Menchú and Ouologuem become swindlers, charlatans. Their detractors painted their alleged literary transgressions as evidence of moral turpitude: Conservative media articles claiming to make a last stand for the liberal cause of personal accountability characterized Menchú as a "brazen confabulator" (Krauthammer 122) and a "crafty accomplice" to leftist "agit-prop propaganda" (D'Souza 27, 29). Dinesh D'Souza confides in his diatribe against Menchú that "there were plenty of reasons to be suspicious from the outset of her credibility" (29). Eric Sellin, the most vocal denouncer of the borrowings in *Le Devoir de violence*, similarly reprehends them above all as an act of willful wrongdoing, emphasizing that it is not the fact of imitation or copying but the intent behind them that matters. "Any young writer," he reasons, "has been influenced by other writers and will attempt to emulate what he admires, either consciously or unconsciously. He will, as in the case of such fine writers as Christopher Okigbo, John Pepper Clark, Léopold Sédar Senghor, and others, write 'in the style of' Pound, Yeats, Eliot, Perse, Claudel, or someone else, without his effort being anything more than apprenticeship derivation or the result of a spontaneous kinship" ("The Unknown Voice" 144). Sellin's examples of acceptable copying cite an established practice of imitation as a top-down phenomenon, a "spontaneous kinship" between the "young" African writer who emulates others in the natural course of his development and the European or American author whom he invariably admires. Ouologuem's offense lies not in borrowing from European authors (for that is, in fact, what good peripheral writers should do) but in corrupting this harmonious order of influence. Sellin places the qualitative difference between plagiarism and progress in the category of intention, as evidenced in his closing lament that "writers whose impulses have led them to adopt or emulate without malice the rhythms of admired foreign writers may now find themselves accused of having used the tactics employed and promulgated by Yambo Ouologuem" (162).

The ease with which the rhetoric of all these commentaries revives longstanding racist and colonialist stereotypes—Menchú as the shifty Indian, Ouologuem as the treacherous but childlike native—suggests that the historic and epistemic contiguities between the investiture of the self-owning individual as the pillar of capitalist society, and the constitutive exclusion of non-Europeans from its modern brand of personhood, are not so easily dispelled from the multicultural regime of authenticity. The version of truth such rhetoric arrogates to itself—and demands of minority texts—is indexed to this very imbrication: the "truth" of minority literature resides in its collusion in the myth of continuity between author and work, a collusion that, through the claims of an identifiable autonomous subject, succeeds in marshalling a representation of otherness to reaffirm certain axiomatic categories of Western discourse. This explains why the "autobiographical pact," the identification of character and author that Philippe Lejeune distinguishes as the definitive quality of autobiography, makes an appropriate descriptor for the practices of reading associated with minority literature in general, regardless of the genre involved. We can recall, for example, that media coverage of the Stoll-Menchú affair virtually without exception referred to *Me llamo Rigoberta Menchú* as an autobiography and that the first critical reception of *Le Devoir de violence* praised the "truer" Africa it presented to readers (Miller gibes, "This . . . was a 'true' novel, as opposed to others that must have been false" [*Blank Darkness* 219]).[7] The axis of evaluation the autobiographical pact puts in play is not good and bad, but true and false: Under it, "Even if the story is, historically, completely false," Lejeune signals, "it will be on the order of the *lie* . . . and not of fiction" (17).

There are two interrelated points to be advanced from the foregoing overview: First, it makes evident that the order of truth imposed on minority texts pertains to an entire ideological realm in which the ratification of exchange as the basis of social life always relays in the end to a fiction of the self-owning individual, the homo economicus. It constitutes a collective lie of the sort denounced by Nietzsche, a set of worn-out metaphors, "illusions about which one has forgotten that this is what they are" which exert "the obligation to lie according to a fixed convention, to lie herd-like in a style obligatory to all" (47). Indeed Nietzsche, like Adorno, detected in truth the violence of all concepts, which raze the diversity of their objects and conscript them to a flat, unified identity. This leads to my second point: that the dogmatic insistence on truth as the arbitrator of minority discourse is merely a screen for the more fundamental lie of minority as a category of consumption, the obligatory lie that calibrates the non-identity of texts like *Me llamo Rigoberta Menchú* and *Le Devoir de violence* to a commodity-form determined by the fancies of the market. Debates over the rigor of truth in minority representation disregard this larger obligatory lie that conceals the commoditization of social life as a whole, and of which minority literature acts as a supremely malleable symptom.

Voids and Secrets: Critical Signatures of the Truth Effect

Here, it seems to me, existing critical literature on the Menchú and Ouologuem scandals does not go far enough. The major discussions have executed a formidable deconstruction of the regulatory fictions of subjectivity, truth, and authorship, but in the main they have yet to address the way these works, regardless of the type of truth they can be made to project, bear witness to the undisclosed truth of minority literature's base relation to capital. The considerable body of writing on Latin American *testimonio*, prominently in the work of John Beverley, has effectively demonstrated how its formal and paratextual idiosyncrasies rupture the ideological endowment through which literature ventriloquizes the bourgeois worldview of the autonomous individual in modern society. Beverley sustains that *testimonio* "allows the entry into literature of persons who would normally, in those societies where literature is a form of class privilege, be excluded from direct literary expression" (*Testimonio* 35). It wrests literary representation from its privileged hegemonic perspective not only in relating firsthand subaltern life experiences, but also in altering the reader's mode of identification with the narrating subject. *Testimonio* is not an authored genre in the traditional sense; rather, it entails collaboration between a marginalized, usually Third-World narrator and an ethnographer or academic who transcribes and edits the story. Furthermore, the narrativized "I" produced in the text by this collaboration does not reflect an individual life but a collective experience: its voice serves as a shifter, "a linguistic function that can be assumed indiscriminately by anyone" (36). Faced with this doubly decentered narrative subject, readers are forced to engage with the person behind the text in a similarly decentered fashion. Unlike autobiography, whose authorial "I," as we have seen, assumes a liberal imaginary of autonomous, self-conscious individuals, *testimonio* assumes a metonymic transference from the individual voice of the text to the community that shares its experience. In Doris Sommer's characterization, the reader does not identify with a narrator like Rigoberta Menchú by taking her place in metaphorical substitution, but rather enacts an "identification-through-relationship, which acknowledges the possible differences among 'us' as components of a centerless whole. This is where we can come in as readers, invited to be (estar) with the speaker rather than to be (ser) her" (39).

Testimonio's crucial rearticulation of the structure and function of narrative voice brings with it a radically different paradigm of readerly identification. Although its content seeks to be read as "real," its textual appearance as such obtains only as an effect of selection, translation, and manipulation, revealing in the final product an untraceable mixture of raw storytelling and literary conceit. Because of the essentially hybrid materialization of the experience it relates and the multiple intersubjective relationships involved—between editor and narrator, editor and reader, and reader and narrator—*testimonio* requires the willing recognition of audiences and institutions, who agree to look at it, as Elzbieta Sklodowska phrases it, with "'testimonio-seeing' eyes" (84). The complex negotiation set in motion by consumers and producers alike to achieve the "certain way of seeing" that makes *testimonio* readable as a true account of subaltern life, in effect throws into question the presumed transparency of all literary voice. By taking textual representation beyond the thematic, formal, and subjective parameters that accredit this transparency (and authorize the hegemonic perspective) as a matter of fact, *testimonio* moves beyond and "against" literature, as Beverley has it; its truth is only the joint effect of the text's creative incitement of the conviction of the reader, and the reader's agreement to believe. This is precisely the truth effect that Algirdas Julien Greimas, in "The Veridiction Contract," saw as a general consequence of the breakdown of self-regulating categories of discourse in the postmodern "age of unbelief": Its effect "is produced through the exercise of . . . a causing-to-appear-to-be-true [which] no longer seeks appropriateness vis-à-vis its referent, but rather trust on the part of the receiver it addresses. It wants the receiver to read it as being true. In turn, the receiver's trust can be acquired only if it corresponds to his expectations. That is, the construction of the simulacrum of truth is greatly conditioned, not directly by the axiological universe of the receiver, but by the sender's view of what the axiological universe is" (657).

Under Greimas's veridiction contract, truth as simulacrum rests upon the text's powers of manipulation: critics have amply discussed, for example, the way Elisabeth Burgos's abridgement and alteration of Menchú's transcript, which she enumerates to readers in her prologue, fashions the most plausible "Rigoberta" for her audience's expectations and desires, as well as the sleight behind Rigoberta's own selection of narrated events, particularly the infamous "secrets" she refuses to tell at several points in the book.[8] Many of the features of *testimonio*'s elaboration of reader fiat as a process of veridiction also correspond to *Le Devoir de violence*, for although the book officially conforms to novelistic protocol, its popularity from the first owes to its ludic violations of discursive propriety. Much as in *testimonio*, the pretended veracity of the text is formally manufactured by knitting together the supposedly raw material of exotic and time-honored accounts of Arab scribes and Songhay griots with an invisible literary contrivance: The book begins with an epic account of the first 800 years of the Nakem empire's history, recounted by a chameleonic narrator who successively assumes the conversational tone of a direct storyteller, quotes a griot, momentarily loses the trail of history in the conflicting versions of "elders" and "chroniclers" (6), and then resumes once again with a direct paraphrase of "the oral tradition of the Africans" filled with specific dates and genealogies (8); the text is interrupted throughout by exclamations of Koranic formula ("God refresh his couch!" [*Dieu rafraîchisse sa couche*]; "God save his soul!" [*Dieu ait son âme*]; "God wills it!" [*Dieu le veut!*] and so on), which punctuate the otherwise dry parade of characters and events with a moralizing, ritualistic inflection. Like Menchú's carefully crafted "I," the voice here acts as a shifter, concatenating a host of authoritative discourses in a performance of direct communication.[9]

Early critics of *Le Devoir de violence* delighted in the patchwork of intertexts that compose its "Africa" through the same disintegration of self-referential authority illuminated by Greimas.[10] The history of the Nakem empire belongs to a maelstrom of competing voices appropriated from countless non-fiction and fictional archives, including the griots and historians of the opening section, and later colonial spoofs like Fritz Shrobenius—a clear caricature of the famed anthropologist Leo Frobenius—who spouts bogus theories of the mythological and metaphysical systems of African art and society to earn himself a chair at the Sorbonne.[11] Savvy reviewers perceived the "real" Africa on offer here as an array of historical perspectives chronicled by Ouologuem and which collectively made up its binding violence. Ouologuem himself disseminated this impression of the quasi-documentary nature of his book, referring repeatedly to its "facts" in interviews and media pieces, and producing for interviewers historical maps and manuscripts he claimed as sources.[12] Much of the opprobrium spurred by the novel's borrowings, in turn, stemmed from the disturbing realization that the original truth effect readers accepted of its narration was supplied not by authentic historical documents teased into fiction, but by the seamless insertion of European fiction, most of it completely unrelated to Africa.[13] This, inextricable as it was from the author's supposed moral shortcomings, precipitated critics' "elation and subsequent deflation" (Sellin, "The Unknown Voice" 138) over the novel: It was as if the honest, gritty—and aesthetically accomplished—version of Africa that Euroamerican audiences had long awaited in colonial and postcolonial fiction were nothing but a figment of the colonial imagination. Under the façade of the original truth effect destroyed by accusations of plagiarism, the only concrete African object to be found was a circuitous illusion of Western referentiality, an imperialist desire. Ouologuem's "true" Africa, as J. Mbelolo ya Mpiku concludes, is "only the expression of a certain 'Afrolatry'" (31); in Randall's assessment, similarly, the "'real' Africa is precisely the one that the West rejects in the form of accusations of plagiarism" (537).

A sustained vein of criticism has read the Ouologuem scandal through this optic of the deconstruction of historical truth, appreciating how *Le Devoir de violence*, as Miller argues, "tells the reader how to look at African history . . . as a void" ("Trait d'union" 114).[14] Miller's analysis of the novel is one of the most compelling of this trend: It draws on an episode near the end of the novel in which the French bishop Henri reveals to the young protagonist Raymond Kassoumi the secret of Africa's destiny of violence, using the analogy of an ancient Chinese game. The game, called "trait d'union," consists of tying two birds together with a long string, then watching as they inevitably collide and destroy one another in the attempt to free themselves. The destructive union of Henri's parable, Miller suggests, serves as a trope for the formal and thematic structure of the novel: all the incidences of union in *Le Devoir de violence*—which he perceives as an "injunction" in the sense of linking, binding, or enjoining (109)—rehearse the mutual bloody corruption of the Chinese game. The many vicious sexual encounters of the characters, "bodies cutting up and cut up, raping and raped," echo the textual "rapes" committed by the prose, which "plugs itself into other texts, borrowing, pillaging, and violating their integrity" (112). Both of these are simultaneously reflected in the violent political interdependencies of the local tyrant Saif and the conniving colonial administrators, who ceaselessly plot each other's assassinations. "The global effect," avers Miller, "is to depict the African past as a purloined, kidnapped and usurped origin, as an originary violence which precludes the autonomy of any given object, leaving only a void" (114).

Miller's conclusions give a good indication of where the analytic of truth effect is bound to lead critical inquiry: It ultimately arrives at a lost object, an irrecuperable origin of the real that structures the endless iterations of truth erected over its abyss. In the *Blank Darkness* version of his essay, Miller refers to the "black hole" of the absent referent of African history which "with all its loss of authority, is the sine qua non of the legend that will emerge" (231). It is significant that Doris Sommer's iconic reading of Menchú's *testimonio* also locates the key of the reader's attempt and failure to reach its truth in a void of narrative, Rigoberta's "secrets." Sommer's essay is one of the most incisive efforts of Latin Americanist criticism of the early 1990s to grapple with the consequences of *testimonio*'s destabilization of literary authority to speak for regional experience; it gestures tentatively toward a critical praxis of solidarity able to extend political participation to the extraliterary and subaltern elements of the genre by adhering to the "respectful distance" in which the testimonial contract—the metonymic process of identification outlined above—trains its metropolitan readers. For Sommer, Rigoberta's secrets offer a primer in such praxis. Her reiterative claims to withhold information about her community and culture, to keep secret "what [she] think[s] no-one should know" (Wright 247), have a metaleptic function: by announcing her resistance to share everything, they incite a desire in the reader that he or she may not have already harbored. The secrets posit a retroactive cause, they "le[t] the fringe of a hidden text show in order to tease us into thinking that the fabric must be extraordinarily complicated and beautiful, even though there may not be much more than fringe to show" (Sommer 34). Sommer's point is that the ultimate truth of testimonial discourse, the core of the difference that legitimizes its authenticity, exists only as a hidden quantity; its secrets are a matter of fabricating voids. It does not matter whether the vaunted refusals of the text actually hold back something beautiful that the reader would like to know, because their real content is their prohibition, the minimum distance required to curtail the appropriative, translational overture of readerly identification. "It is the degree of our foreignness, our cultural difference that would make her secrets incomprehensible to the outsider. We could never know them as she does, because we would inevitably force her secrets into our framework" (34). By holding "at arm's length" (37) the Western ideological edifice that forcibly registers her as the subject of a verifiable, translatable truth, Rigoberta's performance of the secret as unbreachable limit advises us of the stakes of the new post- or anti-literary Latin Americanism *testimonio* is seen to announce. Her silence is "a lesson in the condition of possibility for [a] coalitional politics" (48) that invites readers of the academic north to "be with" minority literature rather than to stand in for it.

My gloss of Miller and Sommer has been oriented to highlight the options truth effect opens up for a more ecumenical understanding of minority literature's dynamics of recognition. Both think assigning Menchú or Ouologuem's unknowable truths to a structural limit point, a void or a "black hole" in the text, is a viable corrective for the colonialist bias that pegs recognition to the obligatory presence of an accountable, self-owning subject. But does this solution answer to the vaster truth disavowed by multiculturalism, under which "respectful" recognition allows capital's universal forces of equivalence—including the university discipline, which is charged with brokering unlike elements as an equalized field of study—to run unchecked?

Alberto Moreiras's analysis of testimonial criticism anticipates this very problem. The optimism that would seize the experiential realm the testimonial voice embeds in literary texts—its "entry into the unguarded possibility of the real" ("The Aura of Testimonio" 207)—as an occasion for the instatement of a new, purely democratic approach to the Latin Americanist object, a hermeneutics of solidarity, ignores the necessary re-literaturization attending disciplinary practice as such. Moreiras points out that, while the voice of *testimonio* indeed stands in a metonymic relation to the community it speaks for, the critic's appeal to that voice, however solidary, is possible only through a metaphoric replacement: Insofar as *testimonio* reauthorizes disciplinary practice through alignment with the unheard voices of its erstwhile exterior, it entails their reabsorption to literary representation. As he puts it, "You can't have a hermeneutics of solidarity without a poetics of solidarity to go with it" (203). Even the most responsible disciplinary vision, one that advocates its own self-effacement in the eventual restitution of its non-identical object, cannot avoid in the course of such an advocacy speaking for the object's silences in all their extraliterary realness.[15] The difficulty lies in articulating the primacy of the indissoluble elements of discourses like *testimonio* without in the act performing a correlate literary reabsorption through which "[c]riticism is thus able to refigure its own aura at the expense of textual reticence and precisely in virtue of its relationship with it" (212). Indeed, this move is perceptible in Sommer's appraisal of Rigoberta's secrets, in which on Moreiras's view "silence, identical to itself, and therefore in itself its own end, has . . . been made to speak, and thus also tropologized as that which is beyond the 'impassible' limit" (212).

The impasse presented by *testimonio*, and by minority literature more broadly, is one variant of the issue brought up in chapter 1, and which has occupied me intermittently throughout this study: What reifications are enabled when the postcolonial (or in other avatars, "*testimonio*," "minority," and so on) becomes a limit, silence, or absence held in reserve as the placeholder for historically contingent antagonisms, over which the theorizing subject now occupies a superior insight? My contention is that the postcolonial handled this way has the effect of absolving critique from its ongoing hand in the conflicts that constitute the "truth" of its object: Disentangled from this constitutive contradiction, it makes silences speak, in Moreiras's terms, and tropologizes them in its own image. The truth effect ultimately gives the same outcome. The limit Sommer or Miller appoint as the text's forbidden real contractually sustains its sought-after object as whatever readers hope and wish to find: Its circumscribed "nothing" re-conscripted to support the critical office, in fact manifests as "anything," which is also the measure of its reification. Rather than pretend an access-through-prohibition to the unrepresentable dimension of minority literature, a better strategy can attempt to read the protest to reification sedimented in its very commodity form, as literature: to "read it, as literature, beyond literature" (Moreiras, "The Aura of Testimonio" 218). I want to approximate this kind of strategy through Adorno's ideas about the truth content of art.

Truth Content

One can no doubt expect a number of objections to a cultural critical reading of Ouologuem and Menchú, especially considering the way *Le Devoir de violence* and *Me llamo Rigoberta Menchú* have been favored by Francophonist/Africanist and Latin Americanist criticism, respectively, as a springboard from which to throw off the yoke of modernist rigidities for freer forms of postcolonial critique. Some early advisories from now-classic commentaries on the intersection of postcolonial and postmodern interpretations of culture will help frame my proposals. In *Reading North by South*, Neil Larsen takes a close look at the Latin Americanist post-literary ethos spawned by *testimonio*, wondering if the rotundness of the much-announced supersession of canon, form, and other concerns suggests, not an overcoming of literature at all, but rather a preservation of its same impulses and jealousies in a new guise, a "countercanonization" which "merely reinforces the canonical hegemony of modernism" (11). This is not to say that the delegitimization of modern standards and criteria of analysis is altogether wrong, Larsen insists, but that the localized attack on the modernist ideological imprimatur—its particular enfolding of form and institution as a naturalized management of Eurocentric priorities—as the total possible realm of literature's stand in politics, obviates the interrogation of deeper and more conflicted circuits of North-South cultural exchange, which are often inherited unheeded by postmodern, postliterary critical platforms. Academic enthusiasm for *testimonio* (and, we can add, for later vicissitudes of the "real thing") inspires a nagging sense that "its existence as a radically new species of literary/postliterary discourse must be postulated in order that the truth of certain other postulates should not be questioned or examined. More concretely, I think that the elevation or countercanonization of the testimonial as postliterary, postrepresentational, and the like, effectively exempts the reader-as-theorist from questioning his or her own dogmatically modernist preconceptions regarding the nature of the 'literary' itself" (10). Larsen's sentiments are echoed in Kwame Anthony Appiah's seminal observations about the "post" of postcolonial and postmodern designators: what easily gets lost in the headlong charge toward the post as a welcome abandonment of the modern and all its bad habits are the multiplex interminglings of African cultural and political agendas with the varying models of valuation handed down from the First World, exchanges in which the market, rather than ideological nuances, are the decisive factor. Indeed, Appiah and Larsen agree that the crucial element crowded out of postmodernism's partnership with postcolonialism is the economic antagonism that joins them, starting with its hesitance to recognize that "modernity has turned every element of the real into a sign, and that sign reads 'for sale'" (Appiah 344). An overhasty break from the modern, taken in hand as a sign of a fresh postcolonial beginning, leaves intact the lingering complicities and expectations of the capitalist machine of coloniality, with the visible consequence that "what the postmodern reader seems to demand of Africa is all too close to what modernism . . . demanded of it. The role that Africa, like the rest of the Third World, plays for Euro-American postmodernism—like its better-documented significance for modernist art—must be distinguished from the role postmodernism might play in the Third World" (356).

Larsen and Appiah reiterate the conclusions of other prominent interventions from the same period by Neil Lazarus, Aijaz Ahmad, and Arif Dirlik about the way postcolonialism's extraction of cultural production from political economic networks of capitalist modernity transposes old asymmetries of empire onto newly covert forms, but their attention is honed on the needs, preferences, and modes of recognition that connect objects of the postcolony differentially to Northern and Southern contexts, including the preferences and modes of recognition of a somewhat old-fashioned idea of art and literature. Again, the argument is not for a wholesale return to modernist ideas about emancipation through art, but for a necessarily speculative acknowledgement that the postmodern tendencies Northern critics detect in the postcolonial do not move beyond the modern in a faithful imitation of their own entropic "space-clearing gesture" (Appiah 348), but reflect interests heterogeneous to or even opposed to that gesture; and furthermore, that the distance between its various trajectories and the horizon of academic postmodernism gives the coordinates of the latter's failure, of the lessons never learned from modernism. If neither the classic categories of authorship and subjectivity, nor the ken the postmodern claims in ousting these categories, has anything trustworthy to tell us about the truth of Ouologuem and Menchú, it may be time to deviate from this pendular track of thought to a deductive account of the ways modernist and postmodernist elements remain enmeshed in the presence of their texts as commodities of the metropolitan culture industry, which can produce a negative of their truth. I think Appiah endorses such a deviation in his stipulation of the minimum difference between postmodern and postcolonial channels of signification, between the "*presence* of the object" imported from the periphery for our (postmodernist) consideration, and its *content*, which "reminds us that the trade is two-way" (343).

The truth one can recuperate from Menchu and Ouologuem's texts, however minor, has to do with the mediation of the two sites Appiah differentiates, the fact of their presence in Western academic and media networks and their content, which in adhering to the constrictions of recognition in those networks also necessarily speaks beyond it, precisely as literature but beyond literature. The two facets of the work are visible within its commodification, in what Adorno called truth content. Adorno saw the paradox of art's political potential in terms amenable to the conundrum of truth in minority literature we have been examining: "namely, how the act of making can cause the apparition of a thing that is not made; how something can be true which is not true in terms of its own concept" (*Aesthetic Theory* 157). As a made thing, a commodity, art claims to offer a picture immediately available for consumption. The immediacy of its contents, which banishes the traces of social mediation from its discrete forms, is necessarily an illusion; yet the very forces of production embedded in the artwork, its irrefutable status as artifact, prove the existence of a reality that runs counter to its pretended wholeness. In other words, the contradiction between the forms of unfreedom necessary to create art under capitalism—particularly art's atomization as another product for exchange—and the false front of being-for-itself conjured in its product, is in fact the cipher of art's revolutionary potential, its truth content. In this sense "the definition of art in terms of illusion is only half-correct: art is true to the degree to which it is an illusion of the non-illusory" (192). Truth content is the historical negation—the "non-illusory"—of art works' illusionary fullness: in tension with its damaged forms, it indirectly posits all those changes necessary for an immediate expression of truth to exist, namely the supersession of the reification of production. In Simon Jarvis's words, truth as "not-made" "would only be fully accessible if production for its own sake, the fetishization of labour, were to come to an end" (105).

Following Adorno's schematics, the truth content of Menchú and Ouologuem's texts obtains in the falseness of their simulation of truth. It is not contained by their "causing-to-appear-to-be-true," or by the deduction of an autonomous subject that would guarantee their truth-saying, but by the dialectical inscription of these forms as the only truths at their disposal, thanks to the contradictions that prevail in society today. The conditions that dictate the strategies at hand for minority literature (e.g., all the subterfuges of voice that create the truth effect of *Me llamo Rigoberta Menchú* and *Le Devoir de violence*), the practical reasons why these techniques and not others are most convincing, plus the ironic excess that spills over their confessional overture to metropolitan audiences, all negate these works' illusion of truth. Through determinate negation, truth content points to the way the injustices of history settle into art's formal matter: as "the crystallization, in art works, of history" (*Aesthetic Theory* 193), it makes the material of art grope at the possibility of a world without contradiction. Art's concealed orientation to a world it cannot yet occupy constitutes a utopia, but a utopia "draped in black," "a recollection of the possible with a critical edge against the real [and] a kind of imaginary restitution of that catastrophe, which is world history" (196).

What the Adornian idea of truth content seeks to foreground, despite all the cynicism scandal has rained on the political import of *Me llamo Rigoberta Menchú* and *Le Devoir de violence*, is the utopian vision figured by their objectives. Rigoberta's secrets, after all, are not in themselves unknowable but something that cannot yet be known, things that could be shared only in a world without death brigades, brutal *ladino* assimilation, or the informal imperialist interventionism that aligns First-World governments and consumers with Third-World regimes. Understanding her life takes time, as she reasons at the end of the book: "Of course, I'd need a lot of time to tell you all about my people because it's not easy to understand just like that. And I think I've given some idea of that in my account" [*Pero yo necesito mucho tiempo para contar algo sobre mi pueblo, porque no se entiende así. Claro, aquí, en toda mi narración yo creo que doy una imagen de eso*] (Wright 247; Burgos 271). As tenable an inference as any is that the time necessary for the whole story to become legible is precisely the historical movement required to change people and society, to make us into adequate interlocutors and, quite literally, to make speaking out less life-threatening.

The Protest of the *Nègre*: Ouologuem's Enslaved Text

Ouologuem seemed to have a similar role in mind for his novel when he explained to interviewers: "My aim is to do violence to the misconceptions of Africans so that we can realize what the real problems are. This is our 'duty to violence'" (Maiangwa 73). The real problem Ouologuem explores implicitly in the content of *Le Devoir de violence* is the singularization of blackness (the *Nègre*) as an ethno-racial obstacle to harmonious postcolonial development. It involves the refusal to recognize France's construction of Africa in the image of its own desire, but also the isolation of worldwide processes of dehumanization under capital as a solely black [*Nègre*] problem. In Ouologuem's estimation, not only is Africa actually France, France is actually Africa: "[T]here are more Negroes in France than there are Blacks in Africa or in the Americas: the slave-laborers, the hoard of people haunted by the SMIG [minimum wage], anonymous inhabitants of this French desert, which is also a miniature Africa" [*Mais il est d'autres Nègres en France que les Noirs d'Afrique ou des Amériques: les gagnes-petits, la horde des gens hantés par le S.M.I.G., anonymes habitants de ce désert français, qui est, lui aussi, une petite Afrique*] (*The Yambo Ouologuem Reader* 212; *Lettre* 10). Ouologuem is articulating here the dynamic Žižek would bespeak decades later: that the recognition of particular cultures relegates to a specific, racialized site capitalism's pandemic enslavement of life everywhere. He elucidates how the *Nègre* becomes the distanced alibi for a worldwide "Negroification" (*The Yambo Ouologuem Reader* 268), disguising that "in point of fact . . . there is no Black issue, only human issues, to which the black man brings a certain color" [*C'est dire qu'il n'y a pas, à proprement parler, de 'problème noir,' mais seulement des problèmes humains, que l'homme noir, par la dérision de sa condition, colorie*] (*The Yambo Ouologuem Reader* 212; *Lettre* 10).

The fictional dismantling of this Black problem in *Le Devoir de violence*—thematically through the viral progression of violence among local elites and colonial invaders, formally in the discursive violence of the work's composition—is supplemented by the much more direct essays of the satirical pamphlet *Lettre à la France nègre*. *Lettre*, published one year after *Le Devoir de violence* and widely considered to be a "blueprint" (Sellin 1971) for its textual and political interventions, offers a series of pointed invectives against the different hypocritical fronts of France's postcolonial foreign policy in Africa, all framed as mocking letters addressed to their respective constituencies. The "*Nègre*" of the title, in addition to meaning "black" is a historical term for "slave": Mangling the discursive codes that attach *Nègre* to the color, comportment, and historic misery of Africans, the book's essays fashion France itself as the privileged incarnation of its attributes.[16] "Letter to Non-Racists," "Letter to Negro Kings Temporarily Residing in France," and "Letter to All Those Who Don't Know What a Negro Is, or Who Have Forgotten What It Means to Be White," interpellate different inhabitants of *la France nègre*, each in their own way slaves to the ideological format of France's self-identification vis-à-vis Africa after colonial rule. The phenomenon of Françafrique, also called *pré de carré* and *coopération*, was commandeered by Charles de Gaulle's paternalistic vision of France's ongoing role as a bastion of civilization in weak nascent republics susceptible to Soviet influence. As Tony Chafer explains, it fostered

> a special kind of relationship, not at all in line with true French Republican ideals, in which the interlinking of state, party and personal interests made it possible to present a set of policies and interventions as serving the wider national interest, that in practice brought nadir benefits to particular interest groups and small sections of the population in both France and Africa. The international prestige of the Gaullist state was enhanced by the group of loyal allies in Africa that looked to France for support and sustenance, while the Gaullist party received much of its funding from the recycling of part of the *coopération* budget, which found its way back to the party's coffers via Africa. (11)

Lettre à la France nègre faults this symbiotic corruption, particularly the allure of foreign lending to African governments that carried the hidden burden of perpetual debt, with "blackening" both societies under the specious mask of a century-long familial conviviality. Ouologuem is sensitive to the ways racist thought, merely cosmetically inverted in Gaullist "anti-racist" policies, deflects consideration of France and Africa's reciprocal degeneration through the spectacularized attention to African poverty and the threat posed by African immigrants to France, an attention latent with colonial stereotypes of sexual depravity and endemic underdevelopment. Blackness—both in the success stories of "black pearls" like Ouologuem, and in the exoticist undercurrents of their recognition—thus becomes a commercial nexus for all the anxieties attending the sordid interdependencies of Françafrique.

The most commented upon of *Lettre*'s missives, "Letter to the Ghostwriters of Famous Writers" [*Lettre aux pisse-copies nègres d'écrivains célèbres*], takes up this intersection of black France with the commodification of African literature by playing sardonically on the double standard through which demands for originality in black writing are tied to an evolutionist perspective on African culture. The polysemy of *Nègre*—a common term for "ghostwriter" as well as "slave," as Christopher Miller first pointed out—is once again critical to Ouologuem's argument. He exploits the historic entanglement of these meanings to characterize the condition of black writers as a type of slavery. They are "copy pissers," menial laborers condemned to churn out stories that, one way or another, will be passed off and sold as the invention of whites. This is so, first, because white culture is premised on a certain correlating idea of non-whiteness, but also because "original" work by black authors is constrained to the preferred framework of Europe's idea of Africa, to which it irreparably responds. Since originality is in fact forbidden to black writing, Ouologuem maintains, the only hope for the liberation of the "black rabble" [*négraille*] author is to turn the tables, to sell as his own the most marketable version of Africa, taken directly from bestsellers. The essay proposes a template from which writers can confect potboilers by stitching together samplings from famous detective novels and bodice rippers, a "denegrifying" device for an assembly-line production [*à la chaine*] of "ONE BILLION NOVELS" [*UN MILLIARD DE ROMANS*] (*The Yambo Ouologuem Reader* 295; *Lettre* 168) without effort:

> By adhering to this formula, dear black-rabble, by composing a new work with an eye towards the demands of the marketplace, to become a *nègre* [ghostwriter] of a famous writer, is to liberate yourself: it is a key to unlocking the boldest and most powerful combinations inherent in a language—which may thereafter be placed at your customers' disposal. It's a little like algebra, but algebra for small children. This algebra does not involve the analysis of objects, but rather the analysis of actions. These actions are not themselves objects in their own right, but they are bound up with the basic structures of our existence—and reveal the innermost spiritual laws of suspense and blood, now made available for consideration [*Sous cette forme, chère*

> *négraille, pour qui exécute ce travail avec une conscience très lucide de la demande du marché, être le nègre d'un écrivain célèbre, c'est se donner, comme une liberté, la clé d'un langage envisagé dans ses puissances combinatoires—mises à la disposition de la clientèle. C'est un peu de l'algèbre, mais de l'algèbre pour petits enfants. Cette algèbre-là n'est pas une analyse d'objet, c'est une analyse d'action. Ces actions elles-mêmes ne sont pas indépendantes, mais concernent des principes structuraux—et révèlent l'opération par laquelle l'esprit du suspense et du sang se considère*]. (*The Yambo Ouologuem Reader* 304; *Lettre* 176–77)

The passage brilliantly demonstrates the multiple levels involved in Ouologuem's excoriation of the black problem. The basic slippage performed by the *Nègre* as at once the slave, ghostwriter, and plagiarist of white texts, is further qualified by the unabashed commodity character of the *négraille*'s key to liberation. The plagiarist's formula—which Ouologuem produces for the reader in a fold-out table full of quotes from popular dime-store detective novels—is "crudely commercial" [*rudement commerciale*]: It cobbles together as through mathematical equation those elements proven to sell as the stuff of *Nègre* originality, reproduced down to each hackneyed, pornographic detail. Its elementary "algebra" becomes an inverted index of that other algebra, which calculates black identity through a series of subtractions and additions of whiteness, reducing it to a quantifiable object ready for exchange. Social reality under the Gaullist regime, Ouologuem suggests in another letter, has become a matter of computation: For De Gaulle himself, "everything seems to take place as if the very formula of his soul was already predetermined by way of a series of complex and precise equations. And, like De Gaulle, each of us may also become a kind of algebraist of his own realities" [*Or, en fait, tout se passe comme si, par Lui, la formule de l'âme se trouvait en quelque sorte déterminée par un agencement complexe, et précis, d'équations différentielles. Ainsi, chacun doit-il trouver comment devenir l'algébriste de sa propre réalité*] (*The Yambo Ouologuem Reader* 282; *Lettre* 112). Thus the illusion of an original, authentic black authorship plagiarism affords is indirectly countered by the reality that makes it saleable: For this reason, the pertinent object of analysis for the *Nègre* is not the composition of his novel but the actions and attitudes that prime it, which are "bound up with the basic structures of our existence." The truth content of the *Nègre* text appears in the denunciation of the social structures that underpin blackness and make its sham into a "true" representation. Posing as a commodity—and, in fact, being a commodity—the text Ouologuem promotes demands a world where the transparency it feigns really could exist.

If, following Adorno, all art enacts an illusion, the sort of art created through plagiarist combinatory performs a double illusion: The falsely immediate vision that denies the objective nature of the work is, in turn, built upon the "false," purloined materials that provide the text's plausibility. This technique of double binding plays out in *Le Devoir de violence* in the epic misery of its characters, whose diegetic enslavement mirrors the similarly "enslaved," stolen prose used to deliver their narrative arc. In one of the novel's most fantastic sequences, the witchdoctor Sankolo relates his travails as a slave sold into a human trafficking ring in the Sahara. Buried alive by the evil Saif after aiding him in a series of poisoning schemes against the French, Sankolo escapes his grave only to be sold to a string of slave-labor chain gangs, transformed into a zombie through the drugs administered by his French and Arab overseers: Along with the other itinerant slaves traded along the desert's outposts, he is prodded on in a trancelike torpor of grueling work and drugs, a living death which is pierced only by occasional orgiastic encounters with prostitutes.

> And for the second time I shall be dead. Cheap labor is needed. Sold without having been bought, I shall work without pay. . . . For Saif's friend Tal Idriss, who will send *his* corpse *here* to work. They've sold me good and proper. An exchange. That's all. An exchange of favors that will drive us all mad, with . . . this frenzy to work in order to possess those sixty sensual women, this drug that is eating away our last fibers . . . The simple souls who countenance and justify the perfidy of man put it down to fetishism. Voodoo. Or some other aberration [*Et pour la deuxième fois je serai mort. Il faut de la main-d'oeuvre à bon marché. Vendu sans avoir été acheté, puisque je sui mort, je travaillerai sans rémunération. . . . Chez l'ami de Saïf, Tall Idriss, lequel enverra son mort ici, travailler. On nous aura proprement vendus. C'est un échange. Voilà tout. Un échange de bons offices, où nous finissons tous fous . . . avec cette rage de travailler pour posséder ces soixante femmes sensuelles à volonté, avec cette drogue qui use nos dernières fibres . . . Les naïfs qui permettent et justifient la ruse des hommes, croient avoir affaire uniquement à du fétichisme. Vaudou. Où je ne sais quelle autre aberration*]. (*Bound to Violence* 100–101; *Lettre* 117–18)

The tale of Sankolo references many of the injustices of Françafrique Ouologuem highlights in *Lettre à la France nègre*. His slavery renders him an exchanged object, a token in the dealings of French and African cooperation. The drugs his masters feed him anesthetize all but his basest human needs, reducing him to a permanent numbness in which only a voracity for women and drugs propels him forward. The careful reader perceives the web of political intrigue and hypocrisy that brings about Sankolo's *mortvivant* state, yet its appearance all too easily corroborates the myth of the *négraille*'s natural heathenness: what is in reality a product of historical forces is shrugged off as evidence of their compulsive primitiveness. Sankolo, like the copy-pissers Ouologuem addresses in the *Lettre*, recognizes that this is "just a nigger's life. Slave. Sold. Bought, sold again, trained. Thrown to the winds . . . They need cheap labor" [*une vie de Nègre. Esclave. Vendu. Acheté, revendu, instruit. Jeté aux quatre vents . . . Il faut de la main-d'oeuvre à bon marché*] (*Bound to Violence* 108; "Le Devoir de violence" 125).

But here, as in many other points of the novel, the plot's clever mimicking of the real circumstances of black authors is itself undermined by the specter of its stolen source materials. An early commentary on *Le Devoir* by Yves Benot singles out the zombie story as one of the book's most improbable moments, "a passage of virtuosity which owes a great deal to Paris and hardly anything, it seems, to Africa," that proves it to be "a greenhouse product, wholly artificial," (quoted in Sellin, "The Unknown Voice of Yambo Ouologuem" 145). Indeed, the frenzied orgies and tortures of Sankolo's adventure belong better in a tawdry piece of Parisian serial literature. Their coruscating disjuncture from the verisimilar illusion of Africa adds another layer to the novel's truth content. All these pieces of the work—the characters' woes, the way the author is manipulated by, and in turn manipulates, the European texts made to speak an African reality—are untrue according to the concepts available to it; their truth is only legible in history's mediation and negation of their simulations, in their "participation in, and determinate critique of, history" (*Aesthetic Theory* 193). None of this is communicated directly by the novel; rather, it gives us a complete picture that could only be legible as such in a world where Ouologuem, his writing, and Africans in general no longer supplied a fetishized "cheap labor" for machines of multinational capital. *Le Devoir de violence* can be seen in this way as a mathematical cipher much like the *Nègre* texts Ouologuem promotes: It is a hieroglyphic, as Adorno wrote, "for which the code has been lost" (*Aesthetic Theory* 183), or rather has yet to materialize.

Menchu's Secrets and the Structure of Anticipation

Given the cryptic style of much of *Me llamo Rigoberta Menchú,* it is perhaps simple to imagine its portrayal of the Maya-Quiché community also as a hieroglyphic. Even apart from the secrets Menchú actively announces to the reader, many of the events recounted and cultural traditions outlined in the book forefend all attempts to align the first-person testimony they give with the kind of precise subject guaranteed by Western truth-telling paradigms. This is not only because of the collective nature of experience and consciousness, disclosed in the first paragraphs, but also because identity itself at many points appears to be a matter of contingency: Spatial, as when Rigoberta's father (Burgos 213) and mother (236) advise their children through the voices of their grandparents, and temporal, as in the overriding preoccupation in the customs of child-rearing and family management with the constant reenactment of the wisdom of the ancestors, the need to stave off cultural extinction by maintaining the presence of the past. If it is true, as Sommer asserts, that the reader must be cut off from certain details of Menchú's culture because his or her understanding, upon becoming privy to them, will inevitably deform and deactivate the truth they have to tell, this alone does not account for the way the text's foreclosures are built into a structure of anticipation. The thrust of Menchú's many descriptions of the beliefs and mores of the Maya-Quiché can be read as a story of a gradual entry into knowledge of its truths patterned on rituals and everyday practices. Maya-Quiché in this sense is not something one *is*, but the essence of a secret that impels one's journey to a certain embodiment of values and ideals of the ancestors, whose total correspondence is still to come. And this is the case not only for secrets between text and reader, but also for those between parents and children, families and neighbors, or the community and the outside world. Menchú's own participation in public discussions during her childhood was conditional upon her respect for the secrets of the adults: "The thing is that Indians have secrets and it's not always a good thing for children to know them. Or not so much that it's not a good thing but because it's not necessary. . . . We respect these different levels in the community" [*Lo que pasa es que el indígena siempre guarda un secreto. Ese secreto, a veces no es conveniente que los hijos lo sepan. No es porque sea inconveniente, sino porque no hay necesidad . . . Son los niveles que respetamos en la sociedad*] (Wright 84; Burgos 110). To grow into a culture as Menchú narrates it means to prove oneself equal to its demands, hailed by what is still hidden to incarnate its principles through the accumulation of experience, in the hope of achieving the fulguration of its ultimate substantiation. Seen this way, the text's secrets hold open the chance that the historical unfolding that envelops them will transform reality itself, making them knowable.

This is precisely the main point of the exposition of the *nahual* in the book's third chapter. Menchú explains that the *nahual*, the "shadow" of each person or a "person parallel to man" [*una persona paralela al hombre*] (Burgos 39) formed from the image of animals, is determined at birth according to the day of the week one is born, but kept a secret from children until adulthood: "We are only told what our *nahual* is when our personalities are formed and our parents see what our behavior is formally. Otherwise, a child might take advantage of his *nahual*. For example, if his *nahual* is a bull, he might like fighting and could say: 'I behave like this because I'm such and such an animal and you must put up with me.' If a child doesn't know his *nahual* he cannot use it as an excuse. He may be compared to the animal, but that is not identifying him with his *nahual*" [*Sólo vamos a saber nuestro nahual cuando ya tengamos una actitud fija, que no varía, sino que ya se sabe esa nuestra actitud. Porque muchas veces se puede uno aprovechar del mismo nahual, si mi nahual es un toro, por ejemplo tendré . . . ganas de pelear con los hermanos. Entonces, para no aprovecharse del mismo nahual, no se le dice a los niños. Aunque muchas veces se les compara a los niños con el animal, pero no es para identificarlo con su nahual*] (Wright 19; Burgos 40). Under the sign of the *nahual*, identity figures as a secret to be revealed at the moment of social fruition, when the child has acquired a steady character; the practice of its withholding ensures the natural incorporation of its features by preventing those of unproven temperament from appropriating it as a mask and mimicking the animal in an false spectacle of its real connection to nature. The realization of the *nahual* in all its sacred nuance, Menchú suggests, occurs through processes of behavior and development rather than the assignment of identity. This is why, although children often favor their animal from a young age, the secret remains intact: The truth of the *nahual* does not lie in the correspondence obtained from birth but in the proper materialization of its attributes, which is individually and historically contingent.

Of course, the secret of the *nahual* is internal to the community Menchú represents, yet everything *testimonio* criticism has concluded about the heterogeneous construction of the truth effect indicates that nothing in this text can be isolated as a mere datum. All items, textual and paratextual, strive for the conviction of the reader. As part of that effort, this secret also mirrors and informs the other secrets the audience cannot know. In fact, the *nahual* chapter finishes with one of Menchú's many caveats to the reader about the things she keeps hidden: "We Indians have always hidden our identity and kept our secrets to ourselves. This is why we are discriminated against. [For us it is often very difficult to say something about ourselves because we know we have to hide it until we can guarantee that our indigenous culture will continue on, that no one can take it away from us. For this reason I cannot explain the *nahual* but there are certain things I can say in general]" [*Nosotros los indígenas hemos ocultado nuestra identidad, hemos guardado muchos secretos, por eso somos discriminados. Para nosotros es bastante difícil muchas veces decir algo que se relaciona con uno mismo porque uno sabe que tiene que ocultar esto hasta que garantice que va a seguir como una cultura indígena, que nadie nos puede quitar. Por eso no puedo explicar el nahual pero hay ciertas cosas que puedo decir a grandes rasgos*]

(Wright 20, translation altered; Burgos 41). The parallel between the two passages involves a refraction of the secret's function. It is Menchú's numen that has to be concealed, yet on the scene of reading she who has not yet shown a constancy of character, who is likely to reduce the *nahual*'s living characteristics to a fixed and exploitable entity, is the reader. These paired-up secrets represent one of the moments where the truth content of the work, as a dialogue between its formal and historical elements, the aesthetic and the ideological, is most palpable: Here, the truth readers discover in Rigoberta's intimate portrait of indigenous life is handed over, but only in terms that negate it. We can perceive that the very circumstances surrounding this portrait as artifact—the threat to the survival of Maya-Quiché culture, the continuing onslaught of discrimination unleashed against it at any given moment—compose the elements of its illusion of truth, which are indexed to the contradictions attending its reception. This is not only to say through analogy that we, like the children of Menchú's community, will be ignorant of our relation to things until we demonstrate a readiness to handle the truth, but also that the two secrets placed in juxtaposition—one framed in a confessional invitation to know her culture, the other in direct refusal—carry the historical force necessary to establish the work's semblant truth and simultaneously to deny it. The book honors its purpose to fulfill a demand—this is its illusion—but all the while espying that no such fulfillment is possible in the present configuration of the world. The secrets, and Menchú's whole narrative, in this very agony admit anticipation for a final and complete revelation. Their structure of anticipation "talk[s] like fairies in tales: if you want the absolute, you shall have it, but only in disguise" (*Aesthetic Theory* 183).

One of the motifs where the historical contradiction embedded in the testimonial form becomes most visible is Menchú's rejection of false identities, disguises that trammel Maya-Quiché identity into a folkloric caricature for the gratification of *ladino* society. Speaking of Guatemalan fiestas, she notes that the birthday of the last king of the Maya, Tecún Umán, is celebrated as a national holiday, while indigenous leaders forbid participation in the festivities. For them, as Menchú explains, this sort of commemoration only serves to gloss over the historical significance of the hero's struggle, rendering it as a stultified icon to be archived in the past rather than the living spirit of a fight for indigenous rights that is far from concluded: "But for us the struggle still goes on today, and our suffering more than ever. We don't want it said that all that happened in the past, but that it exists today, and so our parents don't let us celebrate it. We [don't know the reality] even though the *ladinos* tell it as if it were history" [*Pero para nosotros existe la lucha todavía, y más que todo existe hoy día, entonces nuestros papás no dejan que eso se celebre, porque no sabemos la realidad, aunque los ladinos la cuentan como verdadera historia*] (Wright 204, translation altered; Burgos 229). Menchú is especially attentive to the way representations of indigenous life, however adulatory in appearance, silence the active participation of cultural symbols in the field of historic contingency: Within this field, Tecún Umán is not a dead object of tribute, but a force of memory in the community's ongoing struggle. Against the finalized truth he is compelled to legitimize in national history, Menchú asserts his enduring leadership in shaping a reality that remains inconclusive.

On the reading I am proposing of the truth content of Menchú's *testimonio*, we cannot sever the discrete elements of her exposition of Maya-Quiché culture from the minority commodity form they inhabit: Rather, her protest of the monumentalization of fallen indigenous heroes, like the description of the *nahual*, is directed simultaneously at and against the work that houses it. The topic of identification in particular seems to pose as a thematic plane for this strambotic gaze of the *testimonio*: It offers a subtle instruction in the correct and incorrect modalities of identity, developed throughout the chapter on celebrations. Still explaining national holidays, Menchú remembers that the community sent away elementary school instructors who came to the villages to integrate their children into September 15th independence day festivities, stripping them of their clothing and dressing them in uniforms and shoes, "clothes of all one colour" [*tela de un solo color todos*] (Wright 205; Burgos 230). She draws attention to the symbolic offense of the material, sartorial homogenization of the community's children by which "[they have to] disguise themselves by taking off their own clothes, their costumes" [*se tengan que disfrazar, que dejen sus vestidos, sus trajes*] (Wright 205; Burgos 230). The uniforms, like the ritual homage to Tecún Umán, represent a foreign mask of identification fashioned to the specifications of mainstream *ladino* culture: They suffocate and "disguise" the wearer, in contrast with the community's own markers of identity that, although also unchanging—and even, from a Western perspective, equally suffocating—are authorized through practice. Among the lessons learned from her mother, for example, Menchú emphasizes the sacred nature of women's aprons, which by virtue of being worn constantly, "in the market, in the street, in all her work" [*en el mercado, en la calle, en todo su trabajo*] (Wright 211; Burgos 236), becomes an obligatory, inviolable part of their persona. This symbolics of dress becomes the focus once again of Menchu's distinction between good and bad identity in the last of the celebrations she documents, the administration of beauty pageants in the regional fair of Cobán. As part of the municipality's annual festivities, the mayor organizes a contest to elect one *ladina* and one Indian queen from each town. The administration collects money from the votes, all cast by young *ladino* men from the town proper; thus, the girls are tapped as a veritable business for the government, an investment made overall in the complacent image of authenticity they bring to the festival's folkloric parade.[17] The queens are furnished with costumes and groomed in the proper etiquette for greeting the tourists and officials who will gather to watch their spectacle: "Then they [make them twirl around, act affectionate, greet everyone] so that the public will come and see them, more than anything because of their costumes. There are a whole lot of presentations. I remember that in the months before the fiesta, they fuss over the queens, teaching them how to present themselves because they assume that Indians don't know" [*Entonces, los ponen a los indígenas que den vueltas, que den cariños, que den saludos para que todo el público los presencie, más que todo por el traje. Así van pasando, hacen una serie de presentaciones. Me recuerdo que meses antes que llegue la fiesta, habrá una atención para todas las reinas, para que se les enseñe su forma de presentarse, porque se considera que el indígena no sabe*] (Wright 233, translation altered; Burgos 208).

The description of the parade inevitably takes readers back to the most memorable moments of Burgos's prologue, where she records her impressions of Menchú upon their first meeting in Paris. There too, the Indian girl is emblematized and erased by her costume, the brilliant homespun garments Burgos reproduces in detail for her audience. There too, she is in effect taught to speak, edited and corrected to present only the most pleasing image for her viewers: Burgos shares the procedure she used to convert the transcript of their conversations into the final manuscript, serving as Rigoberta's phantom "double" to suppress certain idiosyncrasies of the spoken narrative, to play up others, to impose a coherent thread and make the story legible but still different enough to coax the text into its proper relationship with the sympathetic reader. The two scenes call to each other, framing the whole *testimonio* like bookends: They offer a cross-section of the testimonial form's entanglement in social processes, by which the thingification of Maya-Quiché culture dialectically signals its opposite. Menchú's sorrow at the treatment of the queens thus becomes an uncanny part of their dialogue: After their performance, the girls turn in their costumes and are dispatched to a cheap hostel in the seedy part of town, left to fend for themselves. This is the saddest part, for Menchú, because "[i]t means that, yes, they think our costumes are beautiful because it brings in money, but it's as if the person wearing them doesn't exist" [*Quiere decir, que el traje sí lo ven bonito porque hace entrar dinero, pero la persona que lo lleva es algo como si fuera nada*] (Wright 209; Burgos 234). Her commentary dissects the dual levels of representation at play in the commodified spectacle of culture: Drawing on Appiah again, we can say it forces us to distinguish between the *presence* of these representations, here in the dresses of the queens but more broadly in the whole narration, as an object made available for contemplation, and the *content,* whose elements conform to the antagonisms that preface the object's consumption. The truth content of Menchu's lamentation for the Indian queens resides in the intervention of this antagonism, the fact that she is able to share her feelings on this topic firsthand with readers of the First World only by way of the same kind of business that *ladino* society uses to manage its indigenous margins.

Conclusion

Perhaps Menchú and Ouologuem's narratives are never as true as when the density of their form becomes a citation of its own reification, when the particles of their illusory truth-telling voice—the emptied shell of native dress, the zombified slave—surface the contradictions that bar any truth-telling for the time being, inviting us to read them as the very script of minority discourse. My adaptation of truth content to the intrigues of minority authorship, as I hope to have made clear, has nothing to do with a straightforward reinstatement of the authority of literary voice or any other modernist dogma, and everything to do with an attempt to reseed critical apparatuses at the minority text's intersections of form and institution, where the reader-as-critic's hand in the conversion from the real to a distanced and wholly recognized, thus saleable, minority identity cannot be theorized away but rather stages the first moment of critique. Only by reconnecting the face of these works' illusion with the historical striations that make them recognizable under the regime of authenticity, can university discourse counteract its own fantasy of engagement: precisely the fantasy by which, in Gareth Williams's phrasing, critics "act as if . . . subalternity were not, in the very practice of cultural exchange, inevitably submitted to discursive commodification, as if the object actually realized itself as something other than exchange-value within the space occupied and delineated by U.S. institutional critical practices" (234). Williams's focus is Latin Americanist *testimonio* criticism, although the same no doubt could be said for a number of Francophonist critics pleased to report the end of historical truth in *Le Devoir de violence*. But insofar as critique is willing to own up to this fantasy, it can renew the challenge initially issued by minority and postcolonial optics of study, which is the challenge I have planted as the defining problematic for Latin Americanist and Francophonist academics who still believe in the viability of the postcolonial concept: namely, to avoid expropriating from the identity traded on under these terms its active participation in the grid of cultural exchange where it is consumed. One must simultaneously avoid making the truth of minority literature vouch for the protection of the autonomous self-owning subject, together with all its colonialist riders, but also avoid converting truth into the negation of the former's claims under the opaque directives of voids or lack. I have tried to show that these alternatives amount to two verses of the same song, both played to drown out the accelerating calcination of all interested parties in minority literature, subjects and objects, under the logic of the money form. However defeatist it may seem to cede the exhaustion of both of these courses, it is the only way to isolate the kernel of hope remaining for a politics of minority literature—the hope that its secrets may yet be revealed, that the *négraille* may yet be unbound. What is visible of the truth content of Menchú and Ouologuem reassures us that, so long as minority works provide a minimum of non-correspondence with the claims of the multicultural metropolis, so long as they have the capacity to rouse scandal, they must still bear witness to the non-illusionary Adorno spoke of. This is their participation in the postcolonial, their minor truth.

Afterword

Commitment to the Negative

What this book has attempted is an intervention in, and a tentative structuring of, the still largely amorphous field of comparative interrogations of the postcolonial concept across non-Anglophone literary and cultural disciplines. The particular historical and critical problematics surrounding Latin Americanist and francophonist engagement with this concept is in no way subsumptive of the various types of connection that span the spectrum of comparative postcolonial studies. Likewise, the issues and texts it has addressed do not come close to exhausting the vast array of commonalities shared by the areas it examines. Instead, they intend to highlight a thread of convergence of disciplinary, aesthetic, and political concerns in what is an infinitely richer plane of potential collaboration between Francophone Studies and Latin Americanism. More than anything, the studies gathered here are offered as an exercise in anticipation: They skeptically endorse the optimism that nowadays recommends comparison as the chosen path along which to invigorate the decrepit—and more often than not imperialist—usages of the postcolonial concept in university discourse.

To my mind, an Adornian outlook on the institutional, aesthetic, and political entanglements involved here provides the right tenor of optimism to take full advantage of the moment augured by postcolonial comparison: Through it, one is exhorted to see the deficiencies and foreclosures of its concept as the final hope for its rehabilitation, not in the elaboration of some better concept but by indexing its poverty to the exterior conditions—including the conditions of academic thought—that, miring it in existing injustice, make it untrue. This is an optimism that recurs to the negative without permitting negativity itself to become a receptacle for thought. It thus departs from other skeptical strains of critique that, cautiously warding off undue appropriation of the heterogeneity of their object, opt for "the direct elevation of negativity, the critique of what merely is, into positivity as if the insufficiency of what is might guarantee that what is will be rid of that insufficiency" (*Negative Dialectics* 393). While negativity, or non-identity, is indeed the nucleus of a responsible, Other-oriented disciplinary practice in the postcolonial era, its incommensurability is not an immutable but a historically determinate obstacle for identity. This is in fact its gift and the basis for optimism, as the last, impassioned argument of *Negative Dialectics* insists: Thought's very perception of its inadequacy to accommodate the other, its sense of despair, is the palpable remnant of hope that thought can and must be transformed. It proves the negative requirement for critique, the realization that total despair is unthinkable.

In this sense, Adorno's tirade against post-war metaphysics applies also to the aura of despair, the "crisis," hanging over twenty-first-century postcolonial studies. For him, nothing is so fearful or complacent as the impulse to hypostatize what lies outside our reach into a positive term: It amounts to the retrofitting of noncompliance to identity, hence an invitation to total despair, since capital loves nothing so much as "to expand its investments, [to] poses[s] itself of the spirit whose own inevitable objectifications spur it to transform them into property, into merchandise" (*Negative Dialectics* 394). A fairer assessment of the trials of identity thinking looming in any discipline's use of the postcolonial, I think, would be difficult to find. Throughout my analyses, I have concurred with Adorno that a preservation of negativity labile enough to key the subject's insufficiencies to the contingent opacities of the object, as an opportunity rather than a state of thought, is available only in experience. The three broad faces of Latin Americanism and Francophone Studies that the preceding chapters have brought to postcolonial inflection—the interrelated ambits of discipline, poetics, and practice—figure loosely as a set of experiences of inadequacy, experiences of the undeconstructible or of wishful thinking, that may deflect thought from staidly appointing its unknown as something over which, however melancholically, it can comfortably keep vigil. Analyzing Latin Americanism together with Francophone Studies illustrates one way in which different fields, although circumstantially opposed in their paths toward the postcolonial optic, still course the same pathologies and anxieties in the experience of the things they study. The obdurate locationism latent in Latin Americanist efforts for postcolonial articulation, no less than Francophone Studies' more unbridled embrace of global visibility, remains subject to capital's merchandising of any object it chooses to calcify under or against the postcolonial label. In very different ways, Glissantian and Lezamian poetics, *mikiliste* and *moderni-*

sta derivations of the Parisian fetish, and Ouologuem and Menchú's minor truths testify to this by drawing us to its contrary: that the truth of the deficiency of thought, the squalor of identity thinking, cannot become a good in itself so long as non-identity continues to materialize its disaccord from under the status quo. For these fields, comparative practice thus foments an accumulation of angles of experience with an eye to dislodging critique from the self-preservationist instinct of discipline, and opening it to the priority of the object.

This may be the first monograph dedicated to a bilateral examination of Latin Americanism and Francophone Studies, but in many ways it merely supports from a new intersection the directions comparative work on issues of postcoloniality, race, and transnationalism is undertaking in other quarters. Françoise Lionnet and Shu-Mei Shih's ambitious endeavors to bring together Francophone Studies, Asian Studies, and Ethnic Studies through the lens of Creolization similarly espouse a commitment to the "negative" of experience by infusing the weary offices of omnipotent theory with the variegated practices of thought sedimented in specific histories of slavery, colonization, and minoritization. Their introduction to *The Creolization of Theory* registers impatience with the logic of despair that has now plagued theory for decades, noting dissatisfaction in particular with the way "The capitalization of the word *Other* raised the term to a universal, theoretical category, detached from its use as a social, economic, and political category that actually refers to new subjects in history" (9). To Creolize theory means to convert it to theory by tethering it to real processes of Creolization in colonial plantation societies and other imperial contexts. It "is open to vernacular grammars, methods, and lexicons in the originary sense of Creolization as a linguistic phenomenon, but also in the sense that it is a living practice that precedes yet calls for theorization while resisting ossification. Creolized theory enables unexpected comparisons and the use of different analytical tools. It can thus make theory more pliable, less rigid, substituting exchange and communication for hegemonization" (31). I do not wish to overstate the parallels between Creolized theory and the present project, but to highlight their basic kernel of correspondence, the vision of critique as a labor made through and against its disjunction from the objective world. Theory is not defunct, Lionnet and Shih suggest, but still to come; its perceived downfall is the occasion for commitment to its innermost goals, which achieve a new visibility by reading their distance from living practices. If comparative practice is similarly able to sway deployments of the postcolonial concept in light of its deficiencies, it may also become solidary with it, in Adorno's words, at the time of its fall (*Negative Dialectics* 408).

Notes

Introduction

1. A number of studies and venues from a decade ago contemplated this "death," including the 2005 conference "The Ends of Postcolonial Theory," held at Princeton University; the 2007 *PMLA* editor's column "The End of Postcolonial Theory?" (Agnani et al.); Vijay Mishra and Bob Hodge's 2005 "What Was Postcolonialism?"; and a 2006 issue of *Postcolonial Text* titled "The Politics of Postcoloniality" (Jeferess, McGonegal, and Milz).

2. This is the sentiment voiced in Sangeeta Ray's entry on postcolonial studies in the 2014 *ACLA* online Report on the State of the Discipline of Comparative Literature: "To think about postcolonial studies is to think in terms of crisis, death, and futurity."

3. In Ania Loomba et al.'s *Postcolonial Studies and Beyond* (2005) and the 2007 *PMLA* roundtable mentioned above, the main consensus is that for postcolonial to remain a useful term, it must "move beyond narrow definitions of postcolonial studies and, frankly, beyond the usual suspects" (Loomba et al. 3). See also Barbara Fuchs and David J. Baker's 2004 issue of *MLQ*, "Postcolonialism and the Past," which challenges the historic parameters of postcolonialism.

4. This book does, in general, use the terms *postcolonialism* and *postcoloniality* as Huggan defines them; however, I do not quote his distinction between them for semantic precision but for the nuances it highlights in the postcolonial's competing regimes of value.

5. As Margaret Majumdar explains, for example, the Organisation Internationale de la Francophonie from the late 1990s on has branded itself as a foil of U.S. hegemony, seeking to represent a French sphere of influence associated with humanitarian ideals and even diversity which, unlike in Francophonie's beginnings, is not tied exclusively to the French language (170–72).

6. In a way, autochthony and globality are meant as a counterpoint to the positions of worldliness and cosmopolitanism outlined by Huggan (*The Postcolonial Exotic* 9–13): Worldliness emphasizes the commitment of metropolitan-based but globally connected intellectuals, while cosmopolitanism describes the commercial savvy of academic immigrants in the metropolis. Autochthony and globality represent a different set of profiles in that the first, regardless of where the autochthonous subject resides or was educated, recurs above all to a native, preferably precolonial, belonging, and the second often involves rejecting identification with the native or ancestral land altogether in favor of a more generic "multicultural" self-fashioning.

7. The context of Moraña's statement is a discussion of how the objectification of Latin America during the generation of the popular "boom" novels is later repeated in successive theoretical "booms," including subaltern studies and postcolonial theory. Sylvia Molloy, similarly, identifies a "magical realist imperative" in postcolonial scholarship on Latin America. See also Richard and Achugar.

8. In the most-discussed single contribution to early debate on the uses of postcolonial studies in Latin Americanism, Jorge Klor de Alva argues against the historical and ideological applicability of the term *postcolonial* for Latin American history.

9. For a thorough review of the origins and development of Francophonie, see Thomas Hale.

10. The status of the French language is one of the thorniest points of contention in the relationship between French and francophone literature and culture. Underlying the resentment many francophone writers express at the mercenary role they are asked to fill in the expansion of publications in French (see, e.g., Mabanckou 2007), there is an assumed equivalence between French nationalism and French language. Jacques Coursil and Delphine Perret signal the anomaly of this attitude compared to other "imperial" European languages, noting that unlike English or Spanish, French is viewed as a national possession (202).

11. Achilles Mbembe, for example, directly links the rejection of postcolonial theory in France to ongoing policies of ethno-racial discrimination supported by the colorless universalism of republican notions of citizenship. See chapter 3.

12. A telling example of this is the controversial *loi du 23 fevrier,* which aims precisely to "'rehabilitate' the colonial project" and highlight through education and cultural initiatives the "civilizing" nature of French empire (Bancel and Blanchard 301–2). The compartmentalized orientation of French approaches to the study of history and culture that tend to dissuade researchers from agreeing that colonial experience has any impact on France itself may go a long way to explain why many of the first publications there to make inroads to a postcolonial perspective focus exclusively on French "colonial memory," as do Bancel and Blanchard's own volumes *La Fracture coloniale* (2005) and *Culture post-coloniale, 1961–2006: traces et mémoire* (2006).

13. The edited volumes of Charles Forsdick and David Murphy, *Francophone Postcolonial Studies* (2005) and *Postcolonial Thought in the French-Speaking World* (2009), for example, are explicitly targeted at claiming a space for Francophone Studies at the table of postcolonial discussion. The past ten years has also seen the inception of the journal *Francophone Postcolonial Studies* and the establishment of

book series dedicated to Francophone and postcolonial viewpoints by both Lexington Books and Liverpool University Press. The notion that Francophone Studies is an exclusively postcolonial field, asserted in the renaming of the Association for the Study of Caribbean and African Literature in French as the Society for Francophone Postcolonial Studies in 2002, or in the decision of the recent Cambridge Introduction to Francophone Literature to omit Belgian and Swiss texts, opens an intense debate about its historical or political determination. If limiting Francophonie to postcolonial writers closes off examination of the nuances of non-French writers' relationships to the language, as Françoise Lionnet argues ("Universalisms and Francophonies"), it also safeguards against the color filter according to which white non-French writers like Samuel Beckett or Jean-Jacques Rousseau are considered French and writers from ex-colonies marked as non-white are categorized francophone, even when the latter are citizens.

14. Indeed, phenomena like the *littérature-monde* movement, as Dominic Thomas suggests, indicate that the French literary institution needs Francophone writers more than they need it ("Intersections and Trajectories"). Lionnet's commentary on the *littérature-monde* manifesto also underlines the multicultural influence on Francophone literature: The task for Francophonie, in her assessment, is to "pluralize" the false univeralism of world literature into a new universal of translation, "the actual ability to translate differences into an acknowledgement of diversity" ("Universalisms and Francophonies" 217).

15. A perusal of mainstream postcolonial studies bibliography from the late 1990s on—in which Latin America is addressed, on average, in one or two out of twenty or more essays—shows Mignolo's work to be included in English-based edited volumes more than that of any other Latin Americanist: Representative examples include *The Pre-Occupation of Postcolonial Studies* (eds. Fawzia Afzal Khan and Kalpana Seshadri-Crooks, 2000), Fredric Jameson and Masao Miyoshi's *The Cultures of Globalization* (2003), Revathi Krishaswamy and John Hawley's *The Postcolonial and the Global* (2008), and more recently, special issues of *Theory, Culture & Society* (2009), and *Postcolonial Studies* (2011) dedicated to decoloniality.

16. The locus of enunciation, or "the disciplinary, geocultural, and ideological space from which discourses of power and resistance are elaborated" (Moraña, Dussel, and Jáuregui "Colonialism and Its Replicants" 3), has become the major conduit, in Latin Americanism, for theorizing the critique of modernity from the perspective of coloniality: The "localization" enacted by the locus of enunciation has as its premise that "world system analysis, postmodern theories, and deconstructive strategies . . . are blind . . . to the epistemic colonial difference and the emergence of border thinking as a new epistemological (or gnoseological) dimension" (Mignolo, *Local Histories/Global Designs* 38).

17. Indeed, for Quijano, Dussel, and Mignolo, the Enlightenment constitutes a secondary and derivative modernity. Mignolo admits that the focus on "first," Iberian colonial, modernity is a result in part of the Latin American perspective: "Since my feelings, education, and thinking are anchored on the colonial legacies of the Spanish and Portuguese empires in the Americas, to 'begin' in the eighteenth century would be to put myself out of the game . . . The Enlightenment comes second in my own experience of colonial histories" (*Local Histories/Global Designs* 19).

18. For the considerable body of criticism inspired by the decolonial paradigm, Latin America is seen to offer a history and critique of colonial power that is both "much longer and more complex than the one generally considered by postcolonial studies" (Moraña, Dussel and Jáuregui, "Colonialism and Its Replicants" 8), and that, unlike postcolonial studies, was not "largely born in the United States and Great Britain, and thus [is not] irremediably bound to the ethical preoccupations of countries with a colonizing past (and present)" (Carballo 253).

19. In Mignolo's estimation, the "irreducibility" of what he calls the "colonial difference" between center and periphery ("The Geopolitics of Knowledge" 231), means that "the critiques of modernity, Western logocentrism, capitalism, Eurocentrism, and the like performed in Western Europe and the United States cannot be valid for persons who think and live in Asia, Africa, or Latin America" (252); the goal of notions like border thinking is to signal new, non-Eurocentric loci of enunciation able to "absorb and displace hegemonic forms of knowledge into the perspective of the subaltern" (*Local Histories/Global Designs* 12).

20. The "decolonial option," prevalent in Mignolo's most recent work, is presented as a kind of third way that refuses to assimilate to either capitalist or socialist positions; because this option "delinks" from the Eurocentric paradigms of these viewpoints, it must "go to the reservoir of ways of life and modes of thinking that have been disqualified by Christian theology since the Renaissance" ("Geopolitics of Sensing" 275). Decoloniality's common recurrence to precolonial or indigenous signifying practices as a basis for counterhegemonic activism, at once inside and outside the Western knowledge/power matrix, has led some commentators to address the logical flaws in Mignolo's contradictory desire, as Scott Michaelsen and Scott Cutler Shershow put it, to "have his difference and deny it too" (43).

21. Adorno never addressed language or specific issues of discourse in a dedicated way in more than a few short essays; however, a consistent "theory" about language emerges implicitly in the way it is included in his larger theoretical treatises, in particular in conjunction with his meditations on aesthetics. Adornian critics who have attempted to reconstruct a cohesive dialectic of language from his oeuvre thus impute to it the same characteristics and terminology as those used in the context of art: Simon Jarvis, for example, explains this dialectic as a movement between the "mimetic" and the "discursive" qualities of words; for Samir Ganesha, similarly, the same notion of "expression" that Adorno outlines as the objective voice of art in *Aesthetic Theory* describes the contextual force in language (106).

22. In *Aesthetic Theory*, Adorno advises to think of expression as "ordinary things and situations in which historical processes and functions have been sedimented, endowing them with the potential to speak" (163).

Chapter 1

1. Because the original Marxist objections to postcolonial theory have been amply documented by most publications dealing with postcolonial studies, I refrain from summarizing them here. The most cited interventions in debates from the early 1990s, by Aijaz Ahmad, Arif Dirlik, and Anne McClintock, are included in Williams and Chrisman. See also Bartolovich and Lazarus.

2. John Beverley's *Latinamericanism after 9/11*, titled and structured similarly to Lazarus's "Postcolonial Studies after the Invasion of Iraq," dedicates a chapter to *The Exhaustion of Difference* with the purpose of demonstrating that what he deems "deconstructivist" Latin Americanism "depends to some extent on the defeat of the historical Left in Latin America . . . and it remains in some ways fatally tied to that event" (55). Both Beverley's chapter and Moreiras's rebuttal to it (2012) acknowledge that *The Exhaustion of Difference* coincided with and helped to shape the emergence of a radical Latinamericanist practice loosely described, in Kate Jenckes's phrasing, as "New Latin Americanism." Specifically, I think one can locate in the double articulation of hybridity the theoretical precursor of Moreiras's adaptation in later work to Derrida's notion of the passive decision (see, in particular, Moreiras 2004).

3. All of the double strategies cited here are indebted to W. E. B. Du Bois's original formulation of double consciousness; however, as Vilashini Cooppan has argued, the movement in Du Bois's movement between cosmopolitan and national politics traces a dialectical understanding of the determinate action and interaction of the forms themselves as pivotal to his proposals: it resembles more what Cooppan calls "dialectical formalism" (308–9) than the sort of aporetics these critics embrace.

4. Consider, for example, in "Force of Law": "Every time that something comes to pass or turns out well, every time that we placidly apply a good rule to a particular case, to a correctly subsumed example, we can be sure that Law may find itself accounted for, but certainly not Justice" (16).

5. Moreiras takes the term "critical regionalism" from Kenneth Frampton, via Fredric Jameson (*The Exhaustion of Difference* 303 n. 2); Spivak does not cite the provenance of her use of the term.

6. Moreiras prefers the term "tactical essentialism" for his postulates on hybridity, drawing on Certeau's distinction between tactic and strategy in *The Practice of Everyday Life*. His formulations, then, cannot properly be called strategic. However, considering his close adaptation of Spivak's original program of "strategic essentialism" and recalling that for Certeau the difference between the two concepts lies not in the field of their intervention but rather in the position of those who intervene, for the purposes of my argument here the two terms can reasonably be interpreted as interchangeable.

7. See along these lines also Peter Dews's arguments against deconstruction, which in his words "as an eternal vigilance, as an incessant attempt to escape the illusion of presence . . . cannot learn from its objects but occupies a position of superior insight" (45). More recently, Jacques Rancière has alleged that democracy to come, in keeping with the prioritization of responsibility to an absolute other, actually bends democracy to a total singularity that cannot be consistent with any manifestation of the "people," and thus replaces the dissensus of politics with aporia ("Should Democracy Come?" 282).

8. This point is eloquently made by Lambert Zuidervaart (140–47).

9. It is important also to note what the difference between these theorems owes to the departure Derrida and Adorno each make from Heidegger: Derrida's central Heideggerian engagements in "*Ousia* and *Gramme:* A Note to a Footnote in *Being and Time*" consisted in demonstrating how the thought of Being depended on the presence of the now as non-time and non-space in order to conceive of the

trace, while Adorno's criticisms of Being in *Negative Dialectics* hinge on what he sees as a hypostasizing of the unknowable of Being to nothingness, which gave subjects full domain over Being as something immediately given.

10. Jonathan Short relates the passage directly to Adorno's treatment of Benjamin's aura in *Aesthetic Theory;* he notes that it is to attenuate somewhat the mystical tone of the description that Adorno describes the child's experiences "in terms of their fragile, liminal quality" as "something real, yet not existing in the domain of the fully thinkable" (192).

11. Rodolphe Gasché has also analyzed the way aporia is reconceptualized from its classical understanding as a figure or problem to an experience of thought in Derrida.

12. Of course, Derrida himself rejected the notion of a "turn" in his writing, insisting that "the thinking of the political has always been a thinking of *différance* and the thinking of *différance* always a thinking of the political" (*Rogues* 39).

13. In Derrida's 2001 speech given in acceptance of the Theodor W. Adorno Prize, later published as a book with the title *Fichus*, he envisions his propinquity to Adorno, indeed his "debt" to Adorno, as a hesitation between the "no" of philosophy and the "yes, perhaps" of poetry, music, or essays. Derrida recognizes his own work, particularly the elaborations of democracy, justice, the pardon, and hospitality, as a labor consistent with Adorno's effort to hesitate between the two: "The possibility of the impossible can only be dreamed, but the thought, a completely other thought of the relation between the possible and the impossible, this other thought according to which I have for so long breathed and which has sometimes winded me in my play and in my paths, it has perhaps even more in common with this dream than does philosophy. It would be necessary, from a waking state, to continue to keep watch over the dream" [*La possibilité de l'impossible ne peut être que revée, mais la pensée, une toute autre pensée du rapport entre le possible et l'impossible, cette autre pensée après laquelle depuis si longtemps, je respire et parfois m'essouffle dans mes cours ou dans mes courses, elle a peut-être plus d'affinité que la philosophie même avec ce rêve. Il faudrait, tout en se réveillant, continuer de veiller sur le rêve*] ("La langue de l'étranger" par. 16). Jean-Philippe Deranty's analysis of the speech finds evidence of a renewed kinship between Adorno and Derrida, going so far as to affirm the latter's recognition of the former as an "adoptive father." Deranty also advances the thesis that the public recognition of ties with the first generation of the Frankfurt School (the speech itself is a long reverie on a letter from Benjamin to Adorno's wife shortly before his death) is meant to give way to a reconciliation of that generation's estranged "children": namely, Habermas and other contemporary Frankfurt School theorists and Derrida. All English translations from this speech are my own.

14. Varadharajan's more recent writing on Adorno suggests this sort of universalization, affirming that the postcolonial "has come to be identified with a global commitment to the eradication of suffering and to the making of new worlds . . . any refusal to 'plug in, turn on, and cop out' in these arduous times necessarily partake of the postcolonial as I have described it" ("On the Morality of Thinking" 319).

15. In *Local Histories/Global Designs*, for example, Walter Mignolo adduces Khatibi's bi-langue to a form of border thinking he calls "bilanguaging": despite the ostensible global lens of the discussion—or perhaps because of it—the engagement

with Khatibi does not go beyond the borrowing of terms and themes associated with the author.

16. For an example of Khatibi's engagement with Derrida, see "Lettre ouverte à Jacques Derrida" in *La langue de l'autre*.

17. Farabé is the Creolized combination of Arab, French, and Berber spoken in the Maghreb. For a concise historic explanation of the heteroglossia of this region, see Toumi. Both Syrotinski (chapter 1) and Jane Hiddleston undertake a reading of *Monolingualism* along autobiographical lines.

18. All translations from *Maghreb pluriel* are my own.

19. Mireille Rosello, for example, has studied how for younger Maghrebi writers like Fouad Laroui translation and linguistic corruption are reflections of an essentially globalized existence; unlike Khatibi's generation, twenty-first-century authors harbor no anxiety for a maternal language.

Chapter 2

1. One can establish, as Chiampi does, an even longer genealogy of essayistic "americanismo," stretching back to mid-nineteenth century discussions of civilization and barbarism in Domingo F. Sarmiento's *Facundo* (9). Nevertheless, what all the intellectuals I mention have in common is the attempt to define Spanish America first, within the new hegemonic configuration dominated by the United States starting in 1898, and second, as a racially and culturally mixed entity. For these reasons, Martí's "Nuestra América" founds a genealogy of essay writing that is substantially different from that of the nineteenth century.

2. Alejo Carpentier's marvelous real is one of the best-known interpretations of land and magic as American cultural resources: In the prologue to *El reino de este mundo*, he counters the tired surrealist formulas that intend to create the marvelous through "tricks of prestidigitation" with the real, naturally occurring marvelous observed in the "magic of tropical landscape" or the rituals and cosmogonies of the Caribbean. Alfonso Reyes's "Visión de Anáhuac," in another move common to *indigenista* literature, invokes the common telluric bond twentieth-century Mexicans share with pre-Cortesian inhabitants despite the disappearance of the poetry and other cultural legacies of the latter; Reyes thus legitimizes the national origins of modern-day citizens through "the community of effort to dominate our wild nature [that] unites us with the race of yesterday" [*la comunidad del esfuerzo por domeñar nuestra naturaleza brava [que] nos une con la raza de ayer*] (64). José Vasconcelos's *La raza cósmica* is an adaptation of the influential eugenicist theory of the late nineteenth- and early twentieth-centuries to the realities of mestizo American societies: The "cosmic" race is a final product of the combination of the four existing races, forged by the love and assimilation proper to Latin American cultures.

3. Lezama's characterization as a postcolonial writer is most often carried out under the aegis of neo-baroque or New World baroque critical classifications, in which his work is closely compared with that of fellow Cubans Alejo Carpentier and Severo Sarduy. In Monika Kaup's studies of New World baroque, Lezama is an integral part of an "alternative modernity," a "site-specific hybrid modernity" (128); Lois Parkinson Zamora's *The Inordinate Eye* similarly details how "Carpentier, Lezama

Lima, and Sarduy . . . came increasingly to understand the Baroque as a postcolonial strategy, as an instrument of *contraconquista* (counterconquest) . . . by means of which Latin American artists might define themselves *against* colonizing structures" (120). The edited volume of Parkinson Zamora and Kaup, *Baroque New Worlds*, follows this classification by placing critical essays on Lezama under the section heading "Postcolonial Positions." In a much earlier essay, César Augusto Salgado makes a more direct connection between Lezama and postcolonial studies—although also within the broader category of "New World" baroque—by positing that the transmogrification of baroque forms embraced by works like *La expresión americana* expresses hybridity as Homi Bhabha has theorized it.

4. *La expresión americana* has never been translated; all English translations from this work are my own.

5. The context of Horkheimer and Adorno's definition, a discussion of negation's uses in Jewish religious practice, is analogous to the way negation works in Lezama's poetics: For Jewish patriarchy, they explain, the magic link between name and essence is retained in the prohibition on uttering the name of God. Denying myth through this one magical concession, "places all hope in the prohibition on invoking . . . the finite as the infinite, the lie as truth. The pledge of salvation lies in the rejection of any faith which claims to depict it, knowledge in the denunciation of illusion" (17). Although Hegel recognizes the force of this mechanism, they argue—they take the term *determinate negation* from *Phenomenology of Spirit*—in "finally postulating the known result of the whole process," he resorts once more to mythology.

6. Ulloa and Ulloa's study of myth in *La expresión americana* is concentrated on his reference to Pliny's *Natural History* and the Greek myth of Acteon; both Palmer and Fazzolari offer detailed discussions of myth in *Paradiso* which also focus overwhelmingly on the Greek, Roman, and Judeo-Christian allusions of the novel.

7. The phrase *anthropological imagination* is taken from Amy Fass Emery's important study of these influences in twentieth-century Latin American literature, one of the first to thematize the ironic movement of the gaze of the region's lettered elite from Europe (or the U.S., in the case of Fernando Ortiz) back to their home societies, whose Others became an object of interest for national literature through the anthropological lens.

8. González Echevarría offers a refreshing explanation of Lezama's positioning with regard to more political intellectual currents of mid-century Latin America: "Lezama did not partake of Afrocubanism, nor did he indulge in the exaltation of the white *guajiros* (peasants) as the source of nationality . . . He sought a higher synthesis in which all those cultural components already would have been absorbed, with the result that, unlike Afrocubanism, his work and that of his associates, including the great mulatto poet Gastón Baquero, is devoid of exoticism. This does not mean that Lezama and his group were "pure" poets, or that their art eschewed Cuban social reality or history, but rather that these were interpreted by a hermeneutics seeking to discover their poetic essence" (par. 3).

9. Asturias, as is well known, becomes familiar with the Maya cosmovision of his native Guatemala only through his work translating the *Popol Vuh* into Spanish, carried out under the tutelage of Sorbonne ethnologist George Raynauld;

Mariátegui's defense of indigenous revolution in Peru comes about only after his stint working in Italy; Cuban writers Fernando Ortiz and Lydia Cabrera are deeply indebted to anthropological frameworks in their treatises on transculturation and religious syncretism. Lezama's short piece on Cabrera, "El nombre de Lydia Cabrera," comes closest to associating his poetic idiom of magic and animism to the ethnographic material popular in Cuban literature, exploring the paremiological wisdom of her informant José de Calazán Herrera as a marker of the enchantment of Cuban culture (*Obras Completas* II 530).

10. *La fijeza*, as Guillermo Sucre perhaps best explains it, is "ecstasy of expansion," a standstill which is also "pure dynamism" and as such a fleeting register of the absolute or God (332). Typical moments of *fijeza* in *Paradiso*, for example, involve the contemplation of objects among which "there exists a network of images, in which the poet participates when he conceives them within a coordinate of radiations" [*existe una red de imágenes, participadas por el poeta cuando las concibe dentro de una coordenada de irradiaciones*] (*Obras Completas* II 180).

11. As Lezama affirms in a later essay, "Confluencias," it is man's very access to the image that proves that salvation exists because "if the image were denied to him he would not know resurrection at all" [*si la imagen le fuera negada desconocería totalmente la resurrección*] (*Obras Completas* II 1215).

12. Walter Moser, for example, identifies in *La expresión americana* an alternation between a strategic appeal to the image and an essentialist thesis that "the baroque occupies an absolute centrality in Latin American culture and thus appears as the identifying element par excellence" [*le baroque occupe une centralité absolue dans la culture latino-américaine et apparaît alors comme l'élément identificateur par excellence*] (99). William Egginton, in bringing Lezama's theory of the image together with Spanish baroque theater, denies his exceptionalism which reserves the plutonic agglutination and fragmentation of the image to American baroque, noting its presence as a transatlantic phenomenon (112).

13. Emilio Bejel's sentient discussion of nature and supranature in Lezama's poetry views the latter as "a new reality that fills the vacuum left by the absence of a natural order" (24); poetry creates a new language to replace lost nature, acting in a sense as a second nature (47). Although Bejel's argument is well-documented, I think that it does not account sufficiently for the material participation in poetic creation and in the autochthony posited in *La expresión americana*. The idea of poetry as a second nature, for example, brings along some of the connotations of alienation and classification attendant in Lukács's definition of the term, associations that, as I argue here, Lezama's remarks on landscape seek expressly to avoid.

Chapter 3

1. The Bandung Conference, as Lionnet explains ("Continents and Archipelagos" 1508), provided the first international forum for the political self-refashioning of Pacific island and archipelic states, allowing for the development of a national and transnational discourse based in interrelationship and movement rather than centralized territory. The Tongan anthropologist Epeli Hau'ofa solidified this imagination for Oceanic populations more recently in his influential essay "Our Sea of Islands,"

which replaces the colonial rendering of the Pacific as "islands in a far sea" with the archipelic vision of "a sea of islands," a view committed to seeing social and political networks "in the totality of their relationships" (7). In the francophone Caribbean, Césaire's *Cahier d'un retour au pays natal* first interrogates the history of the Middle Passage, slavery, and colonialism through landscape, seeking in the mornes and volcanoes, as Michael Dash phrases it, to "give an understanding of affective space, to bring out the irrational crushed beneath the thingifying superstructure of the culture of the Metropole" [*faire comprendre l'espace affectif, faire sortir l'irrationnel écrasé sous la superstructure chosifiante de la culture de la métropole*] ("Le cri du Morne" 102). Cesairean geopoetics thus figures as an unavoidable reference for the exploration of landscape in later writers like Simone Schwarz-Bart, Maryse Condé, Patrick Chamoiseau, and Glissant. For discussions of their negotiations of Césaire's landscape, see De Souza, Prieto ("Landscaping Identity"), and Dash ("Le cri du Morne").

2. Antonio Benítez-Rojo's *La isla que se repite* offers an even more evident instance of the archipelago's slippage between textuality and geography. His treatise, like Glissant's later work, is infused with Deleuzian terminology, and it also emphasizes the unique situation of the Caribbean archipelago at the crossroads of different economic and cultural networks of modernity, most saliently in the paradigm of the plantation. However, unlike Glissant, Benítez-Rojo explicitly theorizes from the archipelago's affinity with the model of the rhizome a "certain way" of being singular to Caribbean, specifically Cuban, culture that travels less well outside the parameters of the Hispanic Caribbean. Román de la Campa (chapter 4) has analyzed this limitation of *La isla que se repite* in comparison with *Poétique de la Relation*.

3. Both Balasopoulos and Elisabeth DeLoughrey, for example, convincingly detail the collusion between British colonialism and the proliferation of "Robinsonades"—island adventure tales—that instilled a popular association of the island topos with experimentation, expansionism, and individualism, all qualities that recommended and justified overseas conquest. Mimi Sheller's *Consuming the Caribbean* also takes a thorough look at the way "the imaginative and material structures that span the Atlantic-Caribbean world enabled [the] unequal transformations of one person's sweat and blood into another's sugar, one person's provision ground into another's playground" (13).

4. All quotations from Glissant's untranslated works are preceded by my own English translations.

5. Convincing challenges to Bongie's and Hallward's conclusions have been raised by more sympathetic critics. Celia Britton, for example, points out the limitations of Hallward's rigid interpretation of politics of resistance, which has it that "the only vehicle for progressive politics is the nation-state" ("Globalization and Political Action" 7), and highlights how such a view waylays the ambivalence of Glissant's theories after the *Discours*. Charles Forsdick ("Late Glissant") provides a corrective and supplementary reading of Bongie's account of Glissant's cultural political stance by summarizing the various civic projects and movements Glissant committed to as a public intellectual.

6. The lens of ecology, as a growing number of studies argue, is particularly apposite for scholarship on issues of postcoloniality: as Rob Nixon has convincingly

argued, perspectives from contexts of colonization have the potential to refresh the mostly U.S.-centric framework of environmentalist writing and to redress the ways "nativist" notions of landscape and nature too easily align with discourses of xenophobia, while environmentalism can highlight the relevance of ecological debates—often viewed as the terrain of liberal, elite intellectual classes—for impoverished and/or (de)colonized societies. Jana Evans Braziel similarly remarks on the need to decolonize ecology's humanistic assumption of a central problematic between "man" and nature, noting that "Not all men, or women, have had the privileged position of 'Man'; some, rather, have been defined as and immersed with 'Nature,' hence the coevolution of dominating nature and human beings through racially hierarchized 'Natural Histories' of the colonial era" (111).

7. Nesbitt lays out this process in detail in his Introduction (1–47).

8. Lukács's definition of second nature is cited in Adorno's "The Idea of Natural History," with a corrected translation by Hullot-Kentor (118). I retain the altered translation here.

9. As Celia Britton's book on Glissant and language details (*Edouard Glissant and Postcolonial Theory*), the manipulation of narrative both within and across different novels and treatises—including the alternation of narrative person and voice and the repetition of characters as both diegetic and extradiegetic figures from one narrative to another—is Glissant's main strategy of resistance against the French language from within it. See, in particular, chapter 7.

10. This is the first point of negative dialectics: "Without 'something' there is no thinkable formal logic, and there is no way to cleanse this logic of its metalogical rudiment. The supposition of an absolute form, of 'something at large' that might enable our thinking to shake off that subject matter, is illusionary" (*Negative Dialectics* 135).

11. The passage is evocative of the paintings of Wilfredo Lam analyzed in *Discours antillais* and *La Cohée du Lamentin*, which in baroque manner begin "by filling the canvas" [*par remplir la toile*] ("Lam, l'envol et la réunion" 14), visibly straining against the artwork's borders: Lam's art, notes Glissant, is a "poetics not of the tree but of vegetation, vertical profusion of what surges from memory and explodes in jungle in insular space" [*poétique non pas de l'arbre mais de la végétation, profusion verticale de ce qui surgit de la mémoire et éxplose en jungle dans l'espace insulaire*] (14); the "rehabilitated forms" of the black African world gathered in the work "launch themselves in all directions and conclude . . . in the unpredictability of the vast world relation" [*s'élancent dans toutes les directions et s'achèvent . . . dans l'inattendu de l'énorme relation mondiale*] (15). These reflections of Lam in his poetics serve as a reminder that, as Dash has argued (*Édouard Glissant* 38), the visual arts—particularly in artists like the Chilean painter Enrique Zañartu and Lam, whose work illustrated early editions of Glissant's poetry—are a cortical point of reference for his thought that continues to be overlooked.

12. In a key moment of the *Poétique*, Glissant defines Relation as a "synthesis-genesis that is never complete," within which "The accumulation of examples aims at perfecting a never complete description of the processes of relation, not circumscribing them or giving legitimacy to some impossible global truth" (174). The *Traité* similarly emphasizes the accumulative, poetic nature of Tout-monde, defining it as

"our universe as it changes and endures by changing and, at the same time, the 'vision' that we have of it" [*notre univers tel qu'il change et perdure en échangeant et, en même temps, la "vision" que nous en avons*] (176).

13. Dash ("Île Rocher/Île Mangrove") has analyzed in detail how these three natural forms figure in Glissant's Relation.

14. Conley here characterizes a general shift apparent in Deleuze and Guattari's *What Is Philosophy?* which as the most complete commentary by the authors on art explicitly embraces a nomadic, rather than monadic, model of the artwork's space of intervention.

15. Bongie, for example, finds distinctions like that between common place and commonplace or globalization and globality "suspiciously neat, strangely systematic for such an enemy of 'systematic thinking'" (*Friends and Enemies* 335).

16. Glissant makes this point forcefully in his interview with Dash and Troupe: "Look, look at all the anti-colonial struggles—what have they led to? Look at Algeria. One million dead over eight, ten years. And what was the result? The mess we find there now. Why? Because from the beginning, we waged this liberation struggle with the very same ideas as the colonizer . . . 'Me, *my* power, *my* roots, *my* culture, my this, my that . . .'. . . . And all colonial struggles have been like this. . . . [W] e must enter a system where we begin to understand that we must be ourselves, but that we must be beyond ourselves at the same time. And this is what nobody wants to understand" (52).

17. This point is illustrated, for example, in Benoit Mendelbrot's demonstration of the difficulty of measuring Britain's coastline, which points both to the way variation in scale makes a definitive measurement impossible and to the political dimension of classic, nonrelative frameworks of physics. N. Katherine Hayles offers a superb examination of Mendelbrot's studies of scale (see, in particular, 210–12), as well as of the consequences of chaos theory for the humanities in general.

18. "Distancing, Determining" is the title of a central chapter of the *Poétique* where the full elaboration of Relation's dialectic between infinite and particular begins (141–57).

19. In this sense, the passage uses the register of what Shalini Puri calls "Manifestoes of desire," a mode of writing that, lacking an egalitarian community or society, invokes it through a subjunctive textual performance: Manifestoes of desire "tend to rehearse a utopian community without rehearsing the alternative material conditions necessary to realize such a community" (85). Puri likens this process to Glissant's own notion of forced poetics, elaborated in the *Discours;* as Bongie points out (*Friends and Enemies* 339), the sort of selective recurrence to "early" Glissant that her study carries out is tidy but less than sufficient to decipher the paradoxical movements captured in later moments of "manifesto" like that of the *Martinique biologique*.

20. Nesbitt, for one, closes his discussion by highlighting the "schizophrenic" positions of Michael Hardt and Antonio Negri's *Empire*, which hail to both "postmodern immanence" and Enlightenment-style designs of political subjectivity without mediating the two categories (190), but fails to carry this critique to Glissant's own schizophrenia.

21. Indeed, the movement from "monad" to "nomad" Deleuze and Guattari carry out in *A Thousand Plateaus* qualifies only a slight difference in characteristic: for

works of "nomad art," they explain, "there is no visual model for points of reference that would make them interchangeable and unite them in an inertial class assignable to an immobile outside observer. On the contrary, they are tied to any number of observers, who may be qualified as 'monads' but are instead *nomads* entertaining tactile relations among themselves" (493). Guattari also likens the sort of ecology exercised by eco-art to a monadic work of art, citing Schlegel: "The operators of this crystallization are fragments of a-signifying chains of the type that Schlegel likens to works of art ('A fragment like a miniature work of art must be totally detached from the surrounding world and closed in on itself like a hedgehog.')." (*The Three Ecologies* 36).

Excursus

1. Camille de Toledo's much-cited response to the *littérature-monde* group emphasizes this false sense of prophecy, a comedy of "before and after" [*l'avant et l'après*] that reflects no such aesthetic or institutional rupture in French-language literature. See chapter 1.

2. Christopher L. Miller expresses his doubts about *littérature-monde* in an incisive summary of this perspective: "*Littérature-monde* would be a smart 'pitch' for a Francophone author to use in seeking publication; but for now the status of *littérature-monde* resonates like a prize—a status to be sought" ("Theory and Pedagogy" 47). He wonders, ultimately, "[I]s *littérature-monde* in effect an honorific label, invented by and reserved for a relatively jet-setting elite of writers?" (47). See also Bongie, "(Not) Razing the Walls."

3. A willing "Francosmopolitan" of the sort Moudileno describes can be found in Dany Laferrière's contribution to the *littérature-monde* volume, "Je voyage en français." His essay consists of a series of scenes from hotel rooms in world capitals, underlining his staunchly global identification with the French language.

4. Hargreaves, Forsdick, and Murphy speculate on the similarities between the hyphenated Tout-monde and *littérature-monde* (2010: 4); Prieto explicitly views the parallels as a matter of the manifesto's glissantian parentage.

Chapter 4

An earlier version of chapter 4 was published as "*Mikilistes* and *Modernistas:* Taking Paris to the 'Second Degree.'" *Comparative Literature* 60.4 (2008): 370–88.

1. Harvey invokes the fetish status of Paris through an analysis of Balzac's portrayal of the city, a prelude to his thoroughgoing examination of the city's social and spatial transformation during the nineteenth century. He orients his observation against the danger "that we will interpret the world solely through surface appearances and thereby replicate the fetish in thought" (55).

2. This term, comparable with Francisca Noguerol's more colorful "parisitis," comes from Pedro Salinas (quoted in Noguerol 165).

3. Gondola recounts that, during the red rubber craze of King Leopold's rule, "If villagers failed to collect required quotas or, in some cases, if the quality of rubber was poor, soldiers customarily wiped out whole villages and brought the

right hands of their victims to the white commissioner . . . This happened so much that human hands took on a value of their own, becoming a sort of currency" (*The History of Congo* 68).

4. In her study of leisure in colonial Brazzaville, Phyllis Martin chronicles the avid interest in French clothing styles and housewares among Congolese from the very beginning of colonial administration: using castoffs from officials and explorers, then firsthand items from the growing selection of imports from Europe and Asia, the residents of Brazzaville grafted French fashion onto existing practices of dress and ornament.

5. This chapter moves indiscriminately between the contexts of Kinshasa and Brazzaville because, although the specific factors of marginalization that have led *sapeurs* to migrate are different in each, the hierarchies of accumulation and exhibition and the economic realities of life in Paris are largely the same for both groups. MacGaffey and Bazenguissa-Ganga point out that, although a language barrier keeps Kinshasa and Brazzaville migrant communities largely separated in Paris (Kinois speak Lingala and Congolese from Brazzaville, Lari), the structures and features of their commercial activities are mostly identical ("Vivre et briller" 126).

6. Gondola documents the hybrid origin of the word *mikiliste* as the Lingala *Mikili*, "the plural for *mokili*, the 'world,' [which] has become synonymous for Europe" ("Dream and Drama" 28). With the French suffix *-iste*, he explains, the term specifies one who has travelled to Europe.

7. I am using the term *singularization* as Kopytoff understands it (73–75), a removal or diversion of an object from its field of exchange, which makes the commodity "priceless" either as a sacralized object (too valuable for exchange) or as something worthless. Kopytoff's proposals about the biography of things pivots on the different processes of singularization present in the lifespan of a given object: "an eventful biography of a thing becomes the story of the various singularizations of it, of classifications and reclassifications in an uncertain world of categories whose importance shifts with every minor change in context" (90). This notion is very similar to Arjun Appadurai's ideas about diversion—also useful for my focus here—as an ongoing matrix of commodities' itineraries of value, by which individual objects and classes of objects are pulled into and out of paths of exchange (22–29). Both concepts effectively steer analysis of commoditization away from strict interpretations of market economy and gift economy (11–13) and toward an appreciation of the processual nature of commoditization, particularly in transcultural contexts.

8. MacGaffey and Bazenguissa-Ganga, Gondola, and Thomas all assert the counterhegemonic gesture contained in the closed circuit of fashion and trading among *mikilistes:* The first, for example, see *sape* migrants as "individuals who refuse to abide by the constraints of the global power structure and its alliances between multinational capitalism, Western governments and African dictators" (MacGaffey and Bazenguissa-Ganga, *Congo-Paris* 3); Gondola, similarly, reads *sape* as a "political statement . . . directed toward the West, the former colonizer, as well as toward the authoritative structures of the African state" ("Dream and Drama" 23). Scholars of *modernismo* and of discourses of Paris in Latin American literature more generally have also proposed to read local appropriations of Paris as a postcolonial discourse, noting the way Paris often serves as a site for projections of cultural autonomy. For

Gerard Aching, *modernistas* were "some of the first non-European cultural workers to construct and fix meaning locally by objectifying, assimilating, and thereby deterritorializing the 'center's' cultural signs" (149). Marcy Schwartz's study of Paris in twentieth-century Latin American literature adapts the term "postcolonial" specifically as "a critical position for rearticulating Latin America's geohistorical relationships through their continuing cross-Atlantic intersections" (4). My position, as I hope the argument of this chapter makes clear, is not that these conclusions are false, but that they fail to pinpoint how reading *mikilistes* and *modernistas* as postcolonial becomes a useful exercise.

9. Ramos's focus when he uses this term is the chronicles José Martí wrote in New York, but it is equally, if not more, appropriate for the chronicles Darío, Enrique Gómez Carrillo, and others wrote from Paris.

10. These tourist itineraries advertised in Darío's Paris chronicles, and in fact all the panoramas, spectacles, and exhibitions he describes for his Spanish American readers, can be characterized as a variation of what Ericka Beckman calls "*modernismo*'s import catalogue," signaling the literary techniques—textual accumulation of luxury objects, aesthetic fixation on commodities, and so on—that cite the economic circuits of export and import between Latin America and Europe at the turn of the twentieth century. See chapter 2.

11. Members of rich ranching families from Argentina and Chile, *rastacueros* often settled in Paris for years or even lifetimes, leaving one male relative at home to manage the ranch and periodically send money. They suffered the reputation among French and Latin Americans alike of ostentation, conspicuous consumption, and lack of taste, and can therefore be considered an antithesis to the Latin American migrant author. For a detailed description of the reputation of the *rastacuero*, see Schlickers (122–23).

12. Viñas writes: "Ever more distanced, at each step destroying links with others and with daily history, the aesthetic traveller will isolate himself to give a version of Europe identified with a museum" [*cada vez más distanciado, a cada paso destruyendo nexos con los otros y con la historia cotidiana el viajero estético se quedará a solas para dar una versión de Europa identificada con un museo*] (44).

13. Cristóbal Pera convincingly argues in *Modernistas en París* that the mythification of Paris through *modernismo* allows for the subsequent emergence of a regional identity. By the first decades of the twentieth century, Spanish American literature indeed had begun a demythologization of the cult of Paris: novels like Alberto Blest Gana's *Los trasplantados* (1904) and Ricardo Güiraldes's *Raucho* (1917) promote through the revelations of their frenchified protagonists a rejection of the soulless nature of foreign culture and nostalgia for a return to national roots.

14. The final consecration of the *mikiliste* begins well before he returns from Paris. As I have detailed elsewhere (Hanneken 2008), it depends upon a series of discursive "proofs" of his success in Paris. In Mabanckou's novel *Bleu blanc rouge*, discussed below, we see how the protagonists use letters and photos strategically to "convince" their social circles back home; the paid dedication of popular songs and other patronage of famous local musicians, called *mabanga*, is a much more influential form of self-promotion, and has even cemented a semi-formalized standard of pricing abroad (Trapido 212; See Trapido in general for a thorough treatment of

the economics of *mabanga*). The frequenting of illegal bars, *nganda*, in Paris is also essential to impress and dazzle the local Congolese population, thus relaying home by word of mouth the news of one's conquest abroad. MacGaffey and Bazenguissa-Ganga (*Congo-Paris* 142–53) document the economics of *nganda* in detail.

15. The hierarchical nature of the acquisition of designer clothes, which determines the relative standing of the *sapeur* through the "rank" of his clothing, is essential to the dynamics of *sape* as group phenomenon. Friedman has helpfully pointed out that the ranking of labels incorporates everything from local couture to imported, non-designer garments, to European knock-off and authentic *griffes*. "In Brazzaville one can begin to accumulate lower ranked clothing, non-*griffés*, copies and ordinary ready-to-wear. . . . Copies are not inacceptable but they have a lower rank in the system" (128–29).

16. Martin and Gondola both trace the origins of *sape* to the fascination with European dress among Congolese servants of colonial administrators. Well-dressed servants, as Gondola explains, attested to the successes of colonialism's civilizing mission and thus added to the status of their masters' households ("Dream and Drama" 26). The first generation of Congolese students educated in Paris returned to Kinshasa and Brazzaville in the 1950s, called *existos* because of their enthusiasm for Jean-Paul Sartre's existentialism and the dominant Parisian trends and fashions with which they associated it, further ritualized the cult of dress and exhibition in clubs with the protean characteristics of *sape* clubs that appeared in the mid-1970s (see Gandoulou, *Dandies* 32–45). The phenomenon of migration to Paris among unemployed young men with the pointed purpose of acquiring distinction through dress dates to the 1960s (MacGaffey and Bazenguissa-Ganga, *Congo-Paris* 139), although the trajectory and practices of the *mikiliste* that I describe here are not widespread until the 1980s.

17. "Trying one's body" is a phrase noted by Gondola in his fieldwork: "when we interrogate these 'adventurers' on the goal of their trip to Europe, many respond in Lingala: '*na ye ko meka nzoto*,' which can be translated as 'I came to try my body'" ("Dream and Drama" 30).

18. MacGaffey and Bazenguissa-Ganga report: "Commerce outside the law is called by several names, among them '*bizness*' and '*co-op*.' '*Bizness*' is a distortion of the English word 'business' and is used indiscriminately to describe all clandestine commercial activities" (*Congo-Paris* 56).

19. Gondola highlights the notion of colonial debt as an important factor of *mikiliste* migration, particularly where migrants apply for political asylum: "Since the former colonizer denies them this identity [of political exiles], they make him pay for it politically. The 'colonial debt' is thus a recurring theory which ultimately 'victimizes' all blacks—from the first African who entered into contact with the white man to the *mikiliste* who is handcuffed and turned back to the departure gate—and compensates them" ("Dream and Drama" 35).

20. Although Paris as used by *mikilistes* and *modernistas* shares with the capital analyzed by Bourdieu a "two-faced reality as commodity and symbolic goods" (3), unlike in Bourdieu's theorization Paris here does not use the restricted field of production to swear off economic or political determinants: Paris is not used to conjure away an existing economic autonomy, but rather to summon an autonomy

that is absent. The intrigue of commoditization therefore runs counter to Bourdieu's symbolic capital. This difference also signals, though for different reasons, the departure of this study from the perspective of Pascale Casanova in *The World Republic of Letters*. Casanova traces an international literary history based upon the notion of Paris as the "Greenwich Meridian" of the literary world, a meeting place where authors from all over the world converged to create a universal standard of literature. Her adaptation of Bourdieu's ideas to assert a Parisian literary economy wholly severed from political and economic demands leads to an evolutionist view of global cultural connections: thus, her discussion of Darío, for example, focuses on his discursive exploitation of Paris as a means of "catching up" Latin America to the literary present. See Hanneken 2010 for a further critique of Casanova's reading of *modernismo*.

21. The physical transformation of the body is integral to the *mikiliste*'s convincing metamorphosis. As Gondola details, skin-lightening with hydroquinone simulates the effects of the European climate but also reproduces colonial-era discourses of whitening and evolution; *mikilistes* also manipulate their bodies to look like older, well-established men of standing by eating semolina to grow thick midsections, and cut their hair to mimic the beginning of baldness. All of these treatments create the effect of a life of affluence and leisure, for Gondola making the body into a metaphor for salvation from poverty and racism ("Dream and Drama" 30–31).

22. Susan Buck-Morss signals the parallel sensations of travel and shopping aroused by the panorama, a twinning of optics that is especially pertinent to Spanish American readerships for whom voyage to Europe became tantamount to consumption: panoramas, she explains, would "provid[e] sweeping views that unrolled before the spectators, giving them the illusion of moving through the world at an accelerated rate. The experience corresponded to that of moving along a street of commodity display windows" (*The Dialectics of Seeing* 82).

23. Yvette Guilbert (1865–1944) and Liane de Pougy (1869–1950) were both star performers during the French Belle Époque.

24. Dominic Thomas also suggests that the similarities between *sape* practices and the activities of nineteenth-century dandies can help illuminate the dissimulated forms of resistance to be read therein ("Fashion Matters" 952).

25. Buck-Morss takes this quote from the M_2 version of the 1935 exposé (Benjamin, *Gesammelte Schriften* vol. 5 46–47), but offers her own translation, which I have chosen to preserve here.

26. Diamonds are indeed one of the very first commodities cited by Marx in *Capital* to illustrate his theory of labor value: "Diamonds are of very rare occurrence on the earth's surface, and hence their discovery costs, on an average, a great deal of labour time. . . . According to Eschwege, the total produce of the Brazilian diamond mines for the eighty years, ending in 1823, had not realised the price of one-and-a-half years' average produce of the sugar and coffee plantations of the same country, although the diamonds cost much more labour, and therefore represented more value. With richer mines, the same quantity of labour would embody itself in more diamonds, and their value would fall. If we could succeed at a small expenditure of labour, in converting carbon into diamonds, their value might fall below that of bricks" (47).

27. In their excellent study of the treatment of jewels in Modernist literature, Enda Duffy and Maurizia Boscagli also comment on the way the "super-commodity" (198) status of diamonds provides a site for the negotiation of mass culture with literary autonomy. They highlight the parallels between the efforts of design discourse to conceal the ornamentation favored by bourgeois consumerism—which converted precious gems into one more vulgar commodity—and the narrative concealment of jewels in acts of disappearance. In both realms, they assert, these disappearing acts reveal "a barely covert exploration of how the potential relations between elite art and popular forms in the dawning era of the mass-commodity could be staged upon the commodity itself" (195).

28. Rosemary LoDato gives a detailed exposition of the motifs of jewelry in *modernismo*, especially art nouveau symbolics of nature and flowing forms.

29. MacGaffey and Bazenguissa-Ganga write: "This simple order, *débrouillez-vous*, was subsequently given to the whole nation by President Mobutu, and has since become associated with all illegal activities: corruption, theft, diamond smuggling and so on" (*Congo-Paris* 54). *Débrouillardise* is in fact such a common part of life that it is often said jokingly to be part of the Congolese constitution. It is, as Catherine Coquery-Vidrovitch notes, the de facto rule of law under the Congolese "nation without a state": "The Congolese have a joke about this: they live on article 14 of the constitution, which in fact consists of only 13 articles. The fourteenth is the well-known *débrouillardise* (how to manage with nothing) article" (247).

30. Trapido explores the etymological connections of *mabanga* to the ethos of *kobeta libanga*. While the term *mabanga* (literally, "stones"), in the context of musical patronage, draws from the euphemism of "throwing stones" ("a musician who cites a patron is said to 'throw'—*kobwaka*—him"), it also partakes more broadly of the discourse of *débrouillardise:* "But certain informants also linked *mabanga* to the idea of 'breaking stone'—*kobeta libanga*—a phrase denoting work but also hustling and the ideology of amoral resourcefulness which Congolese have elevated to a kind of credo as the state has fallen away around them" (205).

31. I am necessarily generalizing a set of conditions that have varied widely over the past three decades of artisanal mining in Lunda province. De Boeck (in particular, "*Garimpeiro* Worlds") traces the way the nature of informal economy, and the miners' relationship to commodities and money, changes from the 1980s to the 1990s as cross-border trading consisting mostly of barter takes on a more organized and more "dollarized" character. My interest in glossing the economy of diamond migration is to draw a general analogy of the types of paths commoditization takes in Congolese interactions with global economies.

32. This appreciation of the danger and animation of dollars and diamonds, as De Boeck details, draws upon a wide range of signifying practices, including paths of initiation to manhood and elderhood such as circumcision, hunting rituals, and the sexual conquest of women ("*Garimpeiro* Worlds" 560), but also sorcery. The "demonic" commodities, it is believed, can possess one with greed, compelling him to sacrifice his relatives through witchcraft in exchange for luck in his mining ("Domesticating Diamonds" 788–89). The precariousness of value in the diamond trade, then, does not have to do simply with the fluctuation of exchange rates but carries out a veritable corruption of the miner's lifeworld by robbing him of his

self-determination: "diamonds and dollars have a terrible effect on people: they make a person lose all sense of self-determination; they turn a person into a thief, a cheat and a liar; they 'eat' or destroy people, for in return for stones one sacrifices one's manhood . . . they cause one to become an animal or a sorcerer . . . breaking down the normal boundaries that characterize the cultural order of life in the village" (1999: 789).

Chapter 5

1. For a detailed treatment of this economy, see Hanneken 2011.

2. My understanding of minority literature here departs from Deleuze and Guattari's theorization of the term in "What Is a Minor Literature?" in that it refers to the way texts are coded and traded on a circuit deemed "minority" according to the way structures of readership in different contexts cathect a variety of markers of marginality, rather than to a subversion of dominant languages in the text itself.

3. Although the cases of Menchú and Ouologuem have received more attention than perhaps any other scandal of minority literature, a number of allegations of pilfering, imposture, and misrepresentation in texts considered "minority" in one way or another have fueled debates over identity and authorship in both the U.S. and the French context. The French literary scene alone has built up a sustained tradition of scandal around postcolonial African, Maghrebi, and *beur* authors, most spectacularly the conviction of Cameroonian writer Calixthe Beyala for plagiarizing the same novel that later won her the Académie Française's Grand prix du roman, and the literary hoax carried out by Jack-Alain Léger, an established white writer who penned a series of popular novels under the name and persona of a young *beur* named Paul Smaïl. A 2006 special issue of *Research in African Literatures* dedicated to textual ownership gathers studies of these and other scandals (Hargreaves, Hitchcott, and Thomas). In the U.S. context, there is the case of *The Education of Little Tree* (1976), an autobiographical tale of a young boy learning the ways of his Cherokee grandparents, which was eagerly adopted by Native American and ecological movements and in 1991 found to have been authored by white supremacist and radical Ku Klux Klan member Asa Carter (Gates); and more recently, the exposé of the memoirs of Margaret B. Jones, *Love and Consequences*, which turned out not to be the life story of a foster child and drug-runner for the Bloods gang in South Los Angeles, but a fiction by a white woman raised in a well-heeled suburb (Rich). In one of the most global scandals of minority text—and instructive of the flexibility of conduits of minoritization as Shih has it—a group of Australian journalists have undertaken a campaign to question the accuracy of *A Long Way Gone*, Ishmael Beah's account of his forced recruitment as a child soldier in Sierra Leone (Sherman).

4. The metaphor of the "negro pearl" is the subject of one of Ouologuem's satirical "letters" to black France in *Lettre à la France nègre*, and also structures the character of Raymond Kassoumi in *Le Devoir de violence*, a character based at least in part on Ouologuem's own experiences. In an address to Charles de Gaulle in *Lettre*, he sarcastically describes hearing from the troubadours of his village "how privileged I was to be allowed to sit upon your [de Gaulle's] knees, and to suck on a gaullipop, which you lavishly bestowed upon me" [*promis à pouvoir toujours jouer*

sur tes genoux, avec, à la bouche, la gaullibacillose galopante que ta libéralité, fort connue, me prodiguerait] (*The Yambo Ouologuem Reader* 213; *Lettre* 15).

5. The success of *Le Devoir de violence* also owed to its repudiation of first-generation postcolonial writing in the mold of Négritude, countering the romanticized depiction of an authentic, precolonial Africa in authors like Senghor and Camera Laye with a narrative universe of relentless depravity, where suffering, violence, and slavery are embedded in political structures by Black chiefs and Arab invaders long before the arrival of white men. This reversal in the propounded image of African authenticity alienated many African critics who found Ouologuem's novel as exaggerated in its nihilism as Négritude literature was in its idealization. Mpiku offers the most developed exposition of the contrast between these two views of Africa and of the negative reaction of the African intellectual community.

6. "Intraconversion" is English's term. English offers a particularly nuanced analysis of the way prizes select and reappoint local and national cultural products for the category of "World" culture, itself intimately tied to multinational capitalism (see chapter 13).

7. D'Souza (27), Krauthammer, and Rohter all refer to *Me llamo Rigoberta Menchú* as an autobiography.

8. Critics of *Me llamo Rigoberta Menchú* have been especially interested in these confessions in Burgos's prologue: She confides to the reader each step of the editorial process, including her decision to correct the grammatical errors "which inevitably occur when someone had just learned to speak a foreign language, [since] it would have been artificial to leave them uncorrected and it would have made Rigoberta look 'picturesque,' which is the last thing I wanted" [*debidos a la falta de conocimiento de alguien que acaba de aprender un idioma, ya que hubiera sido artificial conservarlos y, además, hubiese resultado folklórico en perjuicio de Rigoberta, lo que yo no deseaba en absoluto*] (Wright xx–xxi; Burgos 18). Elzbieta Sklodowska, although her reading examines Miguel Barnet's classic *Biografía de un cimarrón*, offers the most thorough exposition of the oftentimes ironic ways literary devices and editorial interventions construct the testimoniante for consumption.

9. Janis, for example, assigns these interjections the status of shifters, able to "refer to voices or alter-egos of the author and can be used to trace some of [his] authorial selves" (97).

10. It is significant, for example, that Ouologuem's style is often compared to the narrative mode of trickster tales (Lang 398; Wise 2), which also serve as Greimas's central analogy for the discursive mechanisms of veridiction (657).

11. Criticism on *Le Devoir de violence* has commented widely on the significance of Shrobenius (see Mpiku 30–31; Janis 100–101; and Huggan, "Anthropologists and Other Frauds") as a foil for the romantic view of precolonial Africa embraced by Senghor, who substantiated Négritude's attempt to recuperate an authentic native culture with faithful readings of Frobenius. Ouologuem's Shrobenius, in contrast, is a "human crayfish afflicted with a groping mania for resuscitating an African universe . . . which had lost all living reality" (*Devoir* 87). His rendering of the anthropologist as a grotesque, bungling figure is thus emblematic of the "violence" his novel visits on all authoritative models of cultural identity, notably here the self-serving European intellectual tradition and the African who emulates it.

12. In Ouologuem's interview with the *New York Times*, Mel Watkins describes him "ris[ing], sifting through the materials before him to point out specific documents, some six centuries old, to substantiate" the claims his book makes about African history: " 'It is from these documents,' Ouologuem says, 'that many of the facts of my book were taken' " (34). In an exchange published in *Le Figaro Littéraire* during the scandal, Ouologuem once again defends a passage copied from Graham Greene as "a veritable fact, like all the facts reported in my novel" [*un fait véridique, comme tous les faits rapportés par mon roman*] ("Le Devoir de violence"; my translation), making more evident the irony of his framing of the novel's truth effect.

13. The way Ouologuem's detractors singled out passages lifted from modern Western works, as more than one critic has indicated, largely misrepresents the much more comprehensive textual violence of *Le Devoir de violence*, in which a wide and still partially unexplored variety of classical and anonymous works—the Bible, the Koran, and oral narrative of the griots are just the most evident sources—are also parodied in very visible ways, all of which overlap with the text copied from European authors. Aliko Songolo's trenchant reading of the scandal reasons that "[G]iven the extreme variety of 'plundered' texts, one finds oneself in a quandary when it comes to the question of determining the 'true' major source of the novel: is it a contemporary author, André Schwarz-Bart, the Bible, the Qu'ran, the Arabic Chronicles, or the anonymous griot?" (24; translation is from Chaulet-Achour 99). Lang similarly detects borrowings from contemporary African authors in Ouologuem (397).

14. For other variations on this argument, see Lang and Songolo.

15. As Moreiras puts it, "In other words, if the ultimate goal of the discipline is the redemption of the object, so that the object can go back to being fully itself, with no remainder, if the discipline plays itself out in the wager for the self-identity of its object of study, then that self-identity, once accomplished, would void the need for reflection, would abolish the discipline as such" ("Mules and Snakes" 209).

16. If Africans' ancestors really are the Gauls, according to the colonial bromide, if black jazz is the only true music of genius—as the exoticist perspective of Jazz-Age Paris has it—and if de Gaulle really is the black man's "father," "How is it" Ouologuem asks cheekily, "that a White Man can ever really know that he's not a Negro?" (*Lettre* 240).

17. A "business" is exactly what Menchú calls it: "It's like making this Indian girl into a business" [*es como un negocio que hacen con la indígena*] (Wright 208; Burgos 233).

Works Cited

Aching, Gerard. *The Politics of Spanish American Modernismo: By Exquisite Design*. New York: Cambridge UP, 1997. Print.

Achugar, Hugo. "Local/Global Latin Americanisms: 'Theoretical Babbling,' apropos Roberto Fernández Retamar." *The Latin American Cultural Studies Reader*. Ed. Ana Del Sarto, Alicia Rios, and Abril Trigo. Durham, NC: Duke UP, 2004. 669–85. Print.

Adorno, Theodor W. *Aesthetic Theory*. Trans. C. Lenhardt. London: Routledge, 1970. Print.

———. "Commitment." *New Left Review* I.87–88 (1974): 75–89.

———. *Hegel: Three Studies*. Trans. Shierry Weber Nicholsen. Cambridge, MA: MIT Press, 1993.

———. "The Idea of Natural History." Trans. Bob Hullot-Kentor. *Telos* 60 (1984): 111–24. Print.

———. *Minima Moralia: Reflections on a Damaged Life*. Trans. E. Jephcott. New York: New Left Books, 1974. Print.

———. *Negative Dialectics*. Trans. E. B. Ashton. New York and London: Continuum, 1973. Print.

———. "On the Use of Foreign Words." *Notes to Literature* vol. 2. New York: Columbia UP, 1974. 287–91. Print.

———. "Subject and Object." *The Essential Frankfurt School Reader*. Ed. Andrew Arato and Eike Gebhardt. Oxford: Blackwell, 1978. 497–511. Print.

Agnani, Sunil, et al. "Editor's Column: The End of Postcolonial Theory?" *PMLA* 122.3 (2007): 633–51. Print.

Appadurai, Arjun. "Introduction: Commodities and the Politics of Value." *The Social Life of Things. Commodities in Cultural Perspective*. Ed. Arjun Appadurai. Cambridge: Cambridge UP, 1986. 3–63. Print.

Appiah, Kwame Anthony. "Is the Post- in Postmodernism the Post- in Postcolonial?" *Critical Inquiry* 17.2 (1991): 336–57. Print.

Apter, Emily. *The Translation Zone: a New Comparative Literature*. Princeton and Oxford: Princeton UP, 2006. Print.

Arias, Arturo, ed. *The Rigoberta Menchú Controversy*. Minneapolis: U of Minnesota P, 2001. Print.

Artières, Philippe. "Solitaire et Solidaire. Entretien avec Édouard Glissant." *Pour une littérature-monde*. Ed. Michel Le Bris and Jean Rouaud. Paris: Gallimard, 2007. 77–86. Print.

Ashcroft, Bill, Gareth Griffiths, and Helen Tiffin. *The Empire Writes Back: Theory and Practice in Post-Colonial Literatures*. New York: Routledge, 1989. Print.

Bahri, Deepika. *Native Intelligence: Aesthetics, Politics, and Postcolonial Literature*. Minneapolis: U of Minnesota P, 2003.

Balasopoulos, Antonis. "Nesologies: Island Form and Postcolonial Geopoetics." *Postcolonial Studies* 11.1 (2008): 9–26. Print.

Balibar, Etienne. "'Possessive Individualism' Reversed: From Locke to Derrida." *Constellations* 9.3 (2002): 299–317. Print.

Bancel, Nicholas, and Pascal Blanchard. *Culture post-coloniale, 1961–2006: Traces et mémoires coloniales en France*. Paris: Autrement, 2006. Print.

———. "From Colonial to Postcolonial: Reflections on the Colonial Debate in France." *Postcolonial Thought in the French-Speaking World*. Ed. Charles Forsdick and David Murphy. Liverpool: Liverpool UP, 2009. 295–304. Print.

———. *La Fracture coloniale: la société française au prisme de l'héritage colonial*. Paris: La Découverte, 2005. Print.

Barthes, Roland. *The Pleasure of the Text*. Trans. Richard Miller. New York: Hill and Wang, 1975. Print.

Bartolovich, Crystal, and Neil Lazarus. *Marxism, Modernity, and Postcolonial Studies*. Cambridge: Cambridge UP, 2002. Print.

Baudelaire, Charles. *The Painter of Modern Life and Other Essays*. New York: Phaidon, 1995. Print.

Beckman, Ericka. *Capital Fictions: The Literature of Latin America's Export Age*. Minneapolis: U of Minnesota P, 2013. Print.

Bejel, Emilio. *José Lezama Lima: Poet of the Image*. Gainesville: U of Florida P, 1990. Print.

Benítez Rojo, Antonio. *La isla que se repite. El Caribe y la perspectiva posmoderna*. Hanover, NH: Ediciones del Norte, 1989. Print.

Benjamin, Walter. *The Arcades Project*. Trans. Howard Eiland and Kevin McLaughlin. Cambridge: Harvard UP, 1999. Print.

———. *Gesammelte Schriften*. 7 vols. Ed. Rolf Tiedemann and Hermann Schweppenhauser. Frankfurt: Suhrkamp Verlag, 1972. Print.

———. "Theses on the Philosophy of History." *Illuminations: Essays and Reflections*. Ed. Hannah Arendt. Trans. Harry Zohn. New York: Schocken, 1969. 253–64. Print.

Bensmaïa, Réda. *Experimental Nations: Or, the Investigation of the Maghreb*. Trans. Alyson Waters. Princeton and Oxford: Princeton UP, 2003. Print.

———. "Francophonie." *Yale French Studies* 103 (2003): 17–23. Print.

Beverley, John. *Latinamericanism after 9/11*. Durham, NC: Duke UP, 2011.

———. *Una modernidad obsoleta. Estudios sobre el barroco*. Los Teques: Fondo Editorial ALEM, 1997. Print.

———. *Testimonio: On the Politics of Truth*. Minneapolis: U of Minnesota P, 2004. Print.

Bhabha, Homi. *The Location of Culture*. New York and London: Routledge, 1994. Print.

Bongie, Chris. *Friends and Enemies: The Scribal Politics of Post/Colonial Literature*. Liverpool: Liverpool UP, 2008. Print.

———. "(Not) Razing the Walls: Glissant, Trouillot, and the Post-Politics of World 'Literature.'" *Transnational French Studies: Postcolonialism and littérature-monde*. Ed. Alec Hargreaves, Charles Forsdick, and David Murphy. Liverpool: Liverpool UP, 2010. 25–45. Print.

Bourdieu, Pierre. *The Field of Cultural Production*. Ed. Randal Johnson. New York: Columbia UP, 1993. Print.

Braziel, Jana Evans. "Caribbean Genesis: Language, Gardens, Worlds (Jamaica Kincaid, Derek Walcott, Édouard Glissant)." *Caribbean Literature and the Environment: Between Nature and Culture*. Ed. Elizabeth M. DeLoughrey, Renée K. Gosson, and George B. Handley. Charlottesville and London: U of Virginia P, 2005. 110–26. Print.

Bréleur, Ernest, et al. *Manifeste pour les "produits" de haute nécessité*. Paris: Galaade, 2009. Print.

Brennan, Timothy. "Postcolonial Studies and Globalization Theory." *The Postcolonial and the Global*. Ed. Revathi Krishnaswamy and John C. Hawley. Minneapolis: U of Minnesota P, 2008. 37–53. Print.

Britton, Celia M. *Edouard Glissant and Postcolonial Theory: Strategies of Language and Resistance*. Charlottesville, VA: U of Virginia P. 1999. Print.

———. "Globalization and Political Action in the Work of Edouard Glissant." *Small Axe* 30 (2009): 1–11. Print.

Buck-Morss, Susan. *The Dialectics of Seeing: Walter Benjamin and the Arcades Project*. Cambridge: The MIT Press, 1991. Print.

———. *The Origin of Negative Dialectics: Theodor W. Adorno, Walter Benjamin, and the Frankfurt Institute*. New York: The Free Press, 1977. Print.

Burgos, Elisabeth. *Me llamo Rigoberta Menchú y así me nació la conciencia*. Barcelona: Argos Vergara, 1983. Print.

Burke, Donald A., et al, eds. *Adorno and the Need in Thinking. New Critical Essays*. Toronto: U of Toronto P, 2007. Print.

Carballo, Francisco. "Latin America and the Politics of Knowledge: An Introduction." *Postcolonial Studies* 14.3 (2011): 253–57.

Carpentier, Alejo. *El reino de este mundo*. Montevideo: Arca, 1969. Print.

Casal, Julián del. "La última ilusión." *Crónicas habaneras*. La Havana: Universidad Central de las Villas, 1963. 278–83. Print.

Casanova, Pascale. *The World Republic of Letters*. Trans. M. B. DeBevoise. Cambridge: Harvard UP, 2004. Print.

Certeau, Michel de. *The Practice of Everyday Life*. Trans. Steven Rendall. Berkeley: U of California P, 1984. Print.

Chafer, Tony. "Chirac and 'la Françafrique': No Longer a Family Affair." *Modern & Contemporary France* 13.1 (2005): 7–23. Print.

Chamoiseau, Patrick, et al. "Manifeste pour refonder les DOM." *Le Monde* 21 January 2000. 16. Print.

Chiampi, Irlemar. "La historia tejida por la imagen." *La expresión americana*. José Lezama Lima. México: Fondo de Cultura Económica, 2001. 9–33. Print.

Chow, Rey. "The Old/New Question of Comparison in Literary Studies: A Post-European Perspective." *ELH* 71 (2004): 289–311. Print.

Conley, Tom. "A Plea for Leibniz." *The Fold: Leibniz and the Baroque*. Gilles Deleuze. Trans. Tom Conley. Minneapolis: U of Minnesota P, 1993. Print.

Cooppan, Vilashini. "The Double Politics of Double Consciousness: Nationalism and Globalism in the Souls of Black Folk." *Public Culture* 17.2 (2005): 299–318. Print.

Coquéry-Vidrovitch, Catherine. "Nation without a State and State without a Nation: The Case of Africa South of the Sahara." *Nation, State, and the Economy in History*. Ed. Alice Teichova and Herbert Matis. Cambridge: Cambridge UP, 2003. 239–50. Print.

Corcoran, Patrick, Ed. and intro. *The Cambridge Introduction to Francophone Literature*. Cambridge: Cambridge UP, 2007. Print.

Coursil, Jacques. "La catégorie de la relation dans les essais d'Édouard Glissant. Philosophie d'une poétique." *Poétiques d'Édouard Glissant*. Ed. Jacques Coursil. Paris: Presses de l'Université de Paris-Sorbonne, 1999. 85–112. Print.

Coursil, Jacques, and Delphine Perret. "The Francophone Postcolonial Field." *Postcolonial Theory and Francophone Literary Studies*. Ed. H. Adlai Murdoch and Anne Donadey. Gainesville: U of Florida P, 2005. 193–210. Print.

Cruz-Malavé, Arnaldo. *El primitivo implorante: El "sistema poético el mundo" de José Lezama Lima*. Amsterdam: Rodopi, 1994. Print.

Darío, Rubén. *Obras completas*. 5 vol. Madrid: Afrodisio Aguado, 1950–55. Print.

Dash, J. Michael. *Édouard Glissant*. New York: Cambridge UP, 1995. Print.

———. "Île Rocher/Île Mangrove. Éléments d'une pensée archipélique dans l'oeuvre d'Édouard Glissant." *Poétiques d'Édouard Glissant*. Ed. Jacques Coursil. Paris: Presses de l'Université de Paris-Sorbonne, 1999. 17–24. Print.

———. "Le cri du Morne: La Poétique du paysage césarien et la littérature antillaise." *Soleil eclaté. Melanges offerts à Aimé Césaire à l'occasion de son soixante-dixième anniversaire par une équipe internationale d'artistes et de chercheurs*. Ed. Jacqueline Leiner. Tübingen: G. Narr, 1984. 102–10. Print.

Dash, J. Michael, and Quincey Troupe. "Interview with Édouard Glissant." Trans. Hillina Seife. *Black Renaissance* 6.3/7.1 (2006): 49–56. Print.

De Boeck, Filip. "Domesticating Diamonds and Dollars: Identity, Expenditure and Sharing in Southwestern Zaire (1984–1997)." *Development and Change* 29 (1998): 777–810. Print.

———. "*Garimpeiro* Worlds: Digging, Dying, and 'Hunting' for Diamonds in Angola." *Review of African Political Economy* 90 (2001): 549–62. Print.

De la Campa, Román. *Latin Americanism*. Minneapolis: U of Minnesota P, 1999.

Deleuze, Gilles, and Félix Guattari. *A Thousand Plateaus: Capitalism and Schizophrenia*. Trans. Brian Massumi. New York: Continuum, 1988. Print.

———. "What Is a Minor Literature?" *Mississippi Review* 11.3 (1983): 13–33. Print.

———. *What Is Philosophy?* Trans. Hugh Tomlinson and Graham Burchell. New York: Columbia UP, 1994. Print.

DeLoughrey, Elizabeth M. *Routes and Roots. Navigating Caribbean and Pacific Island Literatures*. Honolulu: U of Hawaii P, 2007. Print.

Del Sarto, Ana, Alicia Rios, and Abril Trigo, eds. *The Latin American Cultural Studies Reader*. Durham, NC: Duke UP, 2004. Print.

Deranty, Jean-Philippe. "Adorno's Other Son: Derrida and the Future of Critical Theory." *Social Semiotics* 16.3 (2006): 421–33. Print.

Derrida, Jacques. "Force of Law: The 'Mystical Foundation of Authority.'" *Deconstruction and the Possibility of Justice*. Ed. Drucilla Cornell, Michel Rosenfield, and David Gray Carlson. New York: Routledge, 1992. Print.

———. "La langue de l'étranger." *Le Monde diplomatique*. January 2002: 60 paragraphs. Web. 13 Jan. 2011.

———. *Monolingualism of the Other: Or, the Prosthesis of Origin*. Trans. Patrick Mensah. Stanford: Stanford UP, 1998. Print.

———. *Politics of Friendship*. Trans. George Collins. London, New York: Verso, 1997. Print.

———. *Rogues: Two Essays on Reason*. Trans. Pascale-Anne Brault and Michael Naas. Stanford: Stanford UP, 2005. Print.

———. *Specters of Marx: The State of the Debt, the Work of Mourning and the New International*. Trans. Peggy Kamuf. New York: Routledge, 1994. Print.

De Souza, Pascale. "Gendering Mornes and Volcanoes in French Caribbean Literature." *International Journal of Francophone Studies* 6.3 (2003): 149–64. Print.

De Souza, Pascale, and H. Adlai Murdoch. "Oceanic Dialogues: From the Black Atlantic to the Indo-Pacific." *International Journal of Francophone Studies* 8.2 (2005): 133–46. Print.

De Toledo, Camille. *Visiter le Flurkistan, où les illusions de la littérature-monde*. Paris: Presses Universitaires de France, 2008.

Dews, Peter. "Adorno, Post-Structuralism and the Critique of Identity." *New Left Review* I.57 (1986): 28–44. Print.

D'Souza, Dinesh. "I, Rigoberta Menchú . . . Not!" *The Weekly Standard*. 28 Dec. 1998: 27–29. Print.

Duffy, Enda, and Maurizia Boscagli. "Selling Jewels: Modernist Commodification and Disappearance as Style." *Modernism/Modernity* 14.2 (2007): 189–207. Print.

Egginton, William. "The Corporeal Image and the New World Baroque." *South Atlantic Quarterly* 106.1 (2007): 107–27. Print.

"The Ends of Postcolonial Theory." Princeton University, 2005. Web. 4 April 2011.

English, James. *The Economy of Prestige: Prizes, Awards, and the Circulation of Cultural Value*. Cambridge: Harvard UP, 2005. Print.

Fass Emery, Amy. *The Anthropological Imagination in Latin American Literature*. Columbia: U of Missouri P, 1997. Print.

Fazzolari, Margarita Junco. *Paradiso y el sistema poético de Lezama Lima*. Buenos Aires: Fernando García Cambeiro, 1979. Print.

Forsdick, Charles. "Late Glissant: History, 'World Literature,' and the Persistence of the Political." *Small Axe* 33 (2010): 121–34. Print.

Forsdick, Charles, and David Murphy. *Francophone Postcolonial Studies: A Critical Introduction*. New York: Arnold, 2003. Print.

———. *Postcolonial Thought in the French-Speaking World*. Liverpool: Liverpool UP, 2009. Print.

———. "The Rise of the Francophone Intellectual: The Emergence of a Tradition." *Modern and Contemporary France* 17.2 (2009): 163–75. Print.

Foucault, Michel. "What Is an Author?" *Language, Counter-Memory, Practice. Selected Essays and Interviews*. Ed. Donald F. Bouchard. Trans. Donald F. Bouchard and Sherry Simon. Ithaca: Cornell UP, 1977, 113–38. Print.

Frazer, James. *The Golden Bough: The Roots of Religion and Folklore*. New York: Avenel Books, 1981. Print.

Freud, Sigmund. *Totem and Taboo: Some Points of Agreement between the Mental Lives of Neurotics and Savages*. Trans. James Strachey. New York: W. W. Norton, 1950. Print.

Friedman, Jonathan. "The Political Economy of Elegance." *Culture and History* 7 (1992): 101–25. Print.

Fuchs, Barbara, and David J. Baker. "The Postcolonial Past." *MLQ* 65.3 (2004): 329–40. Print.

Gandoulou, Justin-Daniel. *Au Coeur de la sape: Moeurs et aventures de Congolais à Paris*. Paris: L'Harmattan, 1989. Print.

———. *Dandies à Bacongo. Le culte de l'élégance dans la société congolaise contemporaine*. Paris: L'Harmattan, 1989. Print.

Ganesha, Samir. "Leaving Home: On Adorno and Heidegger." *The Cambridge Companion to Adorno*. Ed. Tom Huhn. Cambridge: Cambridge UP, 2004. 101–28.

Ganguly, Keya. "Adorno, Authenticity, Critique." *Marxism, Modernity, and Postcolonial Studies*. Ed. Crystal Bartolovich and Neil Lazarus. Cambridge: Cambridge UP, 2002. 240–56. Print.

Gasché, Rodolphe. "L'éxperience aporétique aux origines de la pensée." *Études françaises* 38.1–2 (2002): 103–21. Print.

Gates, Henry Louis, Jr. " 'Authenticity,' or the Lesson of Little Tree." *New York Times* 24 Nov. 1991. 1, 26–9. Print.

Gilroy, Paul. *The Black Atlantic: Hybridity and Double Consciousness*. Cambridge: Harvard UP, 1993. Print.

Glissant, Édouard. *Caribbean Discourse. Selected Essays*. Trans. J. Michael Dash. Charlottesville, VA: UP of Virginia, 1989. Print.

———. *Introduction à une poétique du divers*. Paris: Gallimard, 1996. Print.

———. *La Cohée du Lamentin*. Paris: Gallimard, 2005. Print.

———. "Lam, l'envol et la réunion." *CARE* 10 (1983): 14–15. Print.

———. *L'Intention poétique*. Paris: Editions du Seuil, 1969. Print.

———. *Malemort*. Paris: Editions du Seuil, 1975. Print.

———. *Poetics of Relation*. Trans. Betsy Wing. Ann Arbor: U of Michigan P, 1997. Print.

———. *The Ripening*. Trans. Michael Dash. London: Heinemann, 1985. Print.

———. *Soleil de la conscience*. Paris: Seuil, 1956. Print.

———. *Traité du Tout-monde*. Paris: Gallimard, 1997. Print.

Gondola, Didier. "Dream and Drama: The Search for Elegance among Congolese Youth." *African Studies Review* 42.1 (April 1999): 23–48. Print.

———. *The History of Congo*. London: Greenwood Press, 2002. Print.

Goni, Marian Nur. "Baudouin Mouanda immortalise les sapeurs." *Afriscope* 19. 6 Jan. 2011. Web. 11 Dec. 2011.

González Echevarría, Roberto. "Lezama's Fiestas." *Ciberletras* 20 (December 2008). Web. 24 July 2011.

Greimas, Algirdas Julien. "The Veridiction Contract." *New Literary History* 20.3 (1989): 651–60. Print.

Guattari, Félix. *Chaosmosis: An Ethico-Aesthetic Paradigm*. Trans. Paul Bains and Julian Pifanis. Bloomington, IN: Indiana UP, 1995. Print.

———. *The Three Ecologies*. Trans. Ian Pindar and Paul Sutton. New York: Continuum, 2008. Print.

Gugelberger, Georg M., ed. *The Real Thing: Testimonial Discourse and Latin America*. Durham: Duke UP, 1996. Print.

Guyer, Jane I. "Wealth in People and Self-Realization in Equatorial Africa." *Man* 28.2 (1993): 243–65. Print.

Hale, Thomas. "The Manifeste des Quarante-Quatre, Francophonie, la françafrique and Africa: From the Politics of Culture to the Culture of Politics." *International Journal of Francophone Studies* 12.2–3 (2009): 171–201. Print.

Hallward, Peter. *Absolutely Postcolonial: Writing between the Singular and the Specific*. Manchester: Manchester UP, 2001. Print.

Hamacher, Werner. "'Now': Walter Benjamin on Historical Time." *Walter Benjamin and History*. Ed. Andrew Benjamin. New York: Continuum, 2005. 38–68. Print.

Hanneken, Jaime. "Going *Mundial*: What It Really Means to Desire Paris." *MLQ* 71.2 (2010): 129–52. Print.

———. "*Mikilistes* and *Modernistas*: Taking Paris to the 'Second Degree.'" *Comparative Literature* 60.4 (2008): 370–88. Print.

———. "Scandal, Choice, and the Economy of Minority Literature." *Paragraph* 34.1 (2011): 48–65. Print.

Hargreaves, Alec, Charles Forsdick, and David Murphy. "Introduction: What Does Littérature-Monde Mean for French, Francophone and Postcolonial Studies?" *Transnational French Studies: Postcolonialism and littérature-monde*. Ed. Alec Hargreaves, Charles Forsdick, and David Murphy. Liverpool: Liverpool UP, 2010. 1–11. Print.

———. *Transnational French Studies: Postcolonialism and littérature-monde*. Liverpool: Liverpool UP, 2010. Print.

Hargreaves, Alec, Nicki Hitchcott, and Dominic Thomas. "Introduction. Textual Ownership in Francophone African Writing." *Research in African Literatures* 37.1 (2006): vi–ix. Print.

Harvey, David. *Paris, Capital of Modernity*. New York: Routledge, 2003. Print.

Hau'ofa, Epeli. "Our Sea of Islands." *A New Oceania: Rediscovery of Our Sea of Islands*. Ed. E. Waddell, V. Naidu, and E. Hau'ofa. Suva: University of the South Pacific, 1993. 2–18. Print.

Hayles, N. Katherine. *Chaos Bound: Orderly Disorder in Contemporary Literature and Science*. Ithaca and London: Cornell UP, 1990. Print.

Hiddleston, Jane. "Jacques Derrida: Colonialism, Philosophy and Autobiography." *Postcolonial Thought in the French-Speaking World*. Ed. Charles Forsdick and David Murphy. Liverpool: Liverpool UP, 2009. 53–64. Print.

Horkheimer, Max, and Theodor W. Adorno. *Dialectic of Enlightenment: Philosophical Fragments*. Ed. Gunzelin Schmid Noerr. Trans. Edmund Jephcott. Stanford: Stanford UP, 2002. Print.

Huggan, Graham. "Anthropologists and Other Frauds." *Comparative Literature* 46.2 (1994): 113–28. Print.

———. *The Postcolonial Exotic: Marketing the Margins*. London: Routledge, 2001.

Jameson, Fredric. *Late Marxism: Adorno, or, the Persistence of the Dialectic*. New York and London: Verso, 1990. Print.

Janis, Michael. *Africa after Modernism. Transitions in Literature, Media, and Philosophy*. New York: Routledge, 2008. Print.

Jarvis, Simon. *Adorno: a Critical Introduction*. Malden, MA: Polity, 1998. Print.

Jefferess, David, Julie McGonegal, and Sabine Milz. "Introduction: The Politics of Postcoloniality." *Postcolonial Text* 2.1 (2006). Web.

Jenckes, Kate. "The 'New Latin Americanism,' and the End of Regionalist Thinking?" *The New Centennial Review* 4.3 (2004): 247–70. Print.

Johnson, David E. "How (Not) to Do Latin American Studies." *South Atlantic Quarterly* 106.1 (2007): 1–19. Print.

Kaup, Monika. "Neo-Baroque: Latin America's Alternative Modernity." *Comparative Literature* 58.2 (Spring 2006): 128–52. Print.

Khatibi, Abdelkebir. *Amour bilingue*. Paris: Fata Morgana, 1983. Print.

———. "Lettre ouverte à Jacques Derrida." *La langue de l'autre*. New York and Tunis: Les mains secrètes, 1999. 23–33. Print.

———. *Love in Two Languages*. Trans. Richard Howard. Minneapolis: U of Minnesota P, 1990. Print.

———. *Maghreb pluriel*. Paris: Denoel, 1983. Print.

Klor de Alva, Jorge. "Colonialism and Postcolonialism as (Latin) American Mirages." *Colonial Latin American Review* 1–2 (1992): 3–23. Print.

Kopytoff, Igor. "The Cultural Biography of Things: Commoditization as Process." *The Social Life of Things. Commodities in Cultural Perspective*. Ed. Arjun Appadurai. Cambridge: Cambridge UP, 1986. 64–91. Print.

Krauthammer, Charles. "The Case of the Suspect Bios." *Time* 4 Oct. 1999: 122. Print.

Laferrière, Dany. "Je voyage en français." *Pour une littérature-monde*. Ed. Michel Le Bris and Jean Rouaud. Paris: Gallimard, 2007. 87–102. Print.

Lang, George. "Text, Identity, and Difference: Yambo Ouologuem's *Le Devoir de violence* and Ayi Kwei Armah's *Two Thousand Seasons*." *Comparative Literature Studies* 24.4 (1987): 387–402. Print.

Larsen, Neil. *Reading North by South: on Latin American Literature, Culture, and Politics*. Minneapolis: U of Minnesota P, 1995. Print.

Lazarus, Neil. "Postcolonial Studies after the Invasion of Iraq." *New Formations* 59 (2006): 10–22. Print.

Le Bris, Michel, et al. "Toward a 'World-Literature' in French." *Transnational French Studies: Postcolonialism and littérature-monde*. Ed. Alec Hargreaves, Charles Forsdick, and David Murphy. Liverpool: Liverpool UP, 2010. 296–300. Print.

Le Bris, Michel, and Jean Rouaud, eds. *Pour une littérature-monde*. Paris: Gallimard, 2007. Print.

Lejeune, Philippe. *The Autobiographical Pact*. Trans. Katherine Leary. Minneapolis: U of Minnesota P, 1989. Print.

Leo, John. "Nobel Prize for Fiction?" *U.S. News and World Report* 25 Jan. 1999: 17. Print.

Levinson, Brett. "Globalizing Paradigms, or, the Delayed State of Latin American Theory." *South Atlantic Quarterly* 106.1 (2007): 61–82. Print.

———. *Secondary Moderns: Mimesis, History, and Revolution in Lezama Lima's "American Expression."* Lewisburg, PA: Bucknell UP, 1996. Print.

Lévy-Bruhl, Lucien. *Primitive Mentality*. Trans. Lilian Clare. New York: Macmillan, 1923. Print.

Lezama Lima, José. *La expresión americana*. Ed. Irlemar Chiampi. México: Fondo de Cultura Económica, 1993. Print.

———. *La imagen de América Latina*. Caracas: Facultad de Humanidades, Universidad Central de Venezuela, 1988. Print.

———. *Obras completas*. 2 vols. México: Aguilar, 1977. Print.

Lionnet, Françoise. "Continents and Archipelagos: From E Pluribus Unum to Creolized Solidarities." *PMLA* 123.5 (2008): 1503–15. Print.

———. "Universalisms and Francophonies." *International Journal of Francophone Studies* 12.2–3 (2009): 203–221. Print.

Lionnet, Françoise, and Shu-Mei Shih. *The Creolization of Theory*. Durham: Duke UP, 2011. Print.

———. *Minor Transnationalism*. Durham: Duke UP, 2005. Print.

Locke, John. *Two Treatises of Government*. London: Cambridge UP, 1960. Print.

LoDato, Rosemary C. *Beyond the Glitter: The Language of Gems in Modernista Writers Rubén Darío, Ramón Del Valle-Inclán, and José Asunción Silva*. Lewisburg, PA: Bucknell UP, 1999. Print.

Loomba, Ania, et al., eds. *Postcolonial Studies and Beyond*. Durham: Duke UP, 2005. Print.

Lukács, Georg. *The Theory of the Novel*. Trans. Anna Bostock. Cambridge: MIT Press, 1968. Print.

Mabanckou, Alain. *Bleu blanc rouge*. Paris: Présence Africaine, 1998. Print.

———. "Immigration, Littérature-Monde, and Universality: The Strange Fate of the African Writer." *Yale French Studies* 120 (2011): 75–87. Print.

———. "Le chant de l'oiseau migrateur." *Pour une littérature-monde*. Ed. Michel Le Bris and Jean Rouaud. Paris: Gallimard, 2007. 55–66. Print.

MacGaffey, Janet, and Rémy Bazenguissa-Ganga. *Congo-Paris: Transnational Traders on the Margins of the Law*. Bloomington: U of Indiana P, 2000. Print.

———. "Vivre et briller à Paris. Des jeunes Congolais et Zaïrois en marge de la légalité économique." *Politique Africaine* 57 (1995): 24–33. Print.

Majumdar, Margaret. *Postcoloniality: The French Dimension*. New York and Oxford: Berhahn Books, 2007. Print.

Martin, Phylis M. "Dressing Well." *Leisure and Society in Colonial Brazzaville*. Cambridge UP, 1995. Print.

Marx, Karl. *Capital. A Critique of Political Economy*. Trans. Samuel Moore and Edward Aveling. Ed. Frederick Engels. New York: Random House, 1906. Print.

Mbembe, Achille. *Sortir de la grande nuit. Essai sur L'Afrique décolonisée*. Paris: La Découverte, 2010. Print.

Michaelson, Scott, and Scott Cutler Shershow. "Rethinking Border Thinking." *South Atlantic Quarterly* 106.1 (2007): 39–60. Print.

Mignolo, Walter D. "The Geopolitics of Knowledge and the Colonial Difference." *Coloniality at Large: Latin America and the Postcolonial Debate*. Ed. Mabel Moraña, Enrique Dussel, and Carlos A. Jáuregui. Durham and London: Duke UP, 2008. 225–258. Print.

———. "Geopolitics of Sensing and Knowing: On (De)coloniality, Border Thinking, and Epistemic Disobedience." *Postcolonial Studies* 14.3 (2011): 273–83. Print.

———. *The Idea of Latin America*. Malden, MA: Blackwell, 2005. Print.

———. *Local Histories/Global Designs: Coloniality, Subaltern Knowledges, and Border Thinking*. Princeton, NJ: Princeton UP, 2000. Print.

Mignolo, Walter D., and Madina Tlostanova. "The Logic of Coloniality and the Limits of Postcoloniality." *The Postcolonial and the Gobal*. Ed. Revathi Krishnaswamy and John C. Hawley. Minneapolis: U of Minnesota P, 2008. 109–21. Print.

Miller, Christopher L. *Blank Darkness: Africanist Discourse in French*. Chicago: U of Chicago P, 1985. Print.

———. "The Theory and Pedagogy of a World Literature in French." *Yale French Studies* 120 (2011): 33–48. Print.

———. "Trait d'union: Injunction and Dismemberment in Yambo Ouologuem's *Le Devoir de violence*." *Yambo Ouologuem: Postcolonial Writer, Islamic Militant*. Ed. Christopher Wise. London: Lynne Rienner, 1999. 109–20. Print.

Mishra, Vijay, and Bob Hodge. "What Was Postcolonialism?" *New Literary History* 36 (2005): 375–402. Print.

Molloy, Sylvia. "Postcolonial Latin America and the Magic Realist Imperative: A Report to an Academy." *Nation, Language, and the Ethics of Translation*. Ed. Sandra Bermann and Michael Wood. Princeton: Princeton UP, 2005. 370–79. Print.

Montero, Rosa. "Her." *The Rigoberta Menchú Controversy*. Ed. Arturo Arias. Minneapolis: U of Minnesota P, 2001. 76–77. Print.

Moraña, Mabel. "The Boom of the Subaltern." *The Latin American Cultural Studies Reader*. Ed. Ana Del Sarto, Alicia Rios, and Abril Trigo. Durham, NC: Duke UP, 2004. 643–654. Print.

Moraña, Mabel, Enrique Dussel, and Carlos A. Jáuregui. "Colonialism and Its Replicants." *Coloniality at Large: Latin America and the Postcolonial Debate*. Ed. Mabel Moraña, Enrique Dussel, and Carlos A. Jáuregui. Durham and London: Duke UP, 2008. 1–22. Print.

Moraña, Mabel, Enrique Dussel, and Carlos A. Jáuregui, eds. *Coloniality at Large: Latin America and the Postcolonial Debate*. Durham and London: Duke UP, 2008. Print.

Moreiras, Alberto. "The Aura of Testimonio." *The Real Thing: Testimonial Discourse and Latin America*. Ed. Georg M. Gugelberger. Durham: Duke UP, 1996. 192–224. Print.

———. *The Exhaustion of Difference: The Politics of Latin American Cultural Studies*. Durham and London: Duke UP, 2001. Print.

———. "The Fatality of (My) Subalternism. A Response to John Beverley." *The New Centennial Review* 12.2 (2012): 217–46. Print.

———. "A God without Sovereignty. Political Jouissance. The Passive Decision." *The New Centennial Review* 4.3 (2004): 71–108. Print.

———. "Mules and Snakes: On the Neo-Baroque Principle of De-Localization." *Ideologies of Hispanism*. Ed. Mabel Moraña. Nashville: Vanderbilt UP, 2005. 201–229. Print.

Moser, Walter. "La mise à l'essai de l'identité culturelle: Lezama Lima et le discours américaniste." *Études Françaises* 44.1 (2008): 89–110. Print.

Moudileno, Lydie. "Francophonie: Trash or Recycle?" *Transnational French Studies: Postcolonialism and littérature-monde*. Ed. Alec Hargreaves, Charles Forsdick, and David Murphy. Liverpool: Liverpool UP, 2010. 109–23. Print.

———. "La fiction de la migration: Manipulation des corps et des récits *dans Bleu blanc rouge* d'Alain Mabanckou." *Présence Africaine* 163–64 (2001): 182–89. Print.

Moura, Jean-Marc. "French-Language Writing and the Francophone Literary System." *Contemporary French and Francophone Studies* 14.1 (2010): 29–38. Print.

Mpiku, J. Mbelolo. "From One Mystification to Another: 'Négritude' and 'Négraille' in *Le Devoir de violence*." *Yambo Ouologuem: Postcolonial Writer, Islamic Militant*. Ed. Christopher Wise. London: Lynne Rienner, 1999. 23–38. Print.

Murdoch, H. Adlai, and Anne Donadey. *Postcolonial Theory and Francophone Literary Studies*. Tallahassee: UP of Florida, 2005. Print.

Nesbitt, Nick. *Voicing Memory: History and Subjectivity in French Caribbean Literature*. Charlottesville, VA: U of Virginia P, 2003. Print.

Nietzsche, Friedrich. *The Portable Nietzsche*. Ed. Walter Kaufman. New York: Penguin, 1976. Print.

Nixon, Rob. "Environmentalism and Postcolonialism." *Postcolonial Studies and Beyond*. Ed. Ania Loomba et al. Durham: Duke UP, 2005. 233–49. Print.

Noguerol, Francesca. "De parisitis y rastacuerismo: Rubén Darío en Francia." *Estudios en el centenario de Los raros y Prosas profanas*. Ed. Alfonso García Morales. Sevilla: Sectariado de Publicaciones de la Universidad de Sevilla, 1998. 165–88. Print.

Obrist, Hans Ulrich. "Interview with Edouard Glissant." *Point d'Ironie* 29 (2002): 34–39. Print.

Ouologuem, Yambo. *Bound to Violence*. Trans. Ralph Manheim. New York: Harcourt Brace, 1971. Print.

———. "Le Devoir de violence." Letter. *Le Figaro Littéraire* 5 June 1971. Print.

———. *Lettre à la France-nègre*. Paris: Edmond Nalis, 1968. Print.

———. *The Yambo Ouologuem Reader*. Trans. and Ed. Christopher Wise. Trenton: Africa World Press, Inc., 2008. Print.

Palmer, Margarita Mateo. *Paradiso: La aventura mítica*. La Habana: Letras Cubanas, 2002. Print.

Parkinson Zamora, Lois. *The Inordinate Eye: New World Baroque and Latin American Fiction*. Chicago: U of Chicago P, 2006. Print.

Parkinson Zamora, Lois, and Monika Kaup. *Baroque New Worlds: Representation, Transculturation, Counterconquest*. Durham, NC: Duke UP, 2010. Print.

Patai, Daphne. "Whose Truth? Iconicity and Accuracy in the World of Testimonial Literature." *The Rigoberta Menchú Controversy*. Ed. Arturo Arias. Minneapolis: U of Minnesota P, 2001. 270–87. Print.

Pera, Cristóbal. *Modernistas en París*. Oxford: Peter Lang, 1997. Print.

Pérez Firmat, Gustavo. "The Strut of the Centipede: José Lezama Lima and New World Exceptionalism." *Do the Americas Have a Common Literature?* Ed. Gustavo Pérez Firmat. Durham: Duke UP, 1990. 316–32. Print.

Perret, Delphine. *La créolité. Espace de création*. Martinique: Ibis Rouge, 2001. Print.

Prabhu, Anjali. *Hybridity: Limits, Transformations, Prospects*. Albany: SUNY Press, 2007. Print.

Pratt, Mary Louise. "I, Rigoberta Menchú and the 'Culture Wars.'" *The Rigoberta Menchú Controversy*. Ed. Arturo Arias. Minneapolis: U of Minnesota P, 2001. 29–48. Print.

Prieto, Eric. "Edouard Glissant, littérature-monde, and Tout-monde." *Small Axe* 33 (2010): 111–20. Print.

———. "Landscaping Identity in Contemporary Caribbean Literature." *Francophone Post-Colonial Cultures. Critical Essays*. Ed. Kamal Salhi. Lanham: Lexington Books, 2003. 141–52. Print.

Puri, Shalini. *The Caribbean Postcolonial: Social Equality, Post-Nationalism, and Cultural History*. New York: Palgrave, 2004. Print.

Ramos, Julio. *Divergent Modernities: Culture and Politics in Nineteenth-Century Latin America*. Trans. John D. Blanco. Durham: Duke UP, 2001. Print.

Rancière, Jacques. *Dissensus: On Politics and Aesthetics*. Ed. and Trans. Steve Corcoran. New York: Continuum, 2010. Print.

———. "Should Democracy Come? Ethics and Politics in Derrida." *Derrida and the Time of the Political*. Ed. Pheng Cheah and Suzanne Guerlac. Durham, NC: Duke UP, 2009. 274–88.

Randall, Marilyn. *Pragmatic Plagiarism: Authorship, Profit, and Power*. Toronto: U of Toronto P, 2001. Print.

Ray, Sangeeta. "Postcolonial Studies." Ideas of the Decade. *Report on the State of the Discipline of Comparative Literature*. American Comparative Literature Association. 2014. Web.

Reyes, Alfonso. *Visión de Anáhuac*. Madrid: Índice, 1923. Print.

Rich, Motoko. "Tracking the Fallout of (Another) Literary Fraud." *New York Times* 5 March 2008. Web. 20 March 2012.

Richard, Nelly. "Intersecting Latin America with Latin Americanism: Academic Knowledge, Theoretical Practice, and Cultural Criticism." *The Latin American Cultural Studies Reader*. Ed. Ana Del Sarto, Alicia Rios, and Abril Trigo. Durham, NC: Duke UP, 2004. 686–705. Print.

Rohter, Larry. "Tarnished Laureate." *New York Times* 15 Dec. 1998: A1. Print.

Rose, Mark. *Authors and Owners. The Invention of Copyright*. Cambridge, MA and London: Harvard UP, 1993. Print.

Rosello, Mireille. "De la bi-langue de Khatibi à l'a-langue amère de Fouad Laroui: Amour bilingue ou méfiez-vous des parachutistes." *Présence Francophone* 55 (2000): 91–110. Print.

Salgado, César Augusto. "Hybridity in New World Baroque Theory." *The Journal of American Folklore* 112.445 (1999): 316–31. Print.

Salinas, Pedro. "Rubén Darío y la patria." *Ensayos completos*. Madrid: Taurus, 1981. 27–37. Print.

Schlickers, Sabine. "Rastacueros, degenerados y suicidas—o la difícil modernidad en la novela hispanoamerican del fin de siecle." *La modernidad revis(it)ada: Literatura y cultura latinoamericana de los siglos XIX y XX*. Ed. Inke Gunia et al. Berlin: Tranvía, 2000. 119–31. Print.

Schwartz, Marcy. *Writing Paris: Urban Topographies of Desire in Contemporary Latin American Fiction*. Albany: SUNY Press, 1999. Print.

Schwarz, Roberto. *Misplaced Ideas: Essays on Brazilian Culture*. New York: Verso, 1992. Print.

Sellin, Eric. "Ouologuem's Blueprint for *Le Devoir de violence*." *Research in African Literatures* 2.2 (1971): 117–20. Print.

———. "The Unknown Voice of Yambo Ouologuem." *Yale French Studies* 53 (1976): 137–62. Print.

Serrano, Richard. *Against the Postcolonial: "Francophone" Writers at the Ends of French Empire*. Lanham: Lexington Books, 2005. Print.

Sheller, Mimi. *Consuming the Caribbean: From Arawaks to Zombies*. London: Routledge, 2003. Print.

Sherman, Gabriel. "The Fog of Memoir: The Feud over the Truthfulness of Ishmael Beah's *A Long Way Gone*." *Slate.com* 6 March 2008. Web. 20 March 2012.

Shih, Shu-Mei. "Global Literature and the Technologies of Recognition." *PMLA* 119.1 (2004): 16–30. Print.

Short, Jonathan. "Experience and Aura: Adorno, McDowell, and 'Second Nature.'" *Adorno and the Need in Thinking. New Critical Essays*. Ed. Donald A. Burke, et al. Toronto: U of Toronto P, 2007. 181–202. Print.

Sklodowska, Elzbieta. "Spanish American Testimonial Novel: Some Afterthoughts." *The Real Thing: Testimonial Discourse and Latin America*. Ed. Georg M. Gugelberger. Durham: Duke UP, 1996. 84–100. Print.

Sommer, Doris. "Rigoberta's Secrets." *Latin American Perspectives* 18.3 (1991): 32–50. Print.

Songolo, Aliko. "Fiction et Subversion: Le Devoir de violence." *Présence Africaine* 120 (1981): 17–34. Print.

Spivak, Gayatri Chakravorty. *Death of a Discipline*. New York: Columbia UP, 2003. Print.

———. "Deconstructing Historiography." *Selected Subaltern Studies*. Ed. Ranajit Guha and Gayatri Chakravorty Spivak. New York: Oxford University Press, 1988. 3–32.

———. *Other Asias*. Oxford and Malden: Blackwell, 2008. Print.

———. "Poststructuralism, Marginality, Postcoloniality and Value." *Literary Theory Today*. Ed. Peter Collier and Helga Geyer-Ryan. Ithaca: Cornell UP, 1990. 219–44. Print.

Sucre, Guillermo. "Lezama Lima: El logos de la imaginación." *Lezama Lima*. Ed. Eugenio Suárez-Galbán. Madrid: Taurus, 1987. 312–338. Print.

Syrotinski, Michael. *Deconstruction and the Postcolonial*. Liverpool: Liverpool UP, 2007. Print.

Thomas, Dominic. "Fashion Matters: La Sape and Vestimentary Codes in Transnational Contexts and Urban Diasporas." *MLN* 118 (2003): 947–73. Print.

———. "Intersections and Trajectories: Francophone Studies and Postcolonial Theory." *Postcolonial Theory and Francophone Literary Studies*. Ed. H. Adlai Murdoch and Anne Donadey. Tallahassee: UP of Florida, 2005. 235–57. Print.

Toumi, Alawa. "Creolized North Africa: What Do They Really Speak in the Maghreb?" *French Cultural Studies: Criticism at the Crossroads*. Ed. Marie Pierre Le Hir and Dana Strand. Albany, SUNY UP, 2000. 69–80. Print.

Trapido, Joseph. "The Political Economy of Migration and Reputation in Kinshasa." *Africa* 81.2 (2011): 204–25. Print.

Ulloa, Leonor A. and Justo C. Ulloa. "José Lezama Lima: Configuración mítica de América." *MLN* 113.2 (1998): 364–79. Print.

Varadharajan, Asha. *Exotic Parodies: Subjectivity in Adorno, Said, and Spivak*. Minneapolis: U of Minnesota P, 1995. Print.

———. "'On the Morality of Thinking,' or Why Still Adorno." *Adorno and the Need in Thinking. New Critical Essays*. Ed. Donald A. Burke, et al. Toronto: U of Toronto P, 2007. 316–41. Print.

Vasconcelos, José. *La raza cósmica. Misión de la raza iberoamericana, Argentina y Brasil*. Mexico DF: Espasa-Calpe, 1966. Print.

Végső, Roland. "Deconstruction and Experience. The Politics of the Undeconstructible." *A Leftist Ontology: Beyond Relativism and Identity Politics*. Ed. Carsten Strathausen. Minneapolis: U of Minnesota P, 2009. 125–46. Print.

Victor, Gary. "Littérature-monde où liberté d'être." *Pour une littérature-monde*. Ed. Michel Le Bris and Jean Rouaud. Paris: Gallimard, 2007. 315–20. Print.

Viñas, David. *Literatura argentina y realidad política*. Buenos Aires: Jorge Álvarez, 1995. Print.

Vitier, Cintio. *Lo cubano en la poesía*. La Habana: Instituto del Libro, 1970. Print.

Waberi, Abdourahman A. "Ecrivains en position d'entraver." *Pour une littérature-monde*. Ed. Michel Le Bris and Jean Rouaud. Paris: Gallimard, 2007. 67–75. Print.

Watkins, Mel. "Talk with Yambo Ouologuem." *New York Times* Mar. 7 1971. BR7. Print.

Williams, Gareth. "The Fantasies of Cultural Exchange in Latin American Subaltern Studies." *The Real Thing: Testimonial Discourse and Latin America*. Ed. Georg M. Gugelberger. Durham: Duke UP, 1996. 225–53. Print.

Williams, Patrick, and Laura Chrisman. *Colonial Discourse and Postcolonial Theory: A Reader*. New York: Columbia UP, 1994.

Wise, Christopher, ed. *Yambo Ouologuem: Postcolonial Writer, Islamic Militant*. London: Lynne Rienner, 1999. Print.

Wright, Ann, trans. *I, Rigoberta Menchú: An Indian Woman in Guatemala*. Ed. Elisabeth Burgos. London: Verso, 1984. Print.

Zepke, Stephen. *Art as Abstract Machine: Ontology and Aesthetics in Deleuze and Guattari*. New York: Routledge, 2005. Print.

Žižek, Slavoj. "Multiculturalism, or the Cultural Logic of Multinational Capitalism." *New Left Review* I.225 (1997): 28–51. Print.

Zuidervaart, Lambert. "Metaphysics after Auschwitz: Suffering and Hope in Adorno's Negative Dialectics." *Adorno and the Need in Thinking. New Critical Essays*. Ed. Donald A. Burke, et al. Toronto: U of Toronto P, 2007. 133–66. Print.

Index